Automated Network Management Systems

Current and Future Capabilities

Douglas E. Comer

Cisco Systems
San Jose, CA

and

Department of Computer Sciences
Purdue University
West Lafayette, IN

PEARSON

Prentice
Hall

Upper Saddle River, NJ 07458

Library of Congress Cataloging-in-Publication Data

Comer, Douglas.
  Automated network management systems : current and future capabilities / Douglas E. Comer. -- 1st ed.
    p. cm.
  Includes bibliographical references and index.
  ISBN 0-13-239308-5
  1. Computer networks--Management. 2. Computer networks--Management--Automation. I. Title.
  TK5105.5.C58967 2006
  004.6--dc22

                                                                    2006023987

Vice President and Editorial Director, ECS: *Marcia J. Horton*
Executive Editor: *Tracy Dunkelberger*
Editorial Assistant: *Christianna Lee*
Associtate Editor: *Carole Snyder*
Executive Managing Editor: *Vince O'Brien*
Managing Editor: *Camille Trentacoste*
Production Editor: *Craig Little*
Director of Creative Services: *Paul Belfanti*
Creative Director: *Juan López*
Art Director: *Heather Scott*
Cover Art: *KJA-artists.com*
Art Editor: *Xiaohong Zhu*
Manufacturing Manager, ESM: *Alexis Heydt-Long*
Manufacturing Buyer: *Lisa McDowell*
Executive Marketing Manager: *Robin O'Brien*
Marketing Assistant: *Mack Patterson*

 © 2007 Pearson Education, Inc.
Pearson Prentice Hall
Pearson Education, Inc.
Upper Saddle River, NJ 07458

Pearson Prentice Hall™ is a trademark of Pearson Education, Inc.
Cisco is a registered trademark and Cisco ISC, Cisco CDP, and NetFlow are trademarks of Cisco Systems, Incorporated in the United States and other countries. EUI-64 is a trademark of the Institute for Electrical and Electronic Engineers (IEEE). IEEE is a registered trademark of the Institute of Electrical and Electronics Engineers, Inc. Java and Solaris are trademarks or registered trademarks of Sun Microsystems, Inc. in the United States and other countries. Juniper Networks is a registered trademark of Juniper Networks, Inc. in the United States and other countries. Linux is a registered trademark of Linus Torvalds. OpenView is a trademark of the Hewlett-Packard Company. UNIX is a registered trademark of The Open Group in the US and other countries. Windows, Windows NT, Windows CE, and/or other Microsoft products referenced herein are either trademarks or registered trademarks of Microsoft Corporation in the United States and/or other countries. IT Guru is a trademark of OPNET Technologies, Inc.

Additional company and product names used in this text may be trademarks or registered trademarks of the individual companies, and are respectfully acknowledged.

The author and publisher of this book have used their best efforts in preparing this book. These efforts include the development, research, and testing of the theories and programs to determine their effectiveness. The author and publisher make no warranty of any kind, expressed or implied, with regard to these programs or the documentation contained in this book. The author and publisher shall not be liable in any event for incidental or consequential damages in connection with, or arising out of, the furnishing, performance, or use of these programs.

Printed in the United States of America

10 9 8 7 6 5 4 3 2 1

ISBN: 0-13-239308-5

Pearson Education Ltd., *London*
Pearson Education Australia Pty. Ltd., *Sydney*
Pearson Education Singapore, Pte. Ltd.
Pearson Education North Asia Ltd., *Hong Kong*
Pearson Education Canada, Inc., *Toronto*
Pearson Educación de Mexico, S.A. de C.V.
Pearson Education—Japan, *Tokyo*
Pearson Education Malaysia, Pte. Ltd.
Pearson Education, Inc., *Upper Saddle River, New Jersey*

To an automated future

Contents

Preface   **xv**

Chapter 1   The Network Management Challenge   **1**

1.1   *Introduction*   1
1.2   *The Internet And Network Management*   1
1.3   *Internet Structure*   2
1.4   *Managing An Entity*   2
1.5   *Internal And External Policies*   3
1.6   *The State Of Network Management*   3
1.7   *Network Management In The Gartner Model*   4
1.8   *Benefits Of Automation*   4
1.9   *The Lack Of Industry Response*   5
1.10   *Impact On Business*   5
1.11   *Distributed Systems And New Abstractions*   6
1.12   *Remainder Of The Text*   7
1.13   *Summary*   7

PART I   Basics And Definitions

Chapter 2   A Review Of Network Elements And Services   **11**

2.1   *Introduction*   11
2.2   *Network Devices And Network Services*   11
2.3   *Network Elements And Element Management*   12
2.4   *Effect Of Physical Organization On Management*   12
2.5   *Examples Of Network Elements And Services*   13
2.6   *Basic Ethernet Switch*   14
2.7   *VLAN Switch*   15
2.8   *Access Point For A Wireless LAN*   15
2.9   *Cable Modem System*   16
2.10   *DSL Modem System And DSLAM*   17
2.11   *CSU/DSU Used In Wide Area Digital Circuits*   18

2.12   Channel Bank   19
2.13   IP Router   19
2.14   Firewall   20
2.15   DNS Server   20
2.16   DHCP Server   21
2.17   Web Server   22
2.18   HTTP Load Balancer   22
2.19   Summary   23

Chapter 3   The Network Management Problem   25

3.1   Introduction   25
3.2   What Is Network Management?   25
3.3   The Scope Of Network Management   26
3.4   Variety And Multi-Vendor Environments   27
3.5   Element And Network Management Systems   28
3.6   Scale And Complexity   29
3.7   Types Of Networks   31
3.8   Classification Of Devices   31
3.9   FCAPS: The Industry Standard Definition   32
3.10   The Motivation For Automation   33
3.11   Why Automation Has Not Occurred   33
3.12   Organization Of Management Software   34
3.13   Summary   36

Chapter 4   Configuration And Operation   39

4.1   Introduction   39
4.2   Intuition For Configuration   39
4.3   Configuration And Protocol Layering   40
4.4   Dependencies Among Configuration Parameters   43
4.5   Seeking A More Precise Definition Of Configuration   44
4.6   Configuration And Temporal Consequences   44
4.7   Configuration And Global Consistency   45
4.8   Global State And Practical Systems   46
4.9   Configuration And Default Values   46
4.10   Partial State, Automatic Update, And Recovery   47
4.11   Interface Paradigm And Incremental Configuration   48
4.12   Commit And Rollback During Configuration   49
4.13   Automated Rollback And Timeout   50
4.14   Snapshot, Configuration, And Partial State   50
4.15   Separation Of Setup And Activation   51

4.16   *Configuring Multiple Network Elements*   52
4.17   *Summary*   52

Chapter 5   Fault Detection And Correction   55

5.1   *Introduction*   55
5.2   *Network Faults*   55
5.3   *Trouble Reports, Symptoms, And Causes*   56
5.4   *Troubleshooting And Diagnostics*   56
5.5   *Monitoring*   57
5.6   *Baselines*   58
5.7   *Items That Can Be Monitored*   59
5.8   *Alarms, Logs, And Polling*   59
5.9   *Identifying The Cause Of A Fault*   60
5.10   *Human Failure And Network Faults*   62
5.11   *Protocol Layering And Faults*   62
5.12   *Hidden Faults And Automatic Correction*   63
5.13   *Anomaly Detection And Event Correlation*   64
5.14   *Fault Prevention*   64
5.15   *Summary*   65

Chapter 6   Accounting And Billing   67

6.1   *Introduction*   67
6.2   *Business Model And Network Charges*   67
6.3   *Service Level Agreements (SLAs)*   68
6.4   *Service Fees*   68
6.5   *Accounting For Flat-Rate Service*   69
6.6   *Accounting For Use-Based Service*   69
6.7   *Tiered Levels Of Service*   70
6.8   *Exceeding Quotas And Penalties*   70
6.9   *Assessing Financial Penalties*   71
6.10   *Traffic Policing And Strict Enforcement Of Limits*   71
6.11   *Technologies For Limiting The Rate Of Traffic*   72
6.12   *Priorities And Absolute Guarantees*   73
6.13   *Absolute Bandwidth Guarantees And MPLS*   73
6.14   *Relative Bandwidth Guarantees And Priorities*   73
6.15   *Priorities And Types Of Traffic*   74
6.16   *Peering Agreements And Accounting*   74
6.17   *Summary*   75

Chapter 7   Performance Assessment And Optimization   77

7.1   *Introduction   77*
7.2   *Aspects Of Performance   77*
7.3   *Items That Can Be Measured   78*
7.4   *Measures Of Network Performance   78*
7.5   *Application And Endpoint Sensitivity   79*
7.6   *Degraded Service, Variance In Traffic, And Congestion   80*
7.7   *Congestion, Delay, And Utilization   81*
7.8   *Local And End-To-End Measurements   81*
7.9   *Passive Observation Vs. Active Probing   82*
7.10   *Bottlenecks And Future Planning   83*
7.11   *Capacity Planning   83*
7.12   *Planning The Capacity Of A Switch   84*
7.13   *Planning The Capacity Of A Router   84*
7.14   *Planning The Capacity Of An Internet Connection   85*
7.15   *Measuring Peak And Average Traffic On A Link   86*
7.16   *Estimated Peak Utilization And 95th Percentile   87*
7.17   *Relationship Between Average And Peak Utilization   87*
7.18   *Consequences For Management And The 50/80 Rule   88*
7.19   *Capacity Planning For A Complex Topology   89*
7.20   *A Capacity Planning Process   89*
7.21   *Route Changes And Traffic Engineering   94*
7.22   *Failure Scenarios And Availability   94*
7.23   *Summary   95*

Chapter 8   Security   97

8.1   *Introduction   97*
8.2   *The Illusion Of A Secure Network   97*
8.3   *Security As A Process   98*
8.4   *Security Terminology And Concepts   98*
8.5   *Management Goals Related To Security   99*
8.6   *Risk Assessment   100*
8.7   *Security Policies   101*
8.8   *Acceptable Use Policy   102*
8.9   *Basic Technologies Used For Security   102*
8.10   *Management Issues And Security   105*
8.11   *Security Architecture: Perimeter Vs. Resources   105*
8.12   *Element Coordination And Firewall Unification   106*
8.13   *Resource Limits And Denial Of Service   107*
8.14   *Management of Authentication   107*
8.15   *Access Control And User Authentication   108*
8.16   *Management Of Wireless Networks   109*

8.17   Security Of The Network   110
8.18   Role-Based Access Control   111
8.19   Audit Trails And Security Logging   112
8.20   Key Management   112
8.21   Summary   113

PART II   Tools And Platforms

Chapter 9   Management Tools And Technologies   117

9.1   Introduction   117
9.2   The Principle Of Most Recent Change   117
9.3   The Evolution Of Management Tools   118
9.4   Management Tools As Applications   118
9.5   Using A Separate Network For Management   119
9.6   Types Of Management Tools   120
9.7   Physical Layer Testing Tools   121
9.8   Reachability And Connectivity Tools (ping)   122
9.9   Packet Analysis Tools   123
9.10   Discovery Tools   124
9.11   Device Interrogation Interfaces And Tools   126
9.12   Event Monitoring Tools   127
9.13   Triggers, Urgency Levels, And Granularity   127
9.14   Events, Urgency Levels, And Traffic   129
9.15   Performance Monitoring Tools   129
9.16   Flow Analysis Tools   132
9.17   Routing And Traffic Engineering Tools   133
9.18   Configuration Tools   133
9.19   Security Enforcement Tools   134
9.20   Network Planning Tools   134
9.21   Integration Of Management Tools   135
9.22   NOCs And Remote Monitoring   136
9.23   Remote CLI Access   137
9.24   Remote Aggregation Of Management Traffic   138
9.25   Other Tools   140
9.26   Scripting   141
9.27   Summary   141

Chapter 10   Simple Network Management Protocol (SNMP)   **143**

10.1   *Introduction   143*
10.2   *The Remote Management Paradigm And Applications   143*
10.3   *Management Functions And Protocol Definition   144*
10.4   *The Read-Write Paradigm   145*
10.5   *Arbitrary Operations And Virtual Items   146*
10.6   *Standards For Network Management Protocols   146*
10.7   *SNMP Scope And Paradigm   147*
10.8   *Basic SNMP Commands And Optimizations   148*
10.9   *Asynchronous Traps And Event Monitoring   148*
10.10   *Traps, Polling, Bandwidth, And CPU Cycles   149*
10.11   *Management Information Base (MIB) And Variables   150*
10.12   *A Hierarchy Of MIB Variable Names   151*
10.13   *Advantages And Disadvantages Of A Hierarchy   153*
10.14   *Complex Data Aggregates And MIB Tables   154*
10.15   *Granularity Of Aggregate Access   155*
10.16   *Transport Protocols And Interaction   155*
10.17   *Updates, Messages, And Atomicity   156*
10.18   *The Remote Monitoring MIB (RMON)   157*
10.19   *A Manager's View Of MIB Variables   158*
10.20   *Security And The Community String   159*
10.21   *Summary   160*

Chapter 11   Flow Data And Flow Analysis (NetFlow)   **163**

11.1   *Introduction   163*
11.2   *Basic Traffic Analysis   163*
11.3   *The Flow Abstraction   164*
11.4   *The Two Types Of Flows   165*
11.5   *The Purpose Of Flow Analysis   166*
11.6   *Levels Of Flow Aggregation   167*
11.7   *Online And Offline Flow Analysis   168*
11.8   *Examples Of Flow Data Analysis   169*
11.9   *Flow Data Capture And Filtering   171*
11.10   *Packet Inspection And Classification   173*
11.11   *Capture For Online And Offline Analysis   174*
11.12   *Flows Using Packet Content   175*
11.13   *Flows And Optimized Forwarding   175*
11.14   *Flow Data Export   177*
11.15   *Origin Of NetFlow Technology   178*
11.16   *Basic NetFlow Characteristics   178*
11.17   *Extensibility And Templates   179*

11.18 *NetFlow Message Transport And Consequences*   180
11.19 *Effect Of Configuration Choices*   181
11.20 *Summary*   182

Chapter 12   Routing And Traffic Engineering   185

12.1   *Introduction*   185
12.2   *Definitions Of Forwarding And Routing*   185
12.3   *Automation And Routing Update Protocols*   186
12.4   *Routing Basics And Route Metrics*   186
12.5   *Example Routing Update Protocols*   188
12.6   *Management Of Routes*   189
12.7   *The Difficulty Of Route Management*   189
12.8   *Use Of Routing Metrics To Enforce Policy*   190
12.9   *Overcoming Automation*   191
12.10 *Routing And Management Of Quality-of-Service*   192
12.11 *Traffic Engineering And MPLS Tunnels*   193
12.12 *Precomputation Of Backup Paths*   193
12.13 *Combinatorial Optimization And Infeasibility*   195
12.14 *Precomputation And Fast Convergence For IP Routing*   196
12.15 *Traffic Engineering, Security, And Load Balancing*   196
12.16 *Overhead, Convergence, And Routing Protocol Choices*   197
12.17 *OSPF Areas And The Principle Of Hierarchical Routing*   198
12.18 *Management Of Routing And Hidden Problems*   199
12.19 *The Global Nature Of Routing*   200
12.20 *Summary*   201

Chapter 13   Management Scripting   205

13.1   *Introduction*   205
13.2   *Limits Of Configuration*   205
13.3   *Iterative Improvement Using The Upgrade Paradigm*   206
13.4   *Extending Functionality Without An Upgrade Cycle*   207
13.5   *The Traditional Concept Of Scripting*   207
13.6   *Scripts And Programs*   208
13.7   *Stand-Alone Management Scripts*   209
13.8   *CLI, The Unix Expect Program, And Expect Scripts*   210
13.9   *Example Expect Script*   211
13.10 *Management Scripts, Homogeneity, And Expect*   212
13.11 *An Example Stand-Alone Script With Graphical Output*   214
13.12 *Using Scripts As An Extension Mechanism*   223
13.13 *Example Server With Scripting Extensions*   223

13.14 *Example Of Server Extension Points*   225
13.15 *Script Interface Functionality*   226
13.16 *Example Server Extension Script*   227
13.17 *Example Script That Manipulates A Reply*   230
13.18 *Handling Multiple Tasks With A Single Script*   232
13.19 *Script Timing, External Access, And Overhead*   233
13.20 *Summary*   234

PART III   The Future Of Network Management

Chapter 14   Network Automation: Questions And Goals   239

14.1   *Introduction*   239
14.2   *Network Automation*   240
14.3   *Dividing The Problem By Network Type*   241
14.4   *Shortcomings Of Existing Automation Tools*   242
14.5   *Incremental Automation Vs. A Blank Slate*   243
14.6   *Interface Paradigm And Efficiency*   244
14.7   *The Goal Of An Automated Management System*   246
14.8   *Desiderata For An Automated Management System*   248
14.9   *Multiple Sites And Managers*   250
14.10 *Authority Domains And Role-Based Access Control*   250
14.11 *Focus On Services*   251
14.12 *Policies, Constraints, And Business Rules*   251
14.13 *Correlation Of Multiple Events*   253
14.14 *Mapping From Logical To Physical Locations*   253
14.15 *Autonomy, Manual Override, And Policy Changes*   254
14.16 *Summary*   255

Chapter 15   Architectures For Network Management Software   257

15.1   *Introduction*   257
15.2   *Paradigms For Management System Design*   258
15.3   *Characteristics Of A Top-Down Approach*   258
15.4   *Characteristics Of A Bottom-Up Approach*   259
15.5   *Selecting Any Or All In A Bottom-Up Design*   260
15.6   *Weaknesses of The Two Design Paradigms*   260
15.7   *A Hybrid Design Methodology*   261
15.8   *The Critical Need For Fundamental Abstractions*   262
15.9   *An Analogy To Operating Systems*   263
15.10 *Separation Of Management From Elements*   264

15.11 *Mapping From Abstractions To Network Elements*   264
15.12 *Northbound And Southbound Interfaces*   265
15.13 *A Set Of Architectural Approaches*   266
15.14 *Useful Implementation Techniques*   273
15.15 *Late Binding Of A Programmatic Interface*   275
15.16 *Validation Of External Expectations*   276
15.17 *An Architecture Of Orthogonal Tools*   278
15.18 *Summary*   279

Chapter 16   Representation, Semantics, And Information Models   283

16.1   *Introduction*   283
16.2   *Data For Management Software*   283
16.3   *The Issue Of Data Representation*   284
16.4   *Internal Representation And Programming Language*   286
16.5   *The Effect Of Programming Paradigm On Representation*   286
16.6   *Objects And Object-Based Representation*   287
16.7   *Object Representation And Class Hierarchy*   288
16.8   *Persistence, Relations, And Database Representation*   288
16.9   *Representations At Various Points And Times*   289
16.10 *Translation Among Representations*   290
16.11 *Heterogeneity And Network Transmission*   291
16.12 *Serialization And Extensibility*   292
16.13 *The Need For Semantic Specification*   293
16.14 *Semantic Validity And Global Inconsistency*   293
16.15 *Information Models And Model-Driven Design*   294
16.16 *Information And Data Models*   295
16.17 *Class Hierarchies In An Object-Oriented Model*   296
16.18 *Multiple Hierarchies*   298
16.19 *Hierarchy Design And Efficiency*   299
16.20 *Cross-Hierarchy Relationships And Associations*   300
16.21 *Prescriptive Models And Generality*   301
16.22 *Purpose Of Models And Semantic Inference*   303
16.23 *Standardized Information Models*   303
16.24 *Graphical Representation Of Models (UML)*   304
16.25 *The Issue Of Complexity*   306
16.26 *Mapping Objects To Databases And Relations*   307
16.27 *Representation And Storage Of Topology Information*   307
16.28 *Ontology And Data Mining*   309
16.29 *Summary*   309

Chapter 17   Design Tradeoffs

17.1   *Introduction*   313
17.2   *Tradeoffs Involving Scope And Overall Approach*   313
17.3   *Architectural Tradeoffs*   315
17.4   *Engineering Tradeoffs And Costs*   317
17.5   *Tradeoffs In Representation And Semantics*   318
17.6   *Summary*   321

Chapter 18   Open Questions And Research Problems

18.1   *Introduction*   323
18.2   *Fundamental Abstractions For A Management System*   323
18.3   *Separation Of Control And Validation*   324
18.4   *Boundary Between A Network And End Systems*   324
18.5   *Taxonomy Of Network Management Architectures*   325
18.6   *Extent Of Functionality Offered By Existing Systems*   325
18.7   *Management Of Routing And Traffic Engineering*   325
18.8   *Automated Address Assignment*   325
18.9   *Analysis Of Routing*   326
18.10 *Security Policy Enforcement*   326
18.11 *Infrastructure Redesign For Automated Management*   326
18.12 *Peer-To-Peer Propagation Of Management Information*   327
18.13 *Routing Failure Analysis*   327
18.14 *Limits Of Automated Topology Discovery*   327
18.15 *Data Mining Of NetFlow Data*   327
18.16 *Storage Of Network State*   328
18.17 *Anomaly Detection Using Bayesian Filtering*   328
18.18 *Cost Of Protection In Scripting*   328
18.19 *Late-Binding Interface Management Applications*   328
18.20 *Boundary Between Management System And Elements*   329
18.21 *Summary*   329

Bibliography

Index

313

323

331

335

Preface

Network management remains the least understood aspect of networking. Researchers have been successful in devising a set of Internet communication protocols, and the networking industry has developed a diverse set of innovative systems that can process packets at high speed. Meanwhile, network management relies heavily on human ingenuity to diagnose problems and manual intervention to repair problems.

Commercial success has exacerbated the situation. On one hand, increased demand for network services means that networks continue to expand. On the other hand, high demand has created an environment that stimulates vendors to develop innovative products and technologies. Thus, expansion results in significant changes because managers tend to incorporate the latest network elements and mechanisms. Consequently, networks include a diverse set of technologies that have been combined in an ad hoc manner, which means the resulting infrastructure is often haphazard.

Even a small ad hoc network can be difficult to monitor and control. As networks grow larger, however, problems can quickly overwhelm managers. The largest enterprise networks are already so complex that humans cannot handle management tasks. In short, our ability to plan, deploy, configure, control, monitor, measure, and manage large networks is inadequate, and automation is required.

The automation of network management forms the central topic of this book. We examine comprehensive automated management both as an intellectual challenge and a commercially viable endeavor. Chapters consider the problem, review tools and technologies that are available, and examine ways that automation can be extended.

The book is organized into three parts. Following an introduction, Part 1 of the book, Chapters 2 through 8, defines the problem of network management and provides background on the constituent pieces. Chapters 2 and 3 review basic network elements, describe the problem of managing networks, and introduce the industry-standard FCAPS model. Successive chapters each describe one aspect of the FCAPS model.

Part 2 of the book, Chapters 9 through 13, examines tools and technologies that can be used to automate various aspects of management. Examples include discussions of: integrated platforms, SNMP, flow data analysis (NetFlow), routing and traffic management, and management scripting. Instead of presenting commercial products and research prototypes that each handle specific tasks, the chapters focus on concepts.

In the chapter on scripting, for example, concepts are illustrated with an example *expect* script and several example scripts for an extensible DHCP server.

The third part of the the text, Chapters 14 through 18, looks at the future of automation. It lists desirable properties of a comprehensive automated management system and considers possible software architectures that can be used. Later chapters explore the difficult questions of information representation and semantics as well as design tradeoffs. The last chapter presents open questions and research problems.

The text is suitable for both industry and academia. In industry, the material provides an excellent background for network managers that helps define the scope of the task. In an academic setting, the book can be used in an advanced undergraduate or a graduate course. At the undergraduate level, the goal is to educate students about the difficulty of network management tasks and expose them to some of the available tools. At the graduate level, the text provides sufficient background to allow students to undertake research problems.

At either the undergraduate or graduate level, practical hands-on experiments are essential. Undergrads should configure existing network elements manually, and then use tools for configuration and fault monitoring. In addition to mastering concepts, graduate students should gain experience devising, implementing, and measuring automated tools that can handle various aspects of configuration, fault monitoring, flow analysis, or security.

I thank the many people who have contributed to this book. Colleagues at Cisco provided ideas, encouragement, and feedback. Nino Vidovic suggested the project, Dave Oran provided insightful comments, David Bainbridge suggested principles and discussed both semantics and complexity in information models, Fred Serr provided extensive help with the discussion of performance in Chapter 7, Ralph Droms reviewed the outline and several chapters, Thad Stoner provided information on the size of typical enterprise networks, Brian McGovern suggested tools, Jim Brown provided the sample scripts in Chapter 13, and the IP Services Planning group listened to presentations and generated ideas. Finally, Cliff Meltzer invited me to visit Cisco and funded much of the work on the book. Colleagues outside Cisco also contributed, Craig Wills reviewed all chapters and provided many suggestions as did James Cernak. Ethan Blanton wrote the stand-alone monitoring script in Chapter 13. Jennifer Rexford sent several references, and Brent Chapman and Ehab Al-Shaer reviewed parts of the manuscript. In addition to reviewing chapters, Jon Saperia discussed models, hierarchies, and their interactions. Special thanks go to my wife and partner, Christine, whose support, editing, and suggestions make all the difference.

Douglas E. Comer

July, 2006

About The Author

Douglas Comer, Distinguished Professor of Computer Science at Purdue University and Vice President of Research at Cisco Systems Inc.†, is an internationally recognized expert on computer networking, the TCP/IP protocols, and the Internet. The author of numerous refereed articles and technical books, he is a pioneer in the development of networking and systems curricula and laboratories for research and education.

A prolific author, Comer's popular books have been translated into 16 languages, and are used in industry as well as computer science, engineering, and business departments around the world. His landmark three-volume series *Internetworking With TCP/IP* revolutionized networking and network education. His textbooks and innovative laboratory manuals have and continue to shape graduate and undergraduate curricula.

The accuracy and insight of Dr. Comer's books reflect his extensive background in computer systems. His research spans both hardware and software. He has created a complete operating system, written device drivers, and implemented network protocol software for conventional computers as well as network processors. The resulting software has been used by industry in a variety of products.

Comer has created and teaches courses on network protocols and computer technologies for a variety of audiences, including courses for engineers as well as academic audiences. His innovative laboratories allow him and his students to design and implement working prototypes of large, complex systems, and measure the performance of the resulting prototypes. He continues to teach at industries, universities, and conferences around the world. In addition, Comer consults for industry on the design of computer networks and systems.

For over nineteen years, Dr. Comer has served as editor-in-chief of the research journal *Software — Practice and Experience*. He is a Fellow of the ACM, a Fellow of the Purdue Teaching Academy, and a recipient of numerous awards, including a Usenix Lifetime Achievement award.

Additional information can be found at:

www.cs.purdue.edu/people/comer

and information about Comer's books can be found at:

www.comerbooks.com

---

†Comer was a Visiting Faculty in the Network Management Technology Group at Cisco when this book was written.

Other Books From Douglas Comer And Prentice Hall

Internetworking With TCP/IP Volume I: Principles, Protocols and Architectures, 5th edition: 2006, ISBN 0-13-187671-6

The classic reference in the field for anyone who wants to understand Internet technology, Volume I surveys the TCP/IP protocol suite and describes each component. The text covers protocols such as IP, ICMP, TCP, UDP, ARP, SNMP, and RTP, as well as concepts such as Virtual Private Networks and Address Translation.

Internetworking With TCP/IP Volumes II and III: Volume II: Design, Implementation, and Internals (with David Stevens), 3rd edition: 1999, ISBN 0-13-973843-6 **and Volume III: Client-Server Programming and Applications (with David Stevens) Linux/POSIX sockets version:** 2000, ISBN 0-13-032071-4

Volumes II and III continue the discussion of Volume I by considering the implementation of TCP/IP and applications that use TCP/IP.

Network System Design Using Network Processors, Intel IXP 2xxx version: 2006, ISBN 0-13-141792-4

A comprehensive overview of the design and engineering of packet processing systems such as bridges, routers, TCP splicers, and NAT boxes, with a focus on network processor technology.

Computer Networks And Internets, 4th edition: 2004, ISBN 0-13-143351-2

A broad introduction to data communication, networking, internetworking, and client-server applications, including both the hardware and software components that make up computer networks. A CD-ROM is included.

The Internet Book: Everything you need to know about computer networking and how the Internet works, 4th edition: 2006, paperback

A gentle introduction that explains computer networking and the Internet for readers who do not have a technical background. Ideal for someone who wants to become Internet and computer networking literate.

Essentials Of Computer Architecture, 2005, ISBN 0-13-149179-2

An introduction to digital logic and computer organization with emphasis on the relationship between the architecture of a computer and the consequences for programmers.

To order, visit the Prentice Hall Web page at www.prenhall.com/
or contact your local bookstore or Prentice Hall representative.
In North America, call 1-515-284-6751, or send a FAX to 1-515-284-6719.

Chapter Contents

1.1   Introduction, 1
1.2   The Internet And Network Management, 1
1.3   Internet Structure, 2
1.4   Managing An Entity, 2
1.5   Internal And External Policies, 3
1.6   The State Of Network Management, 3
1.7   Network Management In The Gartner Model, 4
1.8   Benefits Of Automation, 4
1.9   The Lack Of Industry Response, 5
1.10   Impact On Business, 5
1.11   Distributed Systems And New Abstractions, 6
1.12   Remainder Of The Text, 7
1.13   Summary, 7

1

The Network Management Challenge

1.1 Introduction

The question of how to effectively manage a communication network has plagued the industry since commercial networks first appeared. Networking equipment must be installed, configured, operated, monitored, and repaired. The underlying copper or fiber infrastructure that connects equipment must be acquired or leased, and customers billed for services. In addition, managers must consider how to protect networks from inadvertent glitches and malicious abuse.

Surprisingly, although the problem of network management has been studied and many technologies have been created to help managers, most management activities still require manual effort — the available technologies are primitive, and human intelligence is used to master the complexity. As a result, an exciting opportunity exists: find ways to build software systems that automate network management tasks. The problem, which forms a focus of our discussion, is intellectually challenging, and the results can be commercially rewarding.

1.2 The Internet And Network Management

The advent of the Internet changed network management in a fundamental way. Unlike the original telephone system in which a large phone company owned and managed an entire network from wires to services, the Internet connects networks that are owned and managed by independent organizations. Thus, instead of concentrating all aspects of network management in a single, centralized phone company, the Internet requires each organization to maintain in-house expertise. As more organizations install data networks, the need for automation becomes pressing.

In the past, the networking research community and networking industry have worked together to solve problems. Early work explored underlying technologies such as signals and modulation, digital encoding, and basics of communication protocols. A second era in networking produced technologies that we use to construct modern communication systems (e.g., Local Area and Wide Area Networks, switches, routers, Internet protocols, and network applications). A third era shifted away from scientific research to more commercial aspects of networking, including Internet Service Providers, contractual agreements that customers sign to obtain service, and agreements that ISPs sign to exchange traffic.

With the urgency and importance of network management, we can predict that:

> *The next era in networking will focus on finding ways to automate the planning, configuration, control, and operation of computer networks and internets.*

1.3 Internet Structure

Understanding why network management is difficult requires us to consider the underlying structure. At one level, the Internet can be viewed as a flat "network of networks" in which a large set of individual packet switching network systems are interconnected by routers. Although the interconnected networks abstraction gives a clear picture, the practical reality is incredibly more complex: networks and routers are divided into subsets, each subset is owned and operated by an administrative entity, and the subsets serve diverse purposes. The situation is further complicated by overlay and tunneling technologies that impose a set of logical connections over a physical network. The term *administrative entity* is purposefully ambiguous because a given entity can be small (e.g., a single individual) or large (e.g., a multi-national corporation), and can use the Internet for its internal business, to support e-commerce, or as the entire basis of a business (e.g., a service provider that offers internet service to others). In terms of the underlying technologies, the structure is also diverse: the edge of the Internet provides connections for end systems such as desktop computers and portable devices, while the core of the Internet provides packet transfer among routers.

1.4 Managing An Entity

The conceptual division of the Internet into administrative entities is important because it implies autonomy — each entity is free to devise and implement its own policies for use. Thus, the notion of ownership forms a key aspect of network management and control:

> *Although devices throughout the entire Internet must cooperate to en-*
> *sure that the network functions correctly, each administrative entity*
> *controls and operates its part of the Internet independently.*

That is, an entity configures, monitors, and controls the switches, routers, and networks that it owns to implement local policy without relying on a universal control scheme. Thus, autonomy offers the freedom to choose policies, but requires that each administrative entity ensures that its policies are enforced.

1.5 Internal And External Policies

We will learn that many issues and details complicate network management. However, one problem arises from the notion of autonomy: the boundaries that exist between administrative entities imply that entities on each side must enforce and coordinate their policies. In a typical corporation, for example, employees are permitted to access internal facilities and services that are not available to users outside the corporation. Thus, corporate policies have rules for "insiders" and "outsiders", and the interaction between the rules causes complexity.

Administrative boundaries present a complex problem for service providers because a provider must establish policies that adhere to contractual agreements with individual customers as well as agreements with other service providers. Thus, when we discuss management of service provider networks, it will be important to remember that much of the complexity arises from administrative boundaries.

1.6 The State Of Network Management

As we will learn, network management is currently in sad shape. Managers† complain that it is difficult to understand operational conditions and traffic, diagnose failures, implement policies, or verify security provisions. Existing tools and protocols provide only basic facilities and do not handle global policies or services that span multiple devices. Instead, each network device is configured and controlled independently, which means that to implement a policy across an entire administrative domain, a manager must configure each individual device to achieve the desired policy. Furthermore, because they are often vendor-specific, current tools cannot easily handle heterogeneous environments and do not interact well with other tools. The point is:

> *Current network management tools focus on individual devices: diag-*
> *nosing a problem or implementing a policy requires a manager to ex-*
> *amine and configure one device at a time.*

---

†Throughout the text, we will use the term *network manager* to refer to a human who engages in activities such as network planning, deployment, operation, measurement, and problem diagnosis or repair; we do not distinguish between *network manager* and *network administrator*.

Furthermore, the networking industry has adopted a paradigm of manual management in which a human manager interacts with a device. We will see that using a human to configure, monitor, and control individual devices is insufficient for two reasons. First, because human interaction is relatively slow, the approach does not scale to accommodate very large networks. Second, and more important, because humans are fallible, the approach does not guarantee consistent implementation of policies across all devices. The point is:

> *Because it relies on humans to control and examine individual devices, the current approach used for network management is insufficient for large networks or networks that have complex policies spanning multiple devices.*

1.7 Network Management In The Gartner Model

Gartner, Inc. has developed a model that rates the maturity of IT processes†. According to the Gartner model, there are four major stages of maturity. With respect to network management, the stages are characterized as:

- Stage 1: Reactive with manual control and response
- Stage 2: Reactive with assistance from automated tools
- Stage 3: Proactive with automation responding to problems
- Stage 4: Adaptive with autonomous systems handling problems

In terms of the Gartner model, network management has reached Stage 2: although tools exist that aid managers in making decisions, actions ultimately rely on humans. The questions are how and when can network management move to Stage 3?

1.8 Benefits Of Automation

Automating network management offers several potential benefits:

- Reduces the time required to perform a given task
- Reduces the probability of human error
- Guarantees consistent policies across an entire network
- Provides accountability for changes

---

†A description of the Gartner Maturity Model for IT Processes can be found online at:
http://www.gartner.com/DisplayDocument?doc_cd=131972

A reduction in the time required for a task is the most obvious benefit, but reducing human error is especially important because many network problems are caused by simple mistakes. Human error is also pertinent to the fourth item — if a change in policy causes errors, a system that records all changes can help identify the cause of the problem.

The third item, guaranteeing consistency, is perhaps the most important. The ad hoc approach currently used to manage networks means that there are few guarantees of consistency. Thus, even a simplistic automation system that replicates a given configuration on multiple devices is beneficial. To guarantee meaningful consistency, however, a system needs to handle more than repetitive, mechanical tasks. That is, meaningful consistency requires the automation of tasks that now require human intelligence.

1.9 The Lack Of Industry Response

Why has the networking industry converged on a manual paradigm for network management? Why haven't software systems been created that automate most management functions? We will see that the problem is extremely complex, and that more research is needed to make automation a reality. From a scientific point of view:

> *Network management is the least-understood aspect of computer networking.*

We will also see that before network management can be automated, a paradigm shift will be required — because the current approach depends on human intelligence, we cannot easily build software to perform the same functions. Thus, before we can build software systems and computer programs that perform network management tasks, we need to look for new ways to represent and store information about networks, new ways to translate policies into configurations, and new ways to gather and analyze information about network operations and performance.

1.10 Impact On Business

What will happen if research and development fails to produce automated management systems? The consequences for business are significant. As networks grow larger, they will become less manageable. In fact, we are already reaching the limits of network size that we can handle with current tools. Service providers find it difficult to install, configure, and control devices and services. Managers of large enterprise networks complain that the networks exceed their ability to handle problems.

The situation is critical because businesses increasingly rely on data networks as the primary link to customers and other businesses. One particular aspect of network management has become inextricably linked to the bottom line: network downtime. For many businesses, the losses that occur while a network is down are staggering. Ironically, as a business grows and its network increases in size, the time required to diagnose and repair problems increases rapidly. Thus, businesses that are most successful bear the most risk. We can summarize:

> *Because businesses increasingly depend on data networks and network sizes are approaching the limits of current management tools, research and development of automated network management systems is crucial.*

1.11 Distributed Systems And New Abstractions

It may seem that the study of network management is part of the more general study of networking. We will learn, however, that devising an automated network management system requires understanding several aspects of Computer Science beyond basic networking. Of course, such an exercise requires familiarity with various network devices and their role in practical networks and the set of parameters that are used to configure such devices. In addition, one must understand how to create the necessary abstractions on which software can be based. Finally, building network management software requires familiarity with concepts from large-scale distributed systems: communicating applications, two-phase commit, and control of concurrent data access.

In fact, when we explore possible approaches to building network management systems and possible architectures for network management software, the focus of attention will shift to system aspects rather than networks and protocols. In particular, we will consider how to collect and handle management data across multiple sites, and see that technologies, such as distributed database systems, can be used to store data needed for many management functions.

One issue in distributed systems is central to the design of automated network management systems: large scale. In addition to including many devices and services, large networks span multiple sites. For example, some networks contain tens of thousands of devices that must be managed. More important, large scale is complicated by heterogeneity — most large networks contain many types of devices.

1.12 Remainder Of The Text

The text is divided into three parts. The first part reviews basics and provides background. Chapters describe an example set of network elements and their role in network systems, characterize the scope and complexity of the network management problem, and give the industry-standard definition of network management functionality. Later chapters in the first part explain each aspect of network management in more detail, and provide specific examples of the functionality required as well as general characteristics.

The second part of the text focuses on existing network management systems by exploring current tools and technologies. Chapters examine the evolution of tools and the interfaces used to manage individual devices, the role and underlying model of the Simple Network Management Protocol, and the analysis of NetFlow data. Finally, Chapter 13 offers a few examples of scripts that are used to manage network devices.

The third part of the text focuses on the future of network management. Chapters list the desirable characteristics of a next-generation system, examine possible architectures, and discuss design tradeoffs. The third part concludes with a set of questions and open problems.

1.13 Summary

Network management is the least-understood aspect of networking and a topic that requires further investigation. This text examines the problem, reviews existing tools and technologies, and outlines possible architectures that can be used to build software systems that automate network management.

Part I

An Introduction To
The Complex Issue Of
Network Management

Chapter Contents

2.1   Introduction, 11
2.2   Network Devices And Network Services, 11
2.3   Network Elements And Element Management, 12
2.4   Effect Of Physical Organization On Management, 12
2.5   Examples Of Network Elements And Services, 13
2.6   Basic Ethernet Switch, 14
2.7   VLAN Switch, 15
2.8   Access Point For A Wireless LAN, 15
2.9   Cable Modem System, 16
2.10   DSL Modem System And DSLAM, 17
2.11   CSU/DSU Used In Wide Area Digital Circuits, 18
2.12   Channel Bank, 19
2.13   IP Router, 19
2.14   Firewall, 20
2.15   DNS Server, 20
2.16   DHCP Server, 21
2.17   Web Server, 22
2.18   HTTP Load Balancer, 22
2.19   Summary, 23

2

A Review Of Network Elements And Services

2.1 Introduction

This brief chapter provides basic background needed to understand automated network management. The chapter presents examples of devices that are used to create networks and the services that a network offers. It reviews basic functionality, and describes some of the parameters that managers can select to configure each device or service. Later chapters continue the discussion by explaining how various aspects of network management apply to the systems presented here.

The point of the chapter is not merely to give facts about network devices and services or to characterize how each system processes packets. Instead, we will look at the aspects that are pertinent to network management. That is, we will concentrate on understanding the constituent parts, facilities, and mechanisms that must be managed (e.g., parameters that managers can assign to initiate and control operation and information a manager can request to examine status).

2.2 Network Devices And Network Services

Items to be managed can be divided into two broad categories: *network devices* (i.e., hardware devices that form the network infrastructure) and *network services* that use the underlying hardware. Services can be divided into three types:

- Application services
- General infrastructure services
- Provisioned services

Application services, such as email and web services, are typically implemented by software running on general-purpose computers (e.g., an email server running on a Linux system). General infrastructure services include mechanisms such as the *Domain Name System* (*DNS*) that handles name translation, the *Dynamic Host Configuration Protocol* (*DHCP*) that handles address assignment during bootstrap, and authentication services that handle validation of communicating entities. Finally, *provisioned services* allow a manager to enforce global policies. Typical provisioned services operate end-to-end (e.g., across an entire network) rather than inside a single device or at a single point. For example, provisioned services include such facilities as an end-to-end *Multi-Protocol Label Switching* (*MPLS*) tunnel and a configuration of all routers in an enterprise to give priority to voice traffic†.

2.3 Network Elements And Element Management

To be precise and avoid confusion, network management systems use the generic term *network element* to refer to any network device or mechanism that can be managed‡. We think of each network element as an independent entity that can be configured and controlled without affecting other elements, and use the term *element management* to refer to the configuration and operation of individual network elements. In particular, when element management is used, creation of an end-to-end service requires a manager to configure each network element along the path.

Of course, a strong relationship exists between element management and service management. For example, a web server application runs on a computer system, which means that a manager must control both the web server program and the underlying hardware system on which it runs. Thus, a manager can reboot the web server program or reboot the underlying computer system.

2.4 Effect Of Physical Organization On Management

Although we describe network elements as logically independent and think of element management as specifying the role of a given element, the physical organization of devices can affect how managers proceed. To understand why, consider circuit multiplexing. In some cases, when a manager leases a digital circuit, a carrier installs a separate physical transmission medium from the source to the destination (e.g., a separate set of copper wires that carry a T1 circuit). In most cases, however, carriers use *Time Division Multiplexing* (*TDM*) technology to transmit data from multiple cir-

---

†Some vendors classify an MPLS tunnel as a *transport service* rather than a generic *provisioned service*.

‡Although we tend to think of a network element as a device, the definition is sometimes extended to services that are integral to the infrastructure (e.g., DNS and DHCP).

cuits across a single underlying transmission medium (e.g., many circuits multiplexed across a single optical fiber). Knowing how circuits are multiplexed across a physical medium allows a manager to better understand and diagnose the cause of problems (e.g., if all circuits multiplexed on a single fiber fail, a manager will concentrate on finding a problem with the fiber rather than looking for problems with individual circuits).

The physical organization of network components is also pertinent to network management. For example, understanding which network components reside in separate cabinets and which components are organized as *blades* (i.e., printed circuit boards) in a device helps managers for two reasons. First, if a failure occurs, knowledge of the physical organization helps a manager determine the cause (e.g., a power supply failure will disable all blades in the chassis, but a blade failure will only disable one). Second, it may be possible to manage an entire chassis rather than each individual blade (e.g., issue a single command to shutdown all blades rather than issuing individual commands to shut down each blade). Thus, when thinking about network management systems, the issue of physical organization cannot be ignored.

2.5 Examples Of Network Elements And Services

The next sections describe examples of network elements and services that can be managed:

- Basic Ethernet switch
- VLAN switch
- Access point for a wireless LAN
- Cable modem system
- DSL modem and DSLAM
- Wide area digital connection (CSU/DSU)
- Channel bank
- IP router
- Firewall
- DNS server
- DHCP server
- Web server
- HTTP load balancer

The text explains the role of each element and service, and lists examples of items visible to the network management system as well as parameters that can be configured (i.e., changed). The examples are chosen to illustrate the diversity that exists in managed devices and to show examples of managed items at various layers of the protocol stack, not to give exact details†. Thus, although we have chosen network elements that are often found in real networks and the managed items we cite are typical, commercial products may include configuration parameters other than those listed and may vary in the way parameters are named or specified.

2.6 Basic Ethernet Switch

A basic *Ethernet Switch* (also called a *Layer 2 Switch*) forms the center of a *Local Area Network* (*LAN*). An Ethernet switch is among the most straightforward devices to manage. Little or no configuration is required because the hardware handles most configuration chores automatically. For example, the Ethernet standard specifies that whenever a device is connected to a switch, the switch detects the connection and negotiates a data speed, choosing the maximum speed that both ends can support. Thus, data speed does not need to be manually configured‡. Similarly, a manager does not need to configure the *MAC address* (i.e., Ethernet address) of connected devices because a switch examines the source address of frames that arrive over each connection and records the MAC address of the computer(s) reachable on that connection.

We can summarize a basic Ethernet switch as follows:

Purpose
Provide packet forwarding among a set of directly-connected devices.

Structure
Typically, a stand-alone device with multiple physical *ports* (usually between 16 and 256) that can each be connected to another device, generally a computer system or an IP router.

Notes
When a device is connected to a port, the two ends can auto-negotiate a data speed to be used.

Configurable Parameters
Each port can be enabled or disabled (i.e., a manager can prevent communication over a port), a manager can set the speed and duplex of the port, and a manager can reset packet counters.

Readable Values
The type and capabilities of the switch (e.g., the make and model, the number of ports, and the maximum speed of a port); status of each port (enabled or disabled, whether a device is connected, current speed); address of all device(s) connected to the port; time since last reboot; identification (e.g., serial number and firmware version); count of packets sent/received, and count of errors detected.

---

†Background on protocol layering can be found in Comer [2006].

‡Although data speed can be configured, a problem arises if one side has a fixed speed and the other attempts to autonegotiate.

2.7 VLAN Switch

A *VLAN switch* extends basic Layer 2 switch technology in one significant way: it allows a manager to partition ports into separate broadcast domains, with each broadcast domain known as a *virtual LAN*. From a packet processing point of view, the definition of a virtual LAN is straightforward: whenever a connected device sends a frame to the *broadcast address*, the switch delivers a copy to all other ports on the same VLAN as the sender. Thus, a VLAN switch appears to operate like a set of independent Layer 2 switches.

Purpose
> Provide packet forwarding among subsets of directly-connected devices.

Structure
> Typically, a stand-alone device with multiple physical *ports* (usually between 16 and 256) that can each be connected to another device, generally a computer system or an IP router.

Notes
> Uses auto-negotiation to determine a data rate to be used (like a basic switch). Only forwards broadcast frames to ports on the same VLAN†.

Configurable Parameters
> In addition to parameters of a basic Ethernet switch, each port can be assigned to a specific VLAN (VLANs are usually numbered 1, 2, 3, ...).

Readable Values
> The same as a basic Ethernet switch plus the VLAN to which each port is currently assigned, and traffic and error counts for each VLAN.

2.8 Access Point For A Wireless LAN

A wireless LAN technology, such as IEEE's *802.11b*, provides wireless network connectivity to a set of computers. A device known as an *access point* forwards packets between wireless devices and a wired network. Typically, an office building equipped to use a wireless LAN has multiple access points that each cover part of the building.

Purpose
> Provide wireless access to a set of (potentially mobile) computers.

Structure
> Typically, a stand-alone system that uses Ethernet to connect to a wired network.

---

†In theory, a VLAN switch does not provide communication between VLANs, but in practice, many switches forward unicast frames if the MAC address is valid.

Notes

Each access point recognizes a name known as a *Service Set IDentifier* (*SSID*); an access point will not accept an incoming packet unless the SSID in the packet header matches the SSID being accepted.

Configurable Parameters

The SSID that the access point will accept can be changed, and a manager can decide whether the access point should broadcast announcements that contain the SSID (potential clients use announcements to find the SSID automatically); the use of security such as the *Wired Equivalent Privacy* (*WEP*) standard can be configured; the IP address of the access point on the wired network can also be changed.

Readable Values

The SSID currently assigned to the access point, the IP address, the number of wireless clients currently associated with the access point, and the MAC address of each associated client.

2.9 Cable Modem System

Cable modem systems use *Data Over Cable Service Interface Specification* (*DOCSIS*) technology developed by *CableLabs* to provide Internet services to a set of subscribers over a cable TV infrastructure (i.e., over the coaxial cable that was initially created to deliver broadcast television signals to subscribers). Although data communications travel over the same copper wiring as television signals, the two operate on separate frequencies. Thus, data services can be managed independent of broadcast television services.

Purpose

Provide Internet access to a set of subscribers over the same coaxial cable that is used to deliver broadcast television channels.

Structure

A *Cable Modem Termination System* (*CMTS*), which resides at the provider's central location, connects to the Internet and also contains multiple *head-end modems* that each communicate with a *tail-end modem* that resides at a customer's site.

Notes

A single CMTS can control up to 5000 tail-end modems. The cable modem technology transfers Ethernet frames (i.e., Layer 2 frames), and subsets of subscribers appear to be on individual physical networks.

Configurable Parameters

In the CMTS: information can be entered that validates specific tail-end modems; the maximum number of subscribers and a maximum data rate can be specified for each subscriber; filters can be set to admit or prohibit certain types of packets; and packet counters can be reset.

Readable Values

The current number of active subscribers, and for each subscriber, the maximum data rate, current status (e.g., enabled or disabled), the count of packets sent/received, and a count of packet errors that have occurred. For each tail-end modem, the MAC address of the modem can be read as well as the status of the connection between the modem and the subscriber's computer.

2.10 DSL Modem System And DSLAM

Telephone companies use *Digital Subscriber Line* (*DSL*) technology to provide Internet services to a set of subscribers over the same copper wiring that is used for conventional voice telephone service. Because DSL uses frequencies other than those used for voice service, data service can be managed independent of voice service.

Purpose

Provide Internet access to a set of subscribers over the same copper wiring that is used to deliver voice telephone communication.

Structure

A head-end modem, which resides at the phone company's central office, connects to a device known as a *DSL Access Multiplexor* (*DSLAM*) and also connects to telephone lines leading to individual subscribers. The DSLAM connects to an ISP network, typically using ATM, and forwards data from each subscriber toward its destination. At each subscriber's premises, a *tail-end modem* connects from the telephone wiring to the subscriber's computer, and acts like a bridge to forward packets over DSL.

Notes

Conceptually, one head-end modem is needed per subscriber.

Configurable Parameters

In the head-end modem, a manager can set a maximum data rate for the subscriber, and can also reset packet counters. A DSLAM can be configured with ATM connections (virtual circuits) that lead to various destinations (typically ISPs), and each customer's modem is configured to map onto one of the ATM connections.

Readable Values

For a head-end modem, whether the modem is currently receiving a signal from the tail-end modem, the maximum data rate, and a count of packets (or cells) sent and received. For a DSLAM, the current configuration of ATM connections and the mapping of subscriber lines to ATM connections.

2.11 CSU/DSU Used In Wide Area Digital Circuits

ISPs and large corporations use digital circuits leased from carriers to provide connections over long distances. Logically, the hardware used at the endpoint of a digital circuit is divided into two units; physically, the two are usually combined into a single device (often a small circuit board that plugs into a switch or router). The device is known as a *Channel Service Unit/Data Service Unit* (*CSU/DSU*).

A CSU/DSU is analogous to a modem for an analog line. However, in addition to encoding data for transmission, a CSU/DSU electrically isolates the leased circuit to protect against voltage spikes or similar problems, and a manager can request that the CSU/DSU perform diagnostic tests to debug problems.

Purpose

Provide the interface between computer equipment and a digital circuit that is leased from a common carrier.

Structure

Either a small stand-alone device or a line card in a switch or router.

Notes

A CSU/DSU may have a *moded interface* in which a manager must either choose to request standard data transmission or diagnostics, but cannot perform both at the same time.

Configurable Parameters

Some CSU/DSU devices operate at a fixed data rate; others must be configured to the data rate of the leased circuit. A manager can enable or disable diagnostic testing.

Readable Values

A CSU/DSU can report the current status of the line, whether the other endpoint is responding, and the results of diagnostic tests.

2.12 Channel Bank

A *channel bank* is used by common carriers or other providers to terminate digital lines from customers and multiplex them onto a high-speed digital circuit. The name arises because a single unit handles a set of lines.

Purpose
> Used by a service provider to terminate a set of digital circuit connections that each lead to a customer.

Structure
> A rack-mounted unit that accepts many individual connections.

Notes
> A channel bank uses time-division multiplexing to combine individual circuits into a single, higher-speed pipe (e.g., multiplex twenty-four T1 circuits onto a single T3 pipe).

Configurable Parameters
> There are two types of parameters: those that refer to individual lines, and those that refer to the entire channel bank and the high-speed upstream connection. Individual connections can be enabled or disabled, as can the upstream connection.

Readable Values
> A channel bank can report the status and uptime of each line and of the upstream connection.

2.13 IP Router

An *IP router* is the fundamental building block used to combine multiple networks into an internet. Each router interconnects multiple (possibly heterogeneous) networks and forwards IP packets among them.

Purpose
> Connect two or more networks to form an internet.

Structure
> A stand-alone device that is managed independently.

Notes
> We use the term *interface* to refer to the hardware in a router that connects to a given network; a router contains multiple interfaces, and forwards datagrams among them.

Configurable Parameters
> Each interface can be assigned a 32-bit IP address and a 32-bit address mask; an interface can be enabled or disabled; routes can be installed; specific routing protocols can be configured; and packet counters can be reset.

Readable Values

The number of interfaces on the router, the current status of each interface, the IP address and address mask assigned to an interface, a count of packets sent and received, and a count of IP packets sent and received.

2.14 Firewall

A security *firewall* is typically placed between the global Internet and an organization's internal networks to prevent unauthorized communication.

Purpose

Keep an organization's network secure by filtering datagrams according to a set of rules.

Structure

Usually implemented by a router, either by software running on the router's CPU or by hardware such as a separate printed circuit card installed in the router.

Notes

Modern firewalls are *stateful* which means the firewall records outgoing connections and automatically accepts packets that are replies for existing connections.

Configurable Parameters

A manager must establish a set of rules that specify exactly which packets to allow and which to deny. A manager can also reset packet counters, and may be able to temporarily disable packet transfer.

Readable Values

The set of filtering rules currently in place, counts of incoming and outgoing packets, and counts of packets that the firewall has rejected in each direction.

2.15 DNS Server

Although most servers for the *Domain Name System* run unchanged for weeks or months at a time, initial configurations must be created, and the configuration must be changed when new computers are added or existing computers are moved.

Purpose

Given a name for a computer, map the name into an IP address.

Structure

Each DNS server operates as an independent entity.

Notes

Each entry in a DNS server (known as a *resource record*) includes a *Time-To-Live* (*TTL*) value that specifies how long the entry can be used.

Configurable Parameters

The address of a server for recursive requests and the set of resource records for the server; each resource record includes a name, a type (e.g., type A specifies the value is an IP address), a value, and a TTL.

Readable Values

A manager can retrieve a specific resource record or all resource records in the server.

2.16 DHCP Server

Like a DNS server, a server for the *Dynamic Host Configuration Protocol (DHCP)* can operate for extended periods without being reconfigured. The configuration is only changed when IP subnet addresses are reassigned.

Purpose

Provide IP addresses and other information needed for communication to a host automatically (usually when the host boots).

Structure

A DHCP server can run in a stand-alone computer or in a router; it is managed as an independent entity.

Notes

A single DHCP server can be configured to hand out addresses on multiple IP subnets; routers can forward requests from hosts on remote networks to the server and can forward responses from the server back to the host. A server is said to *lease* an address to a host; the server specifies a maximum time for the lease, and can choose to allow a host to renew the lease when the time expires.

Configurable Parameters

The set of subnets for which the server honors requests, the IP addresses that are available on each subnet, an address mask, lease time, whether a lease can be renewed, and other information to include in the response. Some servers allow the manager to specify parameters for individual host computers (e.g., to ensure that a specific computer always receives the same IP address).

Readable Values

The number of subnets currently active, the set of IP addresses and the address mask to use on each subnet, the lease times and renewal status for the addresses, additional information to be included in each response, and the addresses currently assigned on a subnet. The server may also provide a count of the requests that have arrived for each subnet.

2.17 Web Server

Perhaps the best-known Internet application, the World Wide Web accounts for a significant percentage of Internet traffic. Technically, a web server is a running process, but the networking industry uses the term *server* to refer to the hardware (e.g., a PC or a Sparc processor) used to run a server process.

Purpose
Provide copies of web pages for display by a browser.
Structure
In theory, a processor that runs a web server can also run other servers. In practice, few managers run multiple types of servers on a single hardware device — the low cost of hardware means that a processor can be dedicated to a server.
Notes
Also see *HTTP Load Balancer* below.
Configurable Parameters
A web server is configured to map the name in an HTTP request into the file name (i.e., path in the file system) where the item is stored. For HTTP requests that correspond to pages that are generated on demand, the name in the request must map onto a program that the server runs to generate the page (by convention, programs are designated with a name such as *cgi-bin*). The server may also be configured to authenticate a user or to use encryption to protect the confidentiality of specified pages. Finally, a manager can reset counters used to report statistics.
Readable Values
A web server stores statistics such as a count of requests received, a count of errors, and a count of data bytes transferred. It may also keep a log of activity.

2.18 HTTP Load Balancer

A load balancer is an essential component of a high-volume web site: the load balancer sits in front of a set of (identical) web servers, and divides incoming requests among the servers. Thus, if the site has N servers, each server handles approximately $1/N$ of the requests.

Purpose

Permit a web site to scale by dividing incoming HTTP requests among a set of servers.

Structure

Usually a stand-alone device that is managed independently.

Notes

Load balancers can communicate with servers using either Layer 2 or Layer 3 protocols; for Layer 3, the load balancer acts like a *Network Address Translator* (*NAT*) device.

Configurable Parameters

A manager can configure the number of servers as well as the address of each. Some load balancers also accept specifications that restrict certain requests to a given subset of servers (e.g., in case only a subset of the servers can generate pages dynamically). A manager can reset packet counters.

Readable Values

The current configuration can be read as well as counters that specify the number of packets sent and received, the number of requests processed, and the number of requests sent to each server.

2.19 Summary

Network management covers two broad categories: services and network elements. Services include applications (e.g., email), infrastructure (e.g., DNS), and provisioned services (e.g., assigning priority to voice traffic across an entire network).

A network element is a device that can be managed independent of other network devices. Element management requires a manager to control one element at a time. Although network elements are logically independent, the physical organization can be pertinent to element management because understanding physical organization can make control and failure diagnosis easier.

We reviewed several network elements and services, and examined examples of parameters that can be configured and values that a manager can extract from each. We conclude that network management includes a wide diversity of managed entities, each of which offers specific values that can be configured or interrogated.

Chapter Contents

3.1   Introduction, 25
3.2   What Is Network Management?, 25
3.3   The Scope Of Network Management, 26
3.4   Variety And Multi-Vendor Environments, 27
3.5   Element And Network Management Systems, 28
3.6   Scale And Complexity, 29
3.7   Types Of Networks, 31
3.8   Classification Of Devices, 31
3.9   FCAPS: The Industry Standard Definition, 32
3.10   The Motivation For Automation, 33
3.11   Why Automation Has Not Occurred, 33
3.12   Organization Of Management Software, 34
3.13   Summary, 36

3

The Network Management Problem

3.1 Introduction

The previous chapter describes the two broad categories of manageable entities: network services and network elements. The chapter gives examples of items from each category, and for each example, lists parameters that a manager can configure and examine.

This chapter continues the discussion by defining basic terminology and characterizing the network management problem. It describes networks that must be managed, and discusses the size and scope of networks and the complexity of the management task. Finally, it concludes by describing the need for automated network management systems. Later chapters expand the discussion by examining various aspects of network management in more detail.

3.2 What Is Network Management?

Perhaps the need for network management arises from the difficulty, imprecision, or complexity that is beyond the capability of automated systems. That is, we can frame a definition of network management that places emphasis on the need for human intervention by saying that network management is an activity that occurs in situations where automation cannot suffice because human judgement is required.

We can take a more optimistic approach, and argue that the need for network management arises merely from the unknown. While this book was being written, for example, an engineer opined to the author that network management is best described as *all the aspects of devising and operating a network that no one knows how to automate.* The engineer observed that once someone discovers a way to automate a management task, vendors incorporate the technology into their products, which means that the task ceases to fall into the purview of a network manager.

Unfortunately, network management covers such a broad range of networks and activities that no short definition can capture the task well. Thus, rather than give a short, precise definition of network management, we will begin with an intuitive idea and use a series of examples to explain and clarify the intuition. The intuition is straightforward:

> *Intuitively, network management encompasses tasks associated with planning, deploying, configuring, operating, monitoring, tuning, repairing, and changing computer networks.*

As we will see, our intuitive definition hides many details, and does not explain the nature or difficulty of the activities.

3.3 The Scope Of Network Management

Where does a network end? Although the question may seem nonsensical, it lies at the heart of network management because the answer defines the scope of management responsibility. That is, once we define the point at which a network ends, we know the boundary beyond which the network manager neither has authority nor control.

It may seem that the network ends with the last network system. However, it does not because end-user systems participate actively in networking. In fact, one of the fundamental principles of a TCP/IP Internet concerns the locus of intelligence:

> *In a TCP/IP Internet, the interior of the network is relatively simplistic; intelligence and application services are concentrated in end-user systems.*

A host computer runs protocol software that understands how to send and receive frames, how to use protocols such as ARP to resolve addresses, and how to use an IP routing table† to forward IP packets. More important, transport protocols (i.e., TCP and UDP) are processed in host computer systems rather than in the switches and routers that constitute the network. In fact, an IP router can forward IP packets without examining or understanding the transport protocols used.

---

†The terms *IP routing table* and *IP forwarding table* are synonymous throughout this text.

Of course, exceptions do exist. Some routers also run servers (e.g., a router might run a DHCP server). Furthermore, intermediate systems, such as NAT devices, parse and modify transport headers. However, the principle holds in the general case.

Having end-systems participate in networking means that network management must encompass such systems. Thus, a network manager may need to check connectivity to a host, configure and control servers running in host computers, and ensure that application programs and protocol software that run in host computers will not cause problems on the network. To summarize:

> *Because end-user systems actively participate in network protocols,*
> *effective network management must extend to such systems.*

The disappointing news is that even in the absence of a network, computer system management is not easy: although it has been studied longer than the problem of network management, the problem of how to manage computer systems effectively remains unsolved.

3.4 Variety And Multi-Vendor Environments

As Chapter 2 illustrates, network management encompasses a wide variety of hardware and services. The chapter also shows that elements and services offer a wide variety of configurable parameters that cross many layers of the protocol stack. The breadth and variety that are present in networks contribute to the overall difficulty of network management. On one hand, because each network is designed to meet the business needs of a specific organization, each represents a unique combination of hardware and software. More important, because the industry has not settled on a small set of network types, a management system must handle an arbitrary combination of hardware and services. On the other hand, because network design involves many choices, including the choice of vendors, it is likely that a given network will contain elements from multiple vendors. For example, consider a network that contains a combination of network elements and application services. Although application services usually run on conventional computer systems, networking equipment vendors do not sell conventional computers and computer vendors do not sell network elements such as switches or routers.

Some of the decisions an organization makes when creating a network can be summarized:

- The set of underlying technologies
- A vendor for each piece of hardware
- A set of services that will be offered
- A hardware platform for each service
- The physical and logical network topologies

The point is:

> *Because each network is designed to meet the needs of a given organ-
> ization and because an organization makes many choices when
> designing a network, a management system must accommodate arbi-
> trary combinations of hardware and services.*

3.5 Element And Network Management Systems

The network management systems offered by most equipment vendors focus on
managing a single network element at a time. That is, a vendor creates each network
element independently, provides the element with a management interface, and allows
customers to coordinate multiple elements. To precisely characterize such systems, we
use the term *Element Management System* (*EMS*), and reserve the more general term
Network Management System (*NMS*) to refer to a system that is capable of managing
and coordinating multiple network elements to make them work together consistently.

Why have vendors concentrated on Element Management Systems? There are
three reasons. First, as we will see, designing a network management system is a non-
trivial intellectual challenge; vendors have tried to design such systems, but have not
been extremely successful. Second, by restricting attention to a single network element,
a vendor can eliminate most of the complexity and concentrate on straightforward tasks
such as monitoring. Third, because networks often contain elements from multiple vendors, a network management system must accommodate other vendors' products and a
given vendor is unlikely to create a system that makes it easy to use competitors' products.

The situation can be summarized:

> *Instead of providing general-purpose Network Management Systems,
> equipment vendors offer Element Management Systems that each focus
> on management of an individual network element.*

Interestingly, the focus on individual network elements has resulted in a paradigm
throughout the industry: when selling a network element, vendors advertise and compare the features and capabilities of the element rather than advertising how the element
meshes with other elements to form a viable network system. In fact, many network
elements are created as self-contained devices rather than as components of a network
system.

3.6 Scale And Complexity

In addition to a variety of equipment and services, network management systems must contend with complexity that arises from large scale. Of course, not all networks are the same size†. Vendors recognize the differences, and design network elements that are appropriate for each size. For example, the smallest Ethernet hubs only accommodate four connections, and run all ports at the same speed. The largest Ethernet switches accommodate hundreds of connections, allow each port to negotiate a speed, and can be expanded by connecting multiple units together.

The smallest networks that correspond to those found in a residence or small business usually consist of one main network element plus wiring and a few supporting hardware items. For example, engineers use the term *SOHO* (*Small Office, Home Office*) to characterize network elements intended for a network with only a few computers. Thus, one might refer to an IP router intended for such an environment as a *SOHO router*.

Intermediate size networks can be found in a business, university, or government organization that has a single campus. For example, at one university, which has approximately 36,000 undergraduate students, the IT organization manages a network that includes classrooms, administrative and faculty offices, and residence halls. Figure 3.1 gives statistics about the university network that help characterize the size.

Quantity	Item
60,000	Registered IP addresses
350	IP Subnets
100	IP Routers
1300	Layer 2 switches (most are Ethernet)
2350	Wireless access points

Figure 3.1 Items in an example university campus network that are managed by the university's IT staff. Additional facilities in departments such as Computer Science are managed independently.

Although exceptions exist, organizations with a single site generally have network sizes that range up to the following:

500	IP Subnets
200	IP Routers
1200	Layer 2 switches
3000	Wireless access points

Companies with multiple sites usually have much larger networks than companies with one site. For example, the network in one multi-national corporation includes:

---

†Typical provider networks are large, but have a relative uniform topology and homogeneous equipment; enterprise networks tend to be smaller, but include a large variety of equipment and services.

8000   IP Subnets
1200   IP Routers
1700   Layer 2 switches
4000   Wireless access points

Interestingly, the network in an ISP does not typically employ a large variety of equipment. For example, a network in an intermediate-size ISP (called a *Tier-2 ISP*) might include:

2000   IP Subnets
400   IP Routers
4000   Layer 2 switches

By comparison, the network in a small ISP (sometimes called a *Mom and Pop shop* or a *Tier 3 ISP*) might contain:

2   IP Subnets
2   IP Routers
2   Layer 2 switches
1   DSLAM

Large size increases the difficulty of network management for several reasons. First, large networks have a greater variety of equipment and services. Second, because a large network spans multiple physical sites, management involves multiple individuals. Third, interrelations among various parts of a large network mean that significantly more data must be considered when assessing performance or diagnosing problems. The point is:

In addition to other factors, larger size makes a network more difficult to manage.

3.7 Types Of Networks

To aid in discussions of management tasks, networks are often classified according to their main purpose. Four categories are typically used:

- Carrier
- Service provider
- Enterprise
- Residence/Consumer

Carrier Network. A *carrier* is a long-distance phone company that owns and operates a very high capacity network that is used to pass Internet traffic among other ISPs. Larger service providers connect to carriers; a carrier connects to other carriers at Internet *peering points.* Carrier networks use data connections with very high throughput, and require equipment that can switch the most packets per second.

Service Provider Network. An *Internet Service Provider* (*ISP*) network is designed to provide transit between individual customers' networks and the Internet. A small ISP connects to a larger ISP; a large ISP connects to a carrier. Service provider networks focus on *aggregation* — data from many subscribers is multiplexed onto a single high-capacity connection that leads toward the center of the Internet.

Enterprise Network. An *enterprise network* is designed to interconnect host computer systems within an organization and to provide those systems with access to the Internet. Unlike traffic on a provider network, most traffic on an enterprise network arises from a computer within the organization (e.g., a desktop computer in an office), and is destined to a computer within the organization (e.g., a server in the data center). Thus, instead of focusing on aggregation, an enterprise network is designed to permit multiple internal conversations to proceed at the same time.

Residence/Consumer Network. A *residential network* consists of one or two computers in a home that connect through a router to an ISP, typically using DSL or cable modem technology.

3.8 Classification Of Devices

In addition to using the above terminology to characterize networks, managers sometimes classify network elements and related hardware as belonging to one of three basic types:

- Core
- Edge
- Access

Although it can be used with arbitrary hardware devices, the terminology is usually applied to IP routers.

A *core router* is designed to operate in the ''center'' of the Internet. That is, a core router is designed for use by a carrier or a large ISP. To handle a high traffic load, a core device operates at high speed, and is optimized to forward traffic as quickly as possible. To achieve the highest possible speed, a core device does not inspect packet contents, check for authorization, or report detailed statistics about traffic. Thus, a network must be designed to check packets before the packets arrive at a core device.

An *edge router* operates in the fringe areas of the Internet, far from the core. Typically, managers interpret *edge* as an enterprise or a residence. An enterprise might use an edge router in its data center to connect multiple subnets, or might use an edge router to connect departments or floors of a building. Edge routers usually offer more functionality, but have lower speed than core routers. For example, an edge router might include a blade that provides the encryption and decryption needed by a VPN connection.

An *access router* provides the connection between the edge and the core. Access routers are typically found in ISPs, and are used to connect the ISP's customers to the rest of the Internet. Access routers often handle tasks such as authentication, intrusion detection, and accounting. Thus, an access router unusually has lower overall throughput than a core router. However, an ISP can use multiple access routers to connect to customers, and then aggregate traffic from the access routers to a smaller set of (possibly one) core routers.

3.9 FCAPS: The Industry Standard Definition

Network management vendors often use the acronym *FCAPS* when discussing network management. The acronym, which is derived from recommendation *M.3400* published by the *International Telecommunications Union (ITU)*†, is expanded into a list of all aspects of network management as Figure 3.2 shows.

Level	Meaning
F	Fault detection and correction
C	Configuration and operation
A	Accounting and billing
P	Performance assessment and optimization
S	Security assurance and protection

Figure 3.2 Items in the FCAPS model of network management and the meaning of each.

---

†The ITU, a standards body that is structured as a consortium of telecommunications companies, has published an entire series of standards that specify how a *Telecommunications Management Network (TMN)* should be configured and operated.

The remaining chapters in this part of the text expand and explain each of the items in the FCAPS model.

3.10 The Motivation For Automation

The discussion above shows that network management is a broad topic that involves many aspects and a myriad of details. One would expect, however, that much of the work can be automated, making it possible to manage large networks without requiring manual intervention. Indeed, it seems that network management is an ideal candidate for automation because the underlying network elements themselves are digital devices inherently capable of computation and communication. Furthermore, because engineers who build network elements are familiar with automated control systems and already design control mechanisms into products, it should be trivial to add the facilities for automated network management.

In addition to the apparent ease of adding automated network management to existing products, a strong economic motivation exists. From a network operator's point of view, current network management is labor-intensive, requires in-house expertise, and because humans are involved, is prone to errors and slow. Human error has become extremely important because the complexity of management tasks continues to increase. For example, consider a firewall configuration that includes hundreds of individual rules. In addition to errors that arise from mistyping configurations, errors can occur because the rule set is too large for a human to remember and understand. Humans also tend to introduce consistency errors — when a large set of devices is configured manually, chances are high that the configurations will be inconsistent. Unfortunately, inconsistencies can remain hidden, and can be difficult to find when problems occur. Because network downtime incurs economic loss, problems that arise from human error are especially important.

In addition to eliminating inconsistencies, automation can reduce economic impact by reducing the downtime needed for upgrades and other changes. In some cases, automated systems can make changes on-the-fly. For example, an intrusion detection system can automatically modify firewall rules to stop a problem that is in progress. Finally, from a networking vendor's point of view, automated network management will increase sales because automation will allow customers to create larger, more complex networks.

3.11 Why Automation Has Not Occurred

Given the strong economic motivation and necessary mechanisms in place to make implementation straightforward, why hasn't an automated network management system been created? As we will see in Part 2 of the text, both the networking industry and the open source community have produced tools that automate some aspects of network management. However, the overall goal of a comprehensive automated system has remained elusive. The reason is fundamental: a lack of abstractions and principles.

Abstractions are needed that allow us to master the complexity without sacrificing understanding. That is, the key does not merely arise from automating the way humans deal with current network elements. Instead, we need new paradigms that permit managers to specify policies and use an automated system to implement the policies.

As an example of why new paradigms are needed, consider configuring firewalls for a site that has multiple Internet connections. Currently a manager must manually configure the firewall rules in each of the routers that has an Internet connection. It may seem that we can automate the task by having the manager specify the rules, give a list of routers, and ask the network management system to install the rules in each of the routers on the list. Although it alleviates some of the manual effort and is less prone to error than having a human enter rules multiple times, having a manager specify rules and specific routers means the interface is low-level. A more efficient approach has the network management system understand where external connections occur, allows a manager to state policies for external communication, and arranges for the network management system to translate policies into rules and install them automatically.

To summarize:

> *Although tools have been devised that automate some aspects of network management, a comprehensive, automated network management system will not be possible until we devise new and better abstractions for network management.*

3.12 Organization Of Management Software

Will we ever be able to create a single, fixed network management system that accepts high-level policy statements and handles all tasks needed to implement arbitrary policies? Many managers argue that such a system is impossible: as networks evolve, requirements change. A fixed system will never be sufficient, they argue, because new types of policies will be needed. For example, a network management system in the 1980's might have included some knowledge of security, but network security has changed dramatically in the succeeding years. Thus, an automated network management system must be able to accommodate new types of policies as well as new policies.

To allow an automated system to remain flexible, a two-level approach has been proposed: a low-level platform that offers a programmable interface and a level of software that uses the low-level platform to translate policies into actions. Figure 3.3 illustrates the concept:

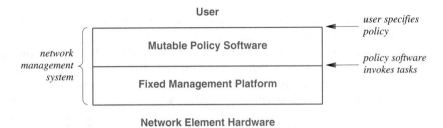

Figure 3.3 The logical organization of a two-level automated network
management system in which the underlying platform supports a
programmable interface and a second level of software implements policy.

As the figure indicates, only the lowest level of the automated system is fixed.
The second layer, which implements policy, can be adapted as new types of policies
arise.

To make the approach flexible, the second level can be structured as a set of
modules that each handle one type of policy. When a manager makes a request, a user
interface directs the request to the appropriate policy module. Flexibility arises because
implementation of a new type of policy can be handled without requiring the underlying
system to change: new policy modules can be added and existing policy modules can be
changed as needed. Figure 3.4 illustrates the structure.

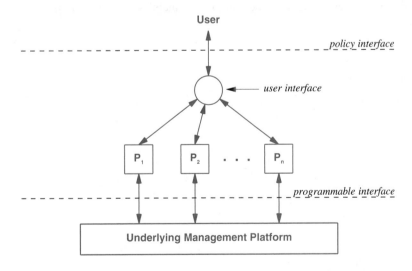

Figure 3.4 A detailed view of the two-level structure for an automated network management system. Policy modules can be changed, and
new policy modules can be added at any time.

It has been pointed out that the two-level approach in Figure 3.4 is analogous to that of an operating system. An operating system provides a fixed kernel that supplies basic functions, and application software uses the operating system to implement more complex functionality. As a further analogy, we can observe that network management systems are in approximately the same state as operating systems were in the early 1960s. Coherent, practical operating systems only became possible after computer scientists devised a new set of abstractions such as processes, files, and directories. In later chapters, we will understand that although the ideas described above provide an overall framework, before coherent, practical network management systems can be built, an analogous set of abstractions must be defined.

3.13 Summary

The problem of network management is difficult for several reasons. In addition to a wide variety of network elements and services with a myriad of parameters, each network is unique and there are few general patterns. Many networks are large, and networks needed by carriers, service providers, and enterprises differ in purpose and functionality. Vendors have concentrated on Element Management Systems.

Automated network management is desirable, and some general properties of an automated system are understood. In particular, to keep an automated system flexible and accommodate future needs, a two-level structure can be used in which a fixed underlying system provides a programmable interface to allow a second level of software to implement policies. However, before an effective and practical automated network management system can be built, new principles and abstractions are needed.

Chapter Contents

4.1   Introduction, 39
4.2   Intuition For Configuration, 39
4.3   Configuration And Protocol Layering, 40
4.4   Dependencies Among Configuration Parameters, 43
4.5   Seeking A More Precise Definition Of Configuration, 44
4.6   Configuration And Temporal Consequences, 44
4.7   Configuration And Global Consistency, 45
4.8   Global State And Practical Systems, 46
4.9   Configuration And Default Values, 46
4.10   Partial State, Automatic Update, And Recovery, 47
4.11   Interface Paradigm And Incremental Configuration, 48
4.12   Commit And Rollback During Configuration, 49
4.13   Automated Rollback And Timeout, 50
4.14   Snapshot, Configuration, And Partial State, 50
4.15   Separation Of Setup And Activation, 51
4.16   Configuring Multiple Network Elements, 52
4.17   Summary, 52

4

Configuration And Operation

4.1 Introduction

Previous chapters introduce terminology and concepts from network management systems, and give examples of network scale. Chapter 2 lists example network elements along with configuration parameters for each, and Chapter 3 argues that the variety of network elements and services contributes to the difficulty of network management. Finally, Chapter 3 introduces the FCAPS model that divides management tasks into five main areas.

This chapter continues the discussion by focusing on one of the most important aspects of FCAPS in more detail: configuration. The chapter explains why an apparently straightforward task such as configuration is complex, and discusses some of the consequences for network management systems. Succeeding chapters each examine one other aspect of the FCAPS model.

4.2 Intuition For Configuration

Because personal computer operating systems and most consumer application software allow a user to configure operations, most computer users have an intuitive understanding of configuration. For example, the operating system on a typical laptop computer allows a user to configure a timeout after which the laptop hibernates to save the battery (e.g., turns off the screen), and a typical browser allows a user to configure the URL of a web page that will be used whenever the user clicks the *Home* button. Configuration of devices and services in a computer network is similar.

We can characterize configuration by stating the general properties listed in Figure 4.1.

1. Configuration is a step that occurs (i.e., must be performed) before a computer system or application program is used.

2. Configuration requires a user (i.e., manager) to make a set of choices that will control the operation of a computer system or the execution of software.

3. Although a configuration can be changed, modifications may require the underlying system to be paused, or shut down and restarted.

4. The interface used for configuration can differ entirely from the interface used when the system runs. In a network, the running system that processes packets may not have a user interface.

Figure 4.1 General properties associated with configuration.

4.3 Configuration And Protocol Layering

Chapter 2 contains examples of network elements and services along with examples of specific configuration parameters. Although the example parameters illustrate the wide variety of configurable items, they do not capture the important conceptual abstractions that underlie configuration. That is, because configuration parameters are merely the mechanism used to achieve a desired result, understanding configuration requires us to understand the ultimate goal. The next sections give examples of the conceptual relationship between configurable items in network elements, layers of a protocol stack, and results that the parameters are used to achieve.

4.3.1 Topology And Layer 2

We said that network elements operating at Layer 2 have relatively few configurable parameters because much of Layer 2 can be handled automatically. However, one key idea emerges when we consider a configurable VLAN switch: configuration can be used to create a topology.

In essence, VLAN configuration is a logical replacement for Layer 1 wiring — instead of creating a topology from a set of basic switches with wiring used to attach a computer to a specific switch, a manager wires all computers to a large VLAN switch and configures the switch to act like a set of separate switches. The chief advantage of using configuration is ease of change: moving a computer from one VLAN to another can be accomplished with a few keystrokes. We will understand why the notion of a configurable topology is important later. The point is:

Creating a set of VLANs and configuring a switch to attach each port to a specific VLAN is equivalent to creating a network topology.

4.3.2 Logical Subnets And Layer 3

Configuration of IP addresses and address masks at Layer 3 is only a detail — the ultimate goal consists of establishing an IP subnet addressing scheme that is correct and makes forwarding efficient. In particular, when configuring IP addresses and address masks in routers, a manager must guarantee that each network is assigned a unique address prefix (and each host is assigned a unique suffix). The important point is:

IP address configuration, which is used to guarantee that each network is assigned a unique prefix, assumes that networks have been defined.

We will understand the significance of the assumption later in the chapter.

Although most networks configure a prefix for each network manually, DHCP protocol software can be used to assign an address to each host automatically. Despite the use of DHCP, manual prefix configuration is needed before assignment because the prefix assigned to a network appears in each address assigned to a host on the network. A DHCP server must itself be configured to know the network prefix before the server can assign addresses to hosts on a network. Thus, we can view DHCP as only assigning host suffixes automatically; the prefix in each assigned address is the prefix that was configured for the network.

4.3.3 Access And Layer 4

Many of the parameters associated with Layer 4 of the protocol stack are assigned automatically. For example, when a client, such as a web browser, contacts a server, the TCP port number that the client uses is assigned automatically by the TCP protocol software that runs in the operating system on the client computer. In addition, network elements such as NAT boxes or load balancers use information found in the Layer 4 protocol headers of packets to build a cache of connections. Thus, a network manager does not usually configure connection information in a NAT device.

Despite automated configuration of items on the forwarding path, some manual configuration of Layer 4 is still needed. Typically, manual configuration focuses on the Layer 4 control path rather than on the data path. That is, configuration information specifies what a system is permitted or is prohibited from doing.

As an example of Layer 4 configuration, consider the access rules configured into a firewall. A typical rule specifies a combination of items such as IP source and destination addresses, a transport protocol type (e.g., TCP), and source and destination protocol port numbers that are to be allowed or denied (i.e., for which packets are permitted to pass or are dropped). Similarly, a NAT system often allows a manager to preconfigure mappings for specific combinations of addresses and protocol port numbers.

The point is:

> *Although the port numbers that Layer 4 protocols use for communication are either selected by server applications or assigned to clients automatically, some network systems allow managers to configure access specifications that involve Layer 4 parameters.*

4.3.4 Applications And Layer 5 (or Layer 7)

Application programs operate at either Layer 5 or 7, depending on whether one uses the 5-layer model that was designed to describe TCP/IP protocols or the less accurate OSI model. In any case, the point is the same: a manager can configure specific applications to operate on specific computers.

As an example, consider the naming service provided by the Domain Name System (DNS). There are two aspects related to configuration of DNS:

- Configuration of client and server software that uses DNS to enable communication
- Configuration of DNS server(s) with specific content

Under the first item, a manager must choose a computer(s) that will run a DNS server, configure the server software to begin running automatically when the computer boots, and configure each server to know the addresses of servers for the parent zone and child zones. In addition, a manager must arrange for other computers in the network to know which computer provides a DNS server (i.e., which computer to contact when name resolution is needed). In cases where DHCP is used to supply the address of a DNS server at boot time, instead of configuring individual computers, the manager merely needs to configure the DHCP server to distribute the correct host addresses.

Under the second item, a manager must supply data for a DNS server to distribute. In particular, a manager must load each DNS server with a set of resource records that specify name bindings, where each name binding consists of a pair *(name, address)*. We can summarize:

In addition to configuring communication among DNS servers and DNS clients, a manager must configure a set of name-to-address bindings.

4.4 Dependencies Among Configuration Parameters

It may seem that the examples in the previous sections each refer to conceptually independent items at one layer of the protocol stack. However, the examples were chosen to illustrate an important point:

Although the management interfaces in network elements allow a manager to configure parameters independently, many parameters are semantically related.

The semantic relationships among parameters complicate configuration. In particular, dependencies among parameters introduce an implicit ordering among choices.

As an example, consider the relationship between configuration of IP subnets at Layer 3 and configuration of topology at Layer 2. We said that a manager must assign a unique IP prefix to each network. For a multi-access broadcast network (e.g., Ethernet), the Internet Protocol relies on ARP to resolve the IP addresses of a next hop to the corresponding MAC address. Because ARP uses broadcast, the definition of *network* is exactly the same as a *broadcast domain*. We also saw that for a network using a Layer 2 switch, the broadcast domain for a given computer corresponds to the set of computers that attach to the same VLAN. Furthermore, a manager can configure an arbitrary port on a switch to be on an arbitrary VLAN. As a result, a semantic dependency exists between topology configuration and subnet configuration: a topology must be configured at Layer 2 before IP prefixes can be assigned at Layer 3.

Although network elements permit configuration parameters to be changed in arbitrary ways, dependencies mean that changing one parameter without changing others can cause errors. For example, if a manager moves a switch port from one VLAN to another without also changing the IP address assigned to the computer, the IP prefix will be incorrect. Similarly, if a manager reconfigures the IP address of a computer without changing the corresponding entry in the DNS database, the DNS server will return an incorrect mapping. We can summarize:

> *Although network elements permit a manager to change arbitrary*
> *configuration parameters, semantic dependencies among parameters*
> *mean that changing a single item without changing dependent items,*
> *possibly at other layers of the protocol stack, can result in a confi-*
> *guration that is globally invalid.*

4.5 Seeking A More Precise Definition Of Configuration

It may seem that a precise, mathematical definition of configuration is straightforward. For example, in our original list of properties in Figure 4.1, property 2 states that a manager must make a set of choices. Mathematically, the manager must specify a binding from a set of values to a set of configurable items. To be more precise, we might specify that a network management system defines a finite (usually small) set of items, and a manager must specify a value for each. To further capture our intuition about configuration, we can specify that the set of possible values for each item is finite and small. In fact, for many items, the network management system explicitly lists all possible choices from which a manager can select (e.g., when configuring a network interface state, the system allows a manager to select *up* or *down*).

It may seem that configuration represents a straightforward mathematical binding:

$$\alpha \rightarrow \beta$$

where β is a K-tuple of items called *variables* that each have a small, finite range of possible values, and α is a K-tuple of values to be bound to the variables. Furthermore, to be *valid*, a binding must be such that the value α_i is in the range of values for variable β_i.

As we have seen, however, semantic dependencies among the set of configuration parameters means that not all combinatorial combinations of values are allowed in practice. The above definition of validity is weak. As we will see in the next section, a definition of configuration also needs to accommodate temporal considerations.

4.6 Configuration And Temporal Consequences

If the notion of binding values to parameters does not adequately capture the concept of network configuration, what does? To understand the problem, consider how a network operates. In general, a manager connects equipment, configures each network element, and then enables network operation. Some configuration parameters merely specify initial conditions that can change once the network becomes operational, and other configuration parameters control how the network operates once packets begin to flow. For example, the initial set of routes configured into routers specify the paths packets will take when a network begins operating. However, the choice of whether to configure a routing update protocol (e.g., RIP or OSPF) determines whether a network will be able to detect and route around link failures.

Because it requires a network manager to imagine how a network will operate in the future, the notion of changes over time complicates configuration. In fact, a manager may need to work backward by envisioning a running network and then imagining a series of steps by which the network reaches the running condition. To envision such steps, a manager must understand how each configuration choice affects the network over time, and must choose values that generate initial conditions that will eventually produce the desired operation. That is, a manager must think about the temporal consequences of each configuration choice.

4.7 Configuration And Global Consistency

In addition to thinking about temporal changes, a network manager must understand how configuration choices interact. That is, a manager must envision the *global state* of the network rather than each individual configuration parameter. In other words, a manager must understand how the values stored in each network element collectively ensure the network achieves desired properties. For example, consider forwarding. To provide Internet connectivity to all hosts, a manager cannot configure one router in isolation, but instead must consider the forwarding state that spans the entire set of routers. Although a manager configures each network element independently, the routes must be globally consistent to guarantee the property that all hosts can reach the Internet.

> *The fundamental goal that a network manager must consider when choosing a configuration is the desired global state of the network; configuration is merely a mechanism that allows one to specify details of an initial state and control changes to the state as time proceeds.*

An important observation regarding state is that multiple valid states can exist. In the example above, for instance, it may be possible to have multiple route configurations which each guarantee that any host can reach the Internet. Thus, a manager cannot know whether a given network element has correct forwarding information without considering the global network state.

> *Because multiple network states can be valid, the validity of the configuration on a single network element can only be assessed relative to the configuration of other network elements.*

4.8 Global State And Practical Systems

As we will see later, the importance of consistency across an entire network influences the design of automated management systems. For now, it is sufficient to understand a key idea: although global state is an essential concept, building software to capture and manipulate global state is impractical. That is, except for trivially small, idle networks, we cannot expect to record the complete state of a network.

Recording global state is impractical for three reasons. First, because a network contains multiple network elements and because each network element is complex, an extraordinary amount of data is needed to represent the entire state of a network. Second, because network state changes over time, capturing global state requires simultaneously capturing state information from all network elements. Third, in addition to relatively static values, global state includes packet queues, which change continuously.

With respect to the large size, one might conclude that forwarding tables constitute the bulk of the state information. However, in addition to forwarding information, network elements contain protocol software, an operating system, device drivers, control and management software, firmware, and other data in memory. Thus, even if we ignore the underlying hardware, a single network element includes an immense amount of state.

The need for simultaneous state capture should be obvious: without a temporal snapshot, the state can be inconsistent. For example, imagine capturing the forwarding tables in routers as routes are changing. If the tables in some elements are captured before the change and the tables in others are captured after the change, the saved data will not represent a valid global state of the network.

Although packets in the network form part of the state, a more significant problem arises from the management data itself: as we will learn in a later chapter, network management systems use the managed network to communicate with network elements. That is, management data flows through the same wires and network elements as user data. Thus, to record the state of multiple network elements requires the transmission of packets (i.e., one cannot "freeze" a network, record the state, and restart the network once the state has been captured).

4.9 Configuration And Default Values

What is the relationship between the configuration a manager specifies for a network element and the initial state of an element? It might seem that except for specifying basic software (e.g., the operating system to run), a manager must completely specify the initial state of an element. In practice, however, only a handful of parameters are needed before a typical network element can function, far fewer parameters than are needed to specify an initial state for the element.

Are configuration parameters merely abbreviations that the management interface expands to cover many items? No. The brevity arises from network vendors' desire to make network configuration as easy as possible. Vendors follow an approach that uses *default* values:

> *Instead of requiring a manager to specify values for all parameters, a management interface begins with a set of default values and allows the manager to override specific values.*

Because it eliminates the opportunity for error, an interface that uses defaults is especially helpful for devices that are managed directly by a human. Ironically, implicit defaults mean that automated software that manages a network element must have knowledge of how the element works.

4.10 Partial State, Automatic Update, And Recovery

We said that although a configuration specifies some of the items in the initial state of a network element, changes to the state occur as the element operates. For example, ARP adds entries to a cache, routing update protocols change routes, and a stateful firewall updates filter rules. Interestingly, the notion of dynamic state change has an important implication:

> *Because the state of a network element or service can change dynamically as the network operates, configuration information alone does not specify network state.*

The ideas that network element state varies over time and that state can depend on traffic in the network are especially important when one considers failure recovery. Reloading a configuration and restarting a network element can only restore partial state information — changes that occur between the time a device is started and the time a failure occurs cannot be recovered.

To further complicate the situation, the hardware in some network elements allows the element to store some or all state information in nonvolatile memory. As a trivial example, consider a VLAN switch that stores port status information in nonvolatile memory, but keeps other configuration data in volatile memory. That is, when a manager configures a port to be *enabled* or *disabled*, the hardware permanently stores the setting so it can be recovered when the hardware reboots. Power cycling such a device nullifies the assignment of ports to VLANs, but allows individual port status to survive unchanged.

> *A network element can use nonvolatile memory to allow some or all state information to survive a power failure.*

4.11 Interface Paradigm And Incremental Configuration

Network elements that use a command-line interface typically allow a manager to enter a series of configuration commands that each make one small change†. That is, each command adds a small *incremental change* to the configuration. To achieve a desired effect, a manager who is using an incremental interface may need to apply multiple commands (e.g., change a value in the forwarding table to use a specific interface and enable the interface). In such cases, encountering an error can complicate the interaction — if an error prevents further progress, a manager may need to undo previous commands in the series.

To help managers master the complexity, some management interfaces allow a series of commands to be viewed as an *atomic unit*. That is, all commands in the set should be applied or none of them should be applied. We use the term *transaction* to describe a set of operations that are to be treated atomically. In cases where a command-line interface offers incremental commands that each perform one small step, a transaction can include a series of many commands. In cases where a command-line interface offers complex commands that each perform many steps, a transaction can consist of a single command. For example, suppose the management interface on a router offers a single command that enables all interfaces. If the command runs as a transaction and a hardware problem prevents one of the interfaces from being enabled, the command reports the error without enabling any of the interfaces. The reasons a transaction interface is important relate to human interaction:

> *Because it relieves a manager from responsibility for undoing partial operations, a management interface that groups operations into transactions is both easy to use and less prone to human error.*

In addition to interfaces that automatically decide how to group commands into transactions, it is possible for an interface to allow a manager to define transactions dynamically. For example, an interface might use braces to denote a transaction as Figure 4.2 illustrates.

It should be obvious that allowing a manager to define the scope of a transaction provides much more flexibility than an interface in which the contents of transactions are predetermined. The downside of permitting managers to specify the boundary of atomicity lies in arbitrary scope: the system must be able to restore the original state if an error occurs while the transaction is being executed.

---

†Some elements use an alternative paradigm in which a manager makes changes to a copy of a configuration, and then loads the entire copy into an element.

transaction *name* {
> *command₁*

> *command₂*

> . . .

> *command*ₙ
} ← *end of transaction*

Figure 4.2 An example syntax that allows a manager to define a transaction that contains multiple commands. Once a definition has been created, the transaction can be invoked by entering the transaction name.

To understand the potential problem, assume a manager has enclosed commands in a transaction that each modify a large data structure (e.g., an ARP cache or a forwarding table). The system must store information needed to recreate the original data structures in case a command in the transaction fails. However, storing a copy of data items requires extra memory. The point is:

Although an interface that allows managers to define transactions is more powerful than an interface in which the definition of transactions is fixed, permitting a manager to define the scope of atomicity means the system must have resources sufficient to back out of arbitrary changes.

Interestingly, network elements differ in the way they implement configuration changes: some elements apply each change immediately, and others require a reboot before a change takes effect. In either case, the consequences of an error can be catastrophic: the element can become unreachable, either immediately or after a reboot. Section 4.13 considers how an automated rollback mechanism can help recover after a catastrophic configuration error.

4.12 Commit And Rollback During Configuration

As an alternative to an interface that defines transactions, some element management systems provide a manager with manual mechanisms for undoing partial configurations. There are two main types:

- Snapshot rollback
- Incremental rollback

The easiest mechanism to understand involves the use of a *snapshot rollback*. Before making configuration changes, a manager takes a snapshot of the configuration (i.e., a snapshot that captures the current state of the network element). The manager then proceeds to enter commands that make changes to the network element. The changes can be extensive (i.e., they can make arbitrary modifications to the network element). Because each command takes effect immediately, a manager can test the system at any time to verify whether the change has produced the desired result. If a manager encounters a problem or decides to forgo any change, the manager instructs the system to use the snapshot to *rollback* the system to its previous state.

The second manual mechanism that element management systems use consists of *incremental rollback*. In essence, an incremental rollback provides a manager with the ability to undo the previous command or transaction. The most significant limit of incremental rollback arises from the number of previous operations that can be rolled back. A system that allows only one previous operation to be undone is less useful than a system that allows an arbitrary number of previous operations to be undone. However, permitting arbitrary rollback requires the system to store information about each previous operation.

4.13 Automated Rollback And Timeout

The concept of rollback can be extended to include a *timeout mechanism*: when a manager initiates a transaction, the system starts a timer. If the transaction fails or does not complete before the timer expires, the system automatically informs the manager that the transaction cannot be completed, and invokes the rollback mechanism to restore the system. Automated rollback is helpful in situations where a transaction requires such a long time to execute that a manager becomes distracted or in situations where an error in the configuration prevents further communication between the element and the manager.

At least one vendor includes automated rollback as part of their management interface. In the vendor's system, if a transaction does not complete within N seconds (default is 75 seconds), the transaction is automatically rolled back.

4.14 Snapshot, Configuration, And Partial State

How much information must be stored for rollback? The answer depends on whether the system stores a copy of all state or merely enough information to restore the state. If a command has an inverse, the inverse command requires much less space than a complete system snapshot. Thus, if a manager moves a switch port from VLAN i to VLAN j, the system can store a rollback command that moves the port from VLAN j to VLAN i. In cases where a management command has no inverse, it may be necessary to store a snapshot of a data structure or of the complete system. For example, when the operating system in a network element is reloaded, so much of the state changes that it is usually easier to restore a snapshot.

The existence of inverse commands determines whether the snapshot or incremental approaches to rollback require more space. Consider a system that permits incremental rollback of N commands. If each command has an inverse, the space taken to store incremental rollback information is Nc, where c is the space required to store one command. If none of the commands has an inverse, however, the system requires space of NS, where S is the size of a complete snapshot. Thus, if commands do not have an inverse, incremental rollback can take significantly more space than requiring a manager to save a snapshot manually.

We can generalize the above discussion: the amount of space required to store a snapshot depends on whether the system stores internal data values or the information needed to recreate the data values. In fact, it may seem that space can be minimized by storing an entire configuration rather than data values.

Some network elements do indeed allow a manager to download a complete configuration in one step rather than enter one piece of configuration at a time. However, we must remember that although it handles many items, configuration information only specifies part of the state information. Thus, it is important to differentiate between rolling back to a previous state and recreating state from partial information.

> *Because configuration files for complex network elements such as routers do not capture all relevant information, rolling back to a previous state cannot be achieved merely by reloading all configuration information.*

4.15 Separation Of Setup And Activation

Some interfaces use an alternative paradigm to avoid problems that arise as configuration changes occur. Instead of applying incremental changes, the interface separates configuration into two complete steps that are known as *setup* and *activation*.

During the setup phase, a manager downloads a set of configuration requests, which an element checks for consistency and correctness without applying the changes. If the requests fail the correctness test, a manager must start again by downloading a revised set of requests. Thus, a manager iterates through revisions until the set of requests satisfies the target element.

Once an element has approved a set of requests, the element allows a manager to *activate* the changes. Because an element can preprocess requests and generate appropriate internal data structures, activation can occur rapidly. In particular, it can be possible for an element that uses activation to install a new configuration without a reboot.

4.16 Configuring Multiple Network Elements

So far, we have concentrated on configuration of a single network element. As we will see later, configuration of services that cross multiple network elements is significantly more complex. For example, an MPLS tunnel can span many routers. Similarly, coordination may be needed between the configuration of network elements and the configuration of services such as DHCP. As a consequence, complex configuration requires that transactions and rollback be coordinated across multiple platforms.

There are two general approaches: *recursive*, in which each element makes a request of another until the transaction can be satisfied, and *iterative*, in which a management system contacts each of the network elements that are needed for a transaction. The recursive approach allows dependencies to be hidden, but can lead to circularity and deadlock. The iterative approach eliminates circularities, but requires the management system to understand all dependencies and interact with each network element.

4.17 Summary

Configuration is one of the most important and difficult aspects of network management. Although configuration occurs at each layer of the protocol stack, semantic dependencies occur among configured items.

Because it specifies initial state and controls operation, configuration is related to the global state of a network. Although many items are configured, the state of a network element can change as the network operates. Furthermore, the validity of a network element's configuration can only be assessed with respect to the global configuration of the network.

A management interface on a network element can permit incremental changes to a configuration; transactions are used to group changes into atomic units. An interface can support snapshot rollback or incremental rollback; the size of saved information for rollback depends on whether each configuration command has an inverse and the number of previous commands that can be undone.

Configuration of services across multiple network elements is significantly more difficult than configuration of a single network element. In a recursive approach, control passes from element to element; in an iterative approach, a manager configures one element at a time.

Chapter Contents

5.1   Introduction, 55

5.2   Network Faults, 55

5.3   Trouble Reports, Symptoms, And Causes, 56

5.4   Troubleshooting And Diagnostics, 56

5.5   Monitoring, 57

5.6   Baselines, 58

5.7   Items That Can Be Monitored, 59

5.8   Alarms, Logs, And Polling, 59

5.9   Identifying The Cause Of A Fault, 60

5.10   Human Failure And Network Faults, 62

5.11   Protocol Layering And Faults, 62

5.12   Hidden Faults And Automatic Correction, 63

5.13   Anomaly Detection And Event Correlation, 64

5.14   Fault Prevention, 64

5.15   Summary, 65

5

Fault Detection And Correction

5.1 Introduction

Earlier chapters in this part of the text introduce the problem of network management and define the FCAPS model. The previous chapter examines a key aspect of FCAPS: configuration.

This chapter considers a second aspect of network management: fault detection and correction. The chapter defines the concept of a network fault, considers how faults occur, and discusses ways network managers detect and correct faults.

5.2 Network Faults

We use the term *network fault* loosely to refer to a wide range of conditions or problems that cause a network to operate incorrectly or to produce undesirable results. In the FCAPS model, faults apply broadly across communication and computational devices and services. Thus, a fault can occur on any type of hardware or software.

In the FCAPS definition, faults encompass problems with packet forwarding (e.g., failure to deliver packets to some destinations), problems with policy administration (e.g., admission of packets that should have been rejected), problems with servers (e.g., a crash), and problems with equipment (e.g., power failures and outages). In short, virtually any problem in the network is classified as a fault.

5.3 Trouble Reports, Symptoms, And Causes

A network manager can learn about a network fault through *trouble reports*. Users provide one source of trouble reports: when network applications fail to perform as expected, a user can send a report to the manager that identifies a problem.

There are two interesting features of trouble reports. First, many trouble reporting systems use the network to send a report from a user to the network manager. In some implementations, a user fills in a form on a web page which is then transmitted to the manager; in others, users send email. Second, a user only reports symptoms (e.g., an application that does not work as the user expects).

Each of the two features has consequences. Using the network to communicate trouble reports means that if a network fault is severe enough to prevent communication, no trouble reports will be received. Relying on users to fill out trouble reports means that the reports often contain ambiguous and confusing statements about symptoms. For example, if a user reports:

My email is not working.

It can mean that email delivery is slow, that a problem on the user's computer has prevented the computer from launching the email application, that the network is disconnected, or that email messages are being bounced back to the user without being delivered. Thus, a trouble report is only a clue — a manager must investigate the problem further to determine whether a network fault has occurred. We can summarize:

> *Because it only list symptoms, a user trouble report contains partial information about a problem; a network manager must translate statements about observed behavior into an underlying cause.*

5.4 Troubleshooting And Diagnostics

We use the term *troubleshooting* to refer to the process of finding the cause of a network problem. Because it can involve careful thought and analysis, troubleshooting is one of the most important network management activities in which humans engage. A manager uses reports of problems to synthesize a hypothesis about a possible cause, investigates to verify the source of the problem, and then effects a repair.

In general, no source of information is sufficient for troubleshooting — diagnosis requires a manager to use all clues available, including reports from equipment, user trouble reports, and diagnostic tools†. Furthermore, because reports of problems often point out general operational problems rather than detailed or specific faults, a manager must relate observed behavior to hardware and software components. Thus, the more a

---

†The second part of the text describes diagnostic tools.

manager knows about the physical and logical structure of the network, the easier it is for the manager to pinpoint the source or causes of a problem.

5.5 Monitoring

How can a manager know whether a network element is behaving correctly? One of the most effective approaches to troubleshooting uses *monitoring*. That is, a manager arranges to measure network elements and network traffic. Usually, network monitoring is performed by an automated software system that collects information continuously and prepares a visual display for the manager. For example, an ISP might use automated software to monitor traffic between the ISP and the Internet. Figure 5.1 illustrates how a display might appear.

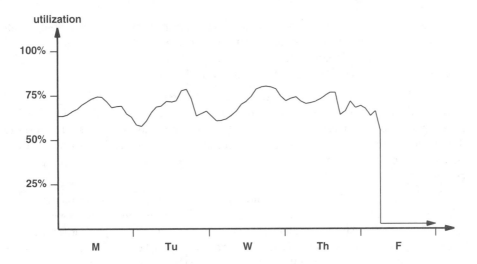

Figure 5.1 Illustration of output from a monitor that shows utilization on a link over a five-day period. The output reveals that on Friday all traffic suddenly dropped to almost zero.

As the figure illustrates, an automated monitoring system can allow a manager to spot a problem quickly (e.g., a sudden cessation in traffic).

5.6 Baselines

It may seem that monitoring provides a quick answer to troubleshooting because the output from a monitor allows a manager to spot a problem quickly. However, there are two drawbacks to monitoring:

- A large network contains many links and devices.
- Normal traffic may have significant variation.

To understand why size is important, recall that a large network can contain thousands of devices. A device such as a router can connect to multiple physical networks, which means that monitoring all possible links produces many thousands of displays similar to the one that Figure 5.1 shows. A network manager cannot possibly examine thousands of such displays.

A second, more serious problem with monitoring arises from the variation in traffic. For example, in many networks, traffic falls to low levels at night and on weekends. Thus, a simplistic automated system that notifies the manager whenever traffic falls below a set threshold will generate many false alarms.

To solve the problem, automated monitoring systems usually follow a statistical approach: the system monitors traffic continuously, but only notifies the manager when traffic appears to be "unusual." That is, instead of setting absolute thresholds, a series of *baseline measurements* are collected, typically over an extended period of time. Once a baseline has been established, measurements of the network can be compared to the baseline.

As an example, assume that a monitoring system collects the number of packets on a link in thirty-minute intervals throughout the week. Once multiple weeks have been collected, a baseline can be computed for each interval (mean and standard deviation). Parameters can be chosen to notify the manager in cases where traffic does not fit the statistical profile (e.g., lies more than one standard deviation from the mean).

The point is:

> *Because traffic on a typical network varies dramatically over time, a monitoring system that uses absolute thresholds provides many false alarms; to be effective, a monitor only alerts a manager when activity differs significantly from a baseline measure.*

5.7 Items That Can Be Monitored

The discussion above focuses on monitoring a single link. However, it is possible to monitor other network devices and facilities. For example, in addition to link monitors, commercial vendors offer systems that monitor:

- Switches
- Routers
- Wide Area Network connections
- Servers (e.g., email, web, and DNS)
- Application software
- Operating systems
- Application gateways
- Printers
- Databases
- Security services and mechanisms

5.8 Alarms, Logs, And Polling

How should monitoring data be represented and communicated? We will see that several approaches can be used. If a network element contains management system facilities (e.g., a separate CPU and software devoted to management tasks), the system can analyze events and generate reports for a manager. If a network element does not contain facilities for network management, a separate computer system can be used to gather and process events from one or more network systems.

Whether events are processed internally by a network element or externally by a separate computer system, a data representation and paradigm are needed. The choice of data representation depends on the size and complexity of the items being communicated (binary, ASCII, or XML have been used). The paradigm depends on the expected frequency of events. The possible approaches are:

- Alarms
- Event logs
- Polling

An *alarm* approach requires the network element to send a report to the management system when a problem is detected. An *event log* records events in a file, possibly in a file accessible over the network. The log file can then be examined offline (e.g., overnight). A *polling* mechanism periodically requests status from a network element.

One of the issues involved in monitoring focuses on the cost of the paradigm and representation. In particular, if management events are sent across the same network as other traffic, the representation and paradigm must be chosen to avoid swamping the network with management traffic.

5.9 Identifying The Cause Of A Fault

Because networks contain many types of devices and services, faults can arise from a variety of sources. For example, the following can cause faults:

- Transmission link failure
- Network element failure
- Software failure
- Protocol failure
- Malicious attack
- Unexpected increase in traffic
- Interface disconnection
- Misconfiguration

Transmission Link Failure. One of the most publicized forms of failure occurs when connectivity is lost when a physical transmission line is cut. Because cable breaks are often associated with construction accidents, the problem is known informally as a *back hoe* type of failure.

In wireless transmission systems, link failures can result from interference as well as from permanent disconnection. For example, an airplane can temporarily block satellite communication or vegetation can block a point-to-point microwave link. For shared wireless links using Wi-Fi technology, interference can arise from radio frequency transmissions or from metal structures. In particular, Wi-Fi introduces an *association* between a mobile computer and a Wi-Fi base station. As a mobile unit moves, the quality of the link can deteriorate to the point of becoming unusable.

Network Element Failure. Individual devices such as routers and switches can fail in several ways. For example, if a central power supply fails, a *complete failure* occurs in which the entire network element ceases operation. Such catastrophic failures are usually easy to detect; it can be more difficult to diagnose a *partial failure* in which some of the components in a device fail and others continue to operate. For example, network elements with multiple chassis or multiple backplanes can fail in such a way that interfaces plugged into one chassis continue to operate but interfaces plugged into another do not.

Software Failure. In general, software systems are more prone to bugs and less reliable than hardware systems. Surprisingly, most network elements include a substantial amount of software, including a special-purpose operating system, device drivers, and protocol stacks. Thus, in addition to application software such as web servers and email systems, network managers handle faults that occur with systems software.

As a special case of software faults, consider software upgrades. Most routers use an operating system, and from time to time, vendors release new versions of their operating system software. In most organizations, routers operate continuously. Thus, a software upgrade must be performed on a "live" network — a manager temporarily stops a router, installs a new version of the software, immediately restarts the router, and watches for problems.

Protocol Failure. Communication protocols are designed to coordinate transmission of data and overcome some network faults. Notably, protocols that communicate routing information can help a network recover from link failure by automatically detecting the failure and changing routes to forward traffic along an alternative path.

Despite being designed to automatically overcome errors, protocols can introduce an additional opportunity for failure. For example, under certain conditions, some routing protocols will create a *routing loop* in which packets are forwarded around a cycle of routers — packets that fall into a routing loop continue around the loop without ever reaching their destination. In other cases, routing protocols can create a *black hole* in which one or more routers do not have a path to certain destinations.

Malicious Attack. Chapter 8 discusses network security in detail. However, we point out here that malicious attacks have become a source of network faults. In particular, *denial-of-service attacks* are designed to disrupt a network and prevent other traffic from getting through.

Unexpected Increase In Traffic. Even if a network does not experience an attack that overwhelms the network with packets, a fault can occur from a sudden increase in legitimate traffic. The phrase *flash crowd* is sometimes used to characterize the situation. For example, immediately after the terrorist attack on the World Trade Center in September 2001, networks at some commercial news agencies were unable to withstand the flood of requests as users scrambled to learn more about the situation. Similar faults can occur if a web site suddenly becomes popular.

Interface Disconnection. Disconnection is a common problem, especially for devices that are accessible to users. In fact, disconnection is so common that many operating systems have a mechanism to alert the user when a network interface detects a loss of connectivity (e.g., a cable has been unplugged). Disconnection can also be a problem in a wiring closet where hundreds of cables plug into switches because humans must identify connections manually — unplugging the wrong cable can inadvertently disconnect a device.

Misconfiguration. Incorrect configuration is a significant cause of network faults. For example, consider a site that uses variable-length subnetting. A correct assignment of subnet numbers requires careful thought that takes into account the bit values assigned when one prefix overlaps another. If a manager follows a simplistic approach of assigning subnet numbers sequentially (i.e., 1, 2, 3, ...), the assignments can lead to ambiguity, a situation where some pairs of hosts are unable to communicate. Unfortunately, subnet ambiguity may not be apparent — the problem only surfaces when a pair of affected hosts attempts to communicate.

5.10 Human Failure And Network Faults

What is the most likely cause of faults? The possible sources of faults listed above does not indicate which faults or causes are most likely to occur. Early items in the list focus on technical aspects of networks that can fail, and items near the end focus on faults caused by humans. When the Internet was still emerging from research labs, hardware and software faults were prevalent. Interestingly, according to a study, human error is now the most significant source of faults [Fox and Patterson 2003]. For example, the study attributes 51% of web site failures to operator error. The authors state:

> *We were a bit surprised to find out that operator error was a leading cause of system problems.*

The observation that human error is the most significant source of faults will be important when we discuss automated network management systems.

5.11 Protocol Layering And Faults

Observe that faults span all layers of the protocol stack. Transmission line disconnection corresponds to a fault at Layer 1. Problems with wireless LAN association and CRC errors occur at Layer 2. Layer 3 faults include ambiguity of subnet addresses or assignment of duplicate addresses. At Layer 4, transport protocols such as UDP can report checksum errors. Finally, application layer faults include server failures.

The presence of faults at each layer of the protocol stack means that diagnosing a fault can require a network manager to understand the protocols at all layers. The point is:

> *Because faults can occur at each layer of the protocol stack, a network manager must be cognizant of the functions of each layer.*

5.12 Hidden Faults And Automatic Correction

Mechanisms that automatically detect and correct faults are intended to make networks easier to operate. However, such mechanisms can have an unintended side-effect: an automated system that overcomes problems can hide symptoms from a network manager and prevent the manager from repairing underlying causes.

As an example of mechanisms that automatically detect and correct problems, consider the combination of bit-error detection techniques and retransmission that protocols offer. To detect bit errors, Ethernet uses a *Cyclic Redundancy Code* (*CRC*) and IP uses a *header checksum*. In each case, error detection involves both a sender and receiver: a sender adds CRC or checksum information to the packet before transmission, and a receiver uses the information to determine whether the packet has been corrupted. If bits of the packet are changed as the packet travels between a sender and receiver, the receiver discards the packet.

A reliable transport protocol, such as TCP, uses acknowledgements and retransmission to handle problems of packet loss. That is, when it transmits a packet, the sending TCP starts a timer. If the timer expires before an acknowledgement arrives specifying that the packet was received, the sending TCP retransmits another copy of the packet and starts the timer again.

It should be obvious how the above mechanisms can combine to hide a network fault. Assume the interface hardware on a network element fails in such a way that it sets one or more of the bits in random packets to zero, and assume the packets contain TCP traffic that is part of a file transfer. The receiver uses the CRC in each packet to verify whether the packet is valid, and discards corrupted packets. When the retransmission timer expires, the sending TCP will send another copy of the packet. If the probability of corruption is less than 1, a copy of the packet will eventually get through, TCP will receive an acknowledgement, and the transfer will proceed.

In the above example, both the user and manager remain unaware of a problem. From a user's point of view, retransmission allows file transfers to proceed (albeit, slowly). From a network manager's point of view, the network may be slow, but is operating. Thus, the underlying problem, loss or severe congestion, can remain hidden.

In the case of retransmission, we observe that the mechanism presents a challenge to managers because the mechanism overcomes a problem without exposing the underlying fault. The point is:

An automated mechanism that overcomes a problem without exposing the underlying fault to a manager can result in a network that operates suboptimally.

5.13 Anomaly Detection And Event Correlation

We have already discussed one of the most important approaches used to identify unusual traffic: link monitoring with baseline measures used to define the norm. The idea can be generalized to events other than those related to traffic: observe the occurrences of an event over a period of time, compute a baseline, and use the baseline to detect abnormal behavior. For example, if a link is up twenty-four hours a day, when the link goes down, the behavior falls outside what is expected.

We use the term *anomaly detection* to refer to the process of comparing events to a baseline, and say that a manager looks for anomalous behavior. Although it can help a network manager spot potential problems, an individual anomaly may not provide sufficient information to identify the underlying cause. Therefore, managers look for ways to combine information about multiple anomalies. The idea is known as *event correlation*.

For example, if a manager observes an anomaly in which a link is down, the manager can only guess the cause. However, if a manager observes that all links leading to a given switch are down, the manager can conclude that the switch has failed. The point is:

> *Correlating multiple anomalies provides a manager with more information than considering each anomaly in isolation.*

We note that a manager can also correlate external events with network failures. For example, if a manager receives a report of a network element being down and a report of an interface on a network element failing immediately after a thunderstorm, the manager is likely to investigate whether the failed items were hit by lightning.

Finally, we note that event correlation can be used at a variety of levels. For example, a manager can correlate events across one service (e.g., correlate all email anomalies) or across multiple services (e.g., email anomalies and web anomalies). Similarly, a manager can correlate anomalies on a single device (e.g., simultaneous anomalies on multiple interfaces) or across multiple devices (e.g., anomalies on a pair of routers).

5.14 Fault Prevention

In the FCAPS definition, the *F* level includes more than fault detection and correction: it also includes *fault prevention*. That is, in addition to correcting a problem, a manager must take steps to prevent the problem from recurring. Furthermore, a manager must identify potential problems that may arise in the future, and take steps to prevent the problems from occurring.

Anticipating faults can be difficult because no manager has knowledge of the future. A later chapter will consider one aspect of problem prevention in detail by examining the question of capacity planning. We will see how managers use traffic statistics to compute the amount of network bandwidth that will be needed in the future.

5.15 Summary

Fault detection and correction require a manager to troubleshoot problems and diagnose the underlying cause. In addition to receiving trouble reports from users, managers rely on automated network monitoring. To eliminate false alarms, monitor output is compared to a baseline; a manager can learn more by correlating anomalies than by considering them individually.

In addition to having each device generate alarms, management systems can use event logs or device polling; the choice of approach and representation depends on the device capabilities and expected traffic.

Network faults can occur at any layer of the protocol stack from physical links to applications; interaction among automated mechanisms from multiple layers can hide problems.

Chapter Contents

6.1   Introduction, 67
6.2   Business Model And Network Charges, 67
6.3   Service Level Agreements (SLAs), 68
6.4   Service Fees, 68
6.5   Accounting For Flat-Rate Service, 69
6.6   Accounting For Use-Based Service, 69
6.7   Tiered Levels Of Service, 70
6.8   Exceeding Quotas And Penalties, 70
6.9   Assessing Financial Penalties, 71
6.10 Traffic Policing And Strict Enforcement Of Limits, 71
6.11 Technologies For Limiting The Rate Of Traffic, 72
6.12 Priorities And Absolute Guarantees, 73
6.13 Absolute Bandwidth Guarantees And MPLS, 73
6.14 Relative Bandwidth Guarantees And Priorities, 73
6.15 Priorities And Types Of Traffic, 74
6.16 Peering Agreements And Accounting, 74
6.17 Summary, 75

6

Accounting And Billing

6.1 Introduction

Earlier chapters in this part of the text introduce basic terminology and provide background. The two previous chapters began a tour of the FCAPS model of network management by discussing configuration and fault detection. This chapter continues the discussion by exploring accounting and billing. Succeeding chapters complete the FCAPS discussion.

6.2 Business Model And Network Charges

Financial accounting is part of all aspects of business. Thus, each computer network needs some form of financial accounting. Computer networks generate capital expenses for equipment and recurring expenses for operation and maintenance; to remain profitable, a group running a network must account for the expenses and devise a method of charging for services that recovers costs.

The FCAPS concept of *accounting* goes beyond merely keeping careful records. It also entails *billing* users for network services. The reason that billing figures prominently into FCAPS arises from the original purpose — the FCAPS model is intended for service providers (i.e., organizations whose main business activity consists of providing networking services to paying customers). In fact, FCAPS was created to describe how to manage telecommunications networks; its application to enterprise networks can be viewed as an extension of the original goal.

Fortunately, FCAPS does not define in detail how accounting should be done nor does it define how billing should be handled. Instead, FCAPS merely specifies that various models of accounting must be supported and that it must be possible to generate bills for use of the network. The staff for each individual network is free to choose an accounting and billing model. Thus, the form of accounting used for an enterprise network can be entirely different than the form used for a service provider network.

6.3 Service Level Agreements (SLAs)

The basis for much of the accounting and billing in a service provider network arises from legal contracts known as *Service Level Agreements* (*SLAs*). A service provider requires each customer to sign an SLA. In addition, a provider creates an SLA for each ISP with which traffic is exchanged (e.g., in addition to signing an SLA with each customer, a Tier-2 provider signs an SLA with at least one Tier-1 provider).

An SLA specifies the network services that will be provided as well as the fees that will be charged for the services. Because it is a contract, an SLA is legally-binding. More important, an SLA contains detailed statements regarding technical aspects of the service to be provided and the relationship between the service provided and fees. Thus, network managers are often involved in drafting or checking the technical specifications in an SLA.

From a network management point of view, an SLA is an important document because it specifies what can be expected. However, expectations of the two parties involved in an SLA differ. From a customer's point of view, an SLA specifies a set of services that must be provided; a customer expects an SLA to guarantee a minimum level of service. From a provider's point of view, an SLA specifies the maximum amount of a service that a customer can use; a provider expects an SLA to provide a bound on the level of service that a customer can obtain. The next sections will consider aspects of each view.

6.4 Service Fees

There are two basic paradigms used to charge customers for Internet access:

- Flat-rate billing
- Use-based billing

As the name implies, *flat-rate billing* refers to a scheme where a customer pays a monthly rate independent of the type or quantity of traffic sent. The alternative, *use-based billing*, refers to a scheme in which the network provider assesses a fee for the quantity of traffic or each time a customer accesses a specific network service.

6.5 Accounting For Flat-Rate Service

The accounting required for flat-rate is usually straightforward, but conditions in an SLA can make it more complex. In the simplest case, a customer is billed for the amount of time that the ISP provides network service. Thus, an ISP can record the number of hours each month that a service is provided, and bill accordingly. If the ISP's connection to the Internet is down for part of the month, the customer's bill is reduced so the customer only pays for the number of hours that service was available.

The terms in an SLA can complicate accounting. For example, some SLAs have a penalty clause that reduces the customer's bill by N dollars for each network outage of more than K minutes, and other SLAs specify that a customer receives a higher discount for outages during working hours than for outages during nights and weekends. Finally, an SLA specifies whether the customer or ISP is responsible for the connection between the customer's premises and the ISP (if the customer is responsible, outages in the connection are not reflected in the billing, but if the ISP is responsible, they are).

We can summarize:

Although the accounting required for flat-rate billing is usually straightforward, a provider or a customer may need to keep detailed records of events such as service disruptions.

6.6 Accounting For Use-Based Service

There are two general approaches employed for use-based service:

- Charging by connection
- Charging by volume

The notion of charging a customer for each *connection* has its roots in the early telephone system, where a customer was charged for each long-distance call. When commercial computer networks first appeared, providers charged for each virtual circuit that a customer created. Thus, each time a customer sent an email message, the customer was charged because the email system created a virtual circuit to transfer the message.

Charging by connection may not have the intended result because computer software can be modified to use a single connection for multiple transfers. For example, to minimize cost in a connection-based scheme, an email system can be configured to batch transfers. That is, the email system opens a single virtual circuit and then transfers multiple email messages across the connection in both directions. To overcome such optimizations, early networks charged for the duration of a connection or the total packets sent over the connection.

Gradually, charging per connection fell out of favor. Most ISPs that employ use-based billing now define *volume of traffic* to be the primary measure of network use. That is, the ISP measures the total number of bits that a customer transmits and receives over a given period of time, and uses the total to compute a bill for the customer.

As the above shows, the accounting required for use-based service is significantly more complex than the accounting needed for flat-rate service. When charging per connection, an ISP must watch each packet, detect the start of a new connection (and later, detect the termination). Even when charging by volume, an ISP must keep a count of packets for each customer, and usually distinguishes between packets sent and packets received. A further accounting complication arises if the SLA specifies only charging for user traffic and not for network control traffic (e.g., updates sent by routing protocols).

6.7 Tiered Levels Of Service

To simplify SLA negotiation, ISPs often use a *tiered* model of service in which the ISP specifies a small set of options from which a customer can choose. For example, Figure 6.1 lists a set of tiered services (in practice, a list of tiered services also contains prices).

Service	Connection Type	Max. Volume Per Month	
		Download	Upload
bronze	dialup	-no limit-	1 GB
silver	DSL (slow)	-no limit-	10 MB
gold	DSL (fast)	-no limit-	20 MB
platinum	T1 line	-no limit-	10 GB

Figure 6.1 Illustration of tiered service offered by an ISP. Instead of negotiating an SLA with individual parameters, each customer chooses one of the tiers.

6.8 Exceeding Quotas And Penalties

What happens if incoming traffic exceeds the level of service specified in the SLA? ISPs follow one of two general approaches that are described in the following sections.

- Accept excess traffic, but charge a financial penalty
- Enforce resource limits by rejecting excess traffic

6.9 Assessing Financial Penalties

The easiest way to handle excessive traffic consists of accepting the traffic, but charging higher fees. That is, instead of viewing tiered service as a set of options from which a customer can choose, an ISP can view the tiers as a fee structure. Each month, the ISP measures the data each customer sends, and uses the list of tiers to determine how much the customer is charged.

Of course, an ISP that bills according to the tier of service must have sufficient capacity to handle unexpected increases. The next chapter will discuss capacity planning, and explain how a network manager anticipates growth.

6.10 Traffic Policing And Strict Enforcement Of Limits

From a network management point of view, strict enforcement of traffic quotas means introducing an extra stage in packet processing. The stage is known as *traffic policing*, and a device that performs enforcement is known as a *traffic policer*. A policer checks incoming traffic, and rejects (i.e., discards) packets that exceed prespecified quotas.

Logically, a separate policer is needed for each customer connection; physically, a policer can be a stand-alone device or, more commonly, can be embedded in a router. In either case, a network manager configures a policer by supplying parameters derived from the SLA.

We can summarize:

> A traffic policer *is a configurable mechanism used to enforce limits on packets from a given source.*

It may seem that a policer should accept packets until a limit is exceeded, and should then discard successive packets. Although such a scheme works well for limits on total volume of traffic, we will learn in the next section that a modification of policing is used to enforce quotas on data rate.

6.11 Technologies For Limiting The Rate Of Traffic

As we noted above, some SLAs specify a maximum rate at which a customer can send or receive traffic. Network managers use a variety of techniques to enforce rate limits, including:

- Low-capacity access connection
- Rate-limiting head-end modem
- Rate-limiting traffic policer

Low-Capacity Access Connection. The simplest mechanism used to limit rate consists of a low-capacity physical connection between a customer and an ISP. For example, a T1 line has a maximum data rate of approximately 1.5 million bits per second (mbps). Instead of specifying a maximum rate of 1.5 mbps in an SLA, an ISP can specify that the connection between the customer and the ISP will be a T1-speed data circuit.

Rate-Limiting Head-End Modem. Modems are needed for *Digital Subscriber Line* (*DSL*) and *cable modem* access technologies. In each case, a *head-end modem* (i.e., a modem located on the provider's premises) has a configuration parameter to control the maximum data rate. Thus, when creating an SLA for a customer, a provider can specify a maximum data rate equal to one of the modem settings. A manager merely configures the modem to the specified setting, and the modem automatically handles the details of limiting the rate to the specified value.

Of course, an ISP can view rate-limiting as a potential source of additional revenue. The network manager monitors each head-end modem to determine if any customer reaches their rate limit. When rate limiting takes over, the ISP contacts the customer to ask if the customer is willing to pay a higher monthly fee to increase the data rate.

Rate-Limiting Traffic Policer. The third mechanism used to limit data rate handles the case where the access technology can deliver data faster than the SLA permits. In such cases, a network manager must employ a traffic policer to limit the rate. Unlike modems that negotiate a rate at which data should be sent to the ISP, a traffic policer handles packets after they arrive at the ISP. Thus, the only way a policer can limit data rate is to discard packets until the desired rate is met.

Interestingly, configuring a traffic policer is more difficult than configuring a rate-limiting modem because a policer uses two parameters: a maximum data rate and a duration over which the rate can be maintained.

To understand why two configuration parameters are needed, we must know that packet traffic tends to come in bursts. During a burst, packets arrive back-to-back, giving the appearance of an extremely high data rate. If it acted too quickly, a policer would discard one or more packets in each burst. So, a policer must average over a period of time that is longer than the burst duration. Thus, a manager must specify a duration as well as a maximum data rate. The point is:

> *A manager can use low-capacity access technology, rate-limiting modems, or a rate-limiting policer to control data rates. To configure a policer, a manager specifies a duration as well as a rate.*

6.12 Priorities And Absolute Guarantees

Although an ISP is interested in limiting the rate at which a given customer sends data, customers usually want the opposite: a minimum guarantee on service. Thus, an SLA can contain language that guarantees functionality, specifically, bandwidth to the Internet. There are two approaches that network managers take in satisfying customers:

- Absolute guarantees on bandwidth
- Relative guarantees in the form of priorities

The former is difficult and expensive to achieve, so ISPs prefer the latter.

6.13 Absolute Bandwidth Guarantees And MPLS

To guarantee a customer a fixed data rate, an ISP must use network elements that allow a manager to configure parameters for specific flows. In general, such technologies use a *connection-oriented approach*; a manager specifies a connection from the customer's entry point, through one or more elements, to the Internet. Each network element along the path must be configured to honor the connection.

The most popular technology that managers currently use to provide absolute guarantees is known as *Multi-Protocol Label Switching* (*MPLS*). MPLS allows a manager to configure a flow from a given customer through the ISP's network and to specify a minimum bandwidth.

6.14 Relative Bandwidth Guarantees And Priorities

To provide a *relative guarantee* on bandwidth, a network manager uses a mechanism known as a *traffic scheduler*. A traffic scheduler accepts incoming packets from multiple flows, applies priorities to determine which packet to accept next, and multiplexes the outgoing packets over a single link.

A network manager configures a traffic scheduler by specifying priorities. For example, a traffic scheduler serving four customers might be configured to assign priorities according to how much a customer pays. Figure 6.2 illustrates one possible assignment.

Customer	Assigned Share
1	20%
2	10%
3	50%
4	20%

Figure 6.2 Illustration of relative bandwidth assignment in which each customer is assigned a percentage of the shared bandwidth.

It may seem that the assignments in the figure are absolute — if the outgoing link operates at 100 mbps, Customer 1 will receive twenty percent of the link or exactly 20 mbps. However, most traffic schedulers divide the currently available bandwidth proportionally. Thus, if some customers are not sending packets at a given time, other customers divide the bandwidth according to their share. In the figure, if Customer 3 temporarily stops sending packets, the bandwidth given to each of the other customers doubles.

6.15 Priorities And Types Of Traffic

It is also possible to use traffic schedulers to assign priorities to types of traffic. Priorities are especially important when real-time traffic is carried over the same network as conventional data because giving priority to real-time traffic avoids delay. For example, a customer can specify that voice traffic (i.e., VoIP) must receive higher priority than traffic from email or web browsing (enterprises often give voice traffic priority internally).

6.16 Peering Agreements And Accounting

When two ISPs peer, the SLA between them usually specifies detailed charges based on traffic destinations. For example, an SLA between a large ISP and a small ISP might specify that if the traffic sent in each direction is the same over a given month, each ISP only pays one-half the cost of the connection (i.e., no money is exchanged), but if the traffic in one direction is more than twenty percent higher than traffic in the other direction, the ISP receiving more traffic must pay a service fee of N dollars. As an alternative, an SLA for a peering arrangement might specify that the charge for traffic depends on the destination. For example, each side of an SLA can specify a charge for *transit traffic* (i.e., traffic that passes through the ISP to another ISP) and a charge for *terminated traffic* (i.e., traffic destined to the ISP's customers).

The primary motivation for an SLA is economic. It can indeed be less expensive to forward an incoming packet internally to a customer than to forward the packet across a peering arrangement to a customer in another ISP. More important, even if costs are the same, an ISP can have an economic motivation for differences in charges: making transit traffic more expensive discourages transit traffic and makes more bandwidth available for customers' traffic. Thus, reducing transit traffic may attract customers because customers receive better service.

Whatever the motivation, accounting must support the scheme specified by an SLA. Thus, a network manager may be asked to keep counts of incoming and outgoing packets for each month or to separate counts of incoming packets for transit and terminated traffic.

6.17 Summary

The FCAPS recommendation includes accounting and billing, but does not specify an exact model. All networks require accounting; billing is primarily used by service providers. Most accounting and billing is derived from Service-Level Agreements (SLAs).

Flat-rate and use-based accounting are each used for charging customers; volume of traffic is the easiest way to assess use. Tiered service requires a manager to track use; traffic that exceeds a tier of service can either be discarded or used to justify billing a customer for a higher level of service.

Data rates can be limited by the access technology (including rate-limiting modems) or by a separate policer. Rate-limiting modems and policers require configuration.

To provide minimum guarantees on bandwidth, a manager must use connection-oriented technologies, such as MPLS; each network element along a path must be configured to enforce guarantees. The alternative to absolute bandwidth guarantees is a relative approach in which a manager configures a traffic scheduler to divide bandwidth proportionally.

Chapter Contents

7.1   Introduction, 77
7.2   Aspects Of Performance, 77
7.3   Items That Can Be Measured, 78
7.4   Measures Of Network Performance, 78
7.5   Application And Endpoint Sensitivity, 79
7.6   Degraded Service, Variance In Traffic, And Congestion, 80
7.7   Congestion, Delay, And Utilization, 81
7.8   Local And End-To-End Measurements, 81
7.9   Passive Observation Vs. Active Probing, 82
7.10 Bottlenecks And Future Planning, 83
7.11 Capacity Planning, 83
7.12 Planning The Capacity Of A Switch, 84
7.13 Planning The Capacity Of A Router, 84
7.14 Planning The Capacity Of An Internet Connection, 85
7.15 Measuring Peak And Average Traffic On A Link, 86
7.16 Estimated Peak Utilization And 95th Percentile, 87
7.17 Relationship Between Average And Peak Utilization, 87
7.18 Consequences For Management And The 50/80 Rule, 88
7.19 Capacity Planning For A Complex Topology, 89
7.20 A Capacity Planning Process, 89
7.21 Route Changes And Traffic Engineering, 94
7.22 Failure Scenarios And Availability, 94
7.23 Summary, 95

7

Performance Assessment And Optimization

7.1 Introduction

Chapters in this part of the text provide general background and define the problem of network management. The three previous chapters explain aspects of the FCAPS model.

This chapter continues the discussion of FCAPS by focusing on evaluation of network performance. Unlike the discussion of monitoring in Chapter 6 that focuses on data needed for accounting and billing, our discussion considers performance in a broader sense. In particular, we examine the important question of how measurements are used for capacity assessment and planning.

7.2 Aspects Of Performance

Three aspects of performance are relevant to network managers. The first two pertain to assessment, and the third pertains to optimization. The aspects can be expressed as determining:

- What to measure
- How to obtain measurements
- What to do with the measurements

Although each aspect is important, the discussion in this chapter emphasizes concepts; a later chapter discusses the SNMP technology that can be used to obtain measurements.

7.3 Items That Can Be Measured

In the broadest sense, a network manager can choose to measure specific entities such as:

- Individual links
- Network elements
- Network services
- Applications

Individual Links. A manager can measure the traffic on an individual link and calculate link utilization over time. Chapter 5 discusses monitoring individual links to detect anomalous behavior; the load on links can also be used in some forms of capacity planning†.

Network Elements. The performance of a network element, such as a switch or a router, is easy to assess. Even basic elements provide statistics about packets processed; more powerful devices include sophisticated internal performance monitoring mechanisms supplied by the vendor. For example, some elements keep a count of packets that travel between each pair of ports.

Network Services. Both enterprises and providers measure basic *network services* such as domain name lookup, VPNs, and authentication service. As with applications, providers are primarily concerned with how the service performs from a customer's point of view.

Applications. The measurement of *applications* is primarily of concern to enterprise networks. An enterprise manager assesses application performance for both internal and external users. Thus, a manager might measure the response time of a company database system when employees make requests as well the response time of a company web server when outsiders submit requests.

7.4 Measures Of Network Performance

Although it would be convenient if managers could use a single value to capture the performance of their networks, no single measure exists. Instead, a set of independent measures are often used to assess and characterize network performance. Five measures are commonly used:

---

†Although link performance is conceptually separate from network element performance, measurement of link performance is usually obtained from network elements attached to the link.

- Latency
- Throughput
- Packet loss
- Jitter
- Availability

Network *latency* refers to the delay a packet experiences when traversing a network, and is measured in milliseconds (ms). The *throughput* of a network refers to the data transfer rate measured in bits transferred per unit time (e.g., megabits per second or gigabits per second). A *packet loss* statistic specifies the percentage of packets that the network drops. When a network is operating correctly, packet loss usually results from congestion, so loss statistics can reveal whether a network is overloaded†. The *jitter* a network introduces is a measure of the variance in latency. Jitter is only important for real-time applications, such as *Voice over IP* (*VoIP*), because accurate playback requires a stream of packets to arrive smoothly. Thus, if a network supports real-time audio or video applications, a manager is concerned with jitter. Finally, *availability*, which measures how long a network remains operational and how quickly a network can recover from problems, is especially important for a business that depends on the network (e.g., a service provider).

7.5 Application And Endpoint Sensitivity

When is a network performing well? How can we distinguish among excellent, good, fair, and poor performance? Some managers think that numbers and statistics alone cannot be used to make a judgement. Instead, they rely on human reaction to gauge performance: a network is performing satisfactorily provided that no user is complaining (i.e., no trouble reports are received).

It may seem that a more precise definition of quality is needed. Unfortunately, network performance cannot be judged easily. In fact, we cannot even define an exact boundary between a network that is *up* and a network that is *down*. The ambiguity arises because each application is sensitive to a certain set of conditions and the performance received by a given pair of endpoints can differ from the performance received by other pairs.

To understand application sensitivity, consider a *remote login* application, a *voice* application, and a *file transfer* application running over the same network. If the network exhibits high throughout and high latency, it may be adequate for file transfer, but unsuitable for remote login. If it exhibits low latency and high jitter, the network may be suitable for remote login, but intolerable for voice transmission. Finally, if it exhibits low delay and low jitter but has low throughput, the network may work well for remote login and voice, but be unsuitable for file transfer.

---

†Loss rates can also reveal problems such as interference on a wireless network.

To understand endpoint sensitivity, observe that latency and throughput depend on the path through a network. The path between a pair of endpoints *(a, b)* can be completely disjoint from the path between another pair of endpoints *(c, d)*. Thus, equipment along the paths can differ, one path can be much longer than the other, or one path can be more congested than the other. Because paths can differ, statements about average behavior are not usually meaningful.

The point is:

Because each application is sensitive to specific network characteristics and the performance that an application observes depends on the path that data travels through a network, a manager cannot give a single assessment of network performance that is appropriate for all applications or all endpoints.

7.6 Degraded Service, Variance In Traffic, And Congestion

Instead of making quantitative statements about network performance, network managers use the term *degraded service* to refer to a situation in which some characteristics of latency, throughput, loss, and jitter are worse than baseline expectations. Of course, degraded service can result from faults such as malfunctioning hardware dropping packets. However, degraded service can also result from performance problems such as nonoptimal routes or route flapping (i.e., routes changing back and forth between two paths).

In many networks, the most significant cause of degraded service is congestion: packets arrive in the network faster than they leave. Congestion often occurs when a given link becomes saturated (e.g., a Layer 2 switch connected to two computers that each send incoming traffic at 1 gbps to a single output port that operates at 1 gbps).

To handle variations in traffic, network elements, such as switches or routers, each contain a packet queue that can accommodate a temporary burst of arrivals. However, if a high-speed burst continues over an extended period of time, the queue fills and the network must discard additional packets that arrive. Thus, congestion raises latency, increases packet loss, and lowers effective throughput. The point is:

In many networks, congestion is a leading cause of degraded performance.

7.7 Congestion, Delay, And Utilization

We said that congestion occurs as a link becomes saturated. The relationship between congestion and degraded performance is crucial because it allows managers to deduce performance from a quantity that is easy to measure: link utilization.

We define utilization as the percentage of the underlying hardware capacity that traffic is currently using, expressed as a value between 0 and 1. When utilization increases, congestion occurs, which raises the delay a packet experiences. As a first order approximation, the effective delay can be estimated by Equation 7.1:

$$D \approx \frac{D_0}{1 - U} \qquad (7.1)$$

where D is the effective delay, U is the utilization, and D_0 is the hardware delay in the absence of traffic (i.e., the delay when no packets are waiting to be sent).

Although it is a first-order approximation, Equation 7.1 helps us understand the relationship between congestion and delay: as utilization approaches 100%, congestion causes the effective delay to become arbitrarily large. For now, it is sufficient to understand that utilization is related to performance; in later sections, we will revisit the question and see how utilization can be used for capacity planning.

7.8 Local And End-To-End Measurements

Measurements can be divided into two broad categories, depending on the scope of the measurement. A *local measurement* assesses the performance of a single resource such as a single link or a single network element. Local measurements are the easiest to perform, and many tools are available. For example, tools exist that allow a manager to measure latency, throughput, loss, and congestion on a link.

Unfortunately, a local measurement is often meaningless to network users because users are not interested in the performance of individual network resources. Instead, users are interested in *end-to-end measurements* (e.g., end-to-end latency, throughput, and jitter). That is, a user cares about the behavior observed from an application on an end system. End-to-end measurements include the performance of software running on end systems as well as the performance of data crossing an entire network. For example, end-to-end measurement of a web site includes measurement of the server as well as the network.

It may seem that the end-to-end performance of a network could be computed from measurements of local resources. Such a computation would be ideal because local measurements are easier to make than end-to-end measurements. Unfortunately, the relationship between local and end-to-end performance is complex, which makes it impossible to draw conclusions about end-to-end performance even if the performance of each network element and link is known. For example, even if the packet loss rate is known for each link, the overall packet loss rate is difficult to compute. We can summarize:

> *Although they are the easiest to obtain, local performance measurements cannot be used to deduce end-to-end performance.*

7.9 Passive Observation Vs. Active Probing

How are networks measured? There are two basic approaches:

- Passive observation
- Active probing

Passive observation refers to a nonintrusive mechanism that obtains measurements without affecting the network or the traffic. A passive observation system can measure a network under actual load. That is, a passive mechanism measures network performance while production traffic is passing through the network.

Active probing refers to a mechanism that injects and measures test traffic. For example, test generators exist that can be used to create many simultaneous TCP connections. Thus, active probing is intrusive in the sense that measurement introduces additional traffic.

In general, passive observation is restricted to local measurement, and active probing is used for end-to-end measurement. In fact, to obtain a more accurate picture of end-to-end performance, external devices are often used as the source of active probes. For example, to test how a web site performs, an active probing mechanism injects web requests at various points in the Internet and measures the response†. Of course, the company that owns and operates the web site may not be able to control the situation because the cause of poor performance may be networks run by ISPs on the path between the test system and the web server. However, active probing can provide a realistic assessment of performance.

To summarize:

> *The only way a manager can obtain a realistic assessment of end-to-end performance is to employ active probing that measures an entire network path plus the performance of applications.*

---

†Commercial companies exist that use active probing to measure performance.

7.10 Bottlenecks And Future Planning

How do network managers use measurement data that is collected? Chapter 5 discusses one use: detection of faults and anomalies. There are two principal uses that arise in the context of performance optimization. The two are related:

- Optimize current network performance
- Optimize future network performance

Optimize Current Network Performance. Managers can maximize performance of a network without upgrading the hardware. To do so, they identify *bottlenecks*. Engineers use the term *bottleneck* to refer to the component or subsystem that is the slowest. The bottleneck in a network can consist of a link that is saturated or a router that is running at capacity. The point of performing bottleneck assessment is to identify links or network elements that are causing performance problems. A bottleneck can be upgraded to improve performance†, or traffic can be rerouted to alternative paths. Unfortunately, as we will see in the next section, bottleneck identification tends to focus on individual network elements when, in fact, most data networks are so complex that no single element forms a bottleneck.

Optimize Future Network Performance. By far the most important and complex use of performance data arises in future planning. A network manager must anticipate future needs, acquire the necessary equipment, and integrate the new facilities into the network before the need arises. As we will see, future planning can be difficult, and requires taking careful and extensive measurements.

7.11 Capacity Planning

We use the term *capacity planning* to refer to network management activities concerned with estimating future needs. In cases of large networks, the planning task is complex. A manager begins by measuring existing traffic and estimating future traffic increases. Once estimates have been generated, a manager must translate the predicted loads into effects on individual resources in the network. Finally, a manager considers possible scenarios for enhancing specific network resources, and chooses a plan as a tradeoff among performance, reliability, and cost.

To summarize:

> *Capacity planning requires a manager to estimate the size of resources that will be needed to meet anticipated load, taking into account a desired level of performance, a desired level of robustness and resilience, and a bound on cost.*

---

†There is no point in upgrading a device that is not a bottleneck.

A major challenge in capacity planning arises because the underlying networks can be enhanced in many ways. For example, a manager can: increase the number of ports on an existing network element, add new network elements, increase the capacity of existing links, or add additional links. Thus, a manager must consider many alternatives.

7.12 Planning The Capacity Of A Switch

Estimating the capacity needed for a switch is among the most straightforward capacity planning tasks. The only variables are the number of connections needed and the speed of each connection. In many cases, the speed required for each connection is predetermined, either by policy, assumptions about traffic, or the equipment to be attached to the switch. For example, an enterprise might have a policy that specifies each desktop connection uses wired Ethernet running at 100 mbps. As an example of equipment, the connection between a switch and a router might operate at 1 gbps.

To plan the capacity of a switch, a manager estimates the number of connections, N, along with the capacity of each. For most switches, planning capacity is further simplified because modern switches employ 10/100/1000 hardware that allows each port to select a speed automatically. Thus, a manager merely needs to estimate N, the number of ports. A slow growth rate further simplifies planning switch capacity — additional ports are only needed when new users or new network elements are added to the network. The point is:

> *Estimating switch capacity is straightforward because a manager only needs to estimate the number of ports needed, and port demand grows slowly.*

7.13 Planning The Capacity Of A Router

Planning router capacity is more complex than planning switch capacity for three reasons. First, because a router can provide services other than packet forwarding (e.g., DHCP), a manager needs to plan capacity for each service. Second, because the speed of each connection between a router and a network can be changed, planning router capacity entails planning the capacity of connections. Third, and most important, the traffic a router must handle depends on the way a manager configures routing. Thus, to predict the router capacity that will be needed, a manager must plan the capacity of surrounding systems and routing services. To summarize:

Estimating the capacity needed for a router requires a manager to estimate parameters for surrounding hardware systems as well as estimate services the router must perform.

7.14 Planning The Capacity Of An Internet Connection

Another capacity planning task focuses on the capacity of a single link between an organization and an upstream service provider. For example, consider a link between an enterprise customer and an ISP, which can be managed by the ISP or the customer. If the ISP manages the link, the ISP monitors traffic and uses traffic increases to encourage the customer to pay a higher fee to upgrade the speed of the link. If the customer manages the link, the customer monitors traffic and uses increases to determine if the link will soon become a bottleneck.

In theory, planning link capacity should be straightforward: use link utilization, an easy quantity to measure, in place of delay, throughput, loss, and jitter. That is, compute the percentage of the underlying link capacity that is currently being used, track untilization over many weeks, and increase link capacity when utilization becomes too high.

In practice, two difficult question arise:

- How should utilization be measured?
- When should link capacity be increased?

To understand why the questions are difficult, recall from the discussion in Chapter 5 that the amount of traffic on a link varies considerably (e.g., is often much lower during nights and weekends). Variations in traffic make measurement difficult because measurements are only meaningful when coordinated with external events such as holidays. Variations make the decision about increasing link capacity difficult because a manager must choose an objective. The primary question concerns packet loss: is the objective to ensure that no packets are lost at any time or to compromise by choosing a lower-cost link that handles most traffic, but may experience minor loss during times of highest traffic? The point is:

Because link utilization varies over time, when upgrading a link, a manager must decide whether the objective is to prevent all packet loss or compromise with some packet loss to lower cost.

7.15 Measuring Peak And Average Traffic On A Link

How should a link be measured? The idea is to divide a week into small intervals, and measure the amount of data sent on the link during each interval. From the measurements, it is possible to compute both the maximum and average utilization during the week. The measurements can be repeated during successive weeks to produce a baseline.

How large should measurement intervals be? Choosing a large interval size has the advantage of producing fewer measurements, which means management traffic introduces less load on links, intermediate routers, and the management system. Choosing a small interval size has the advantage of giving more accuracy. For example, choosing the interval size to be one minute allows a manager to assess very short bursts; choosing the interval size to be one hour produces much less data, but hides short bursts by averaging all the traffic in an hour.

As a compromise, a manager can choose an interval size of 5, 10, or 15 minutes, depending on how variable the manager expects traffic to be. For typical sites, where traffic is expected to be relatively smooth, using a 15-minute interval represents a reasonable choice. With 7 days of 24 hours per day and 4 intervals per hour, a week is divided into 672 intervals. Thus, measurement data collected over an entire week consists of only 672 values. Even if the procedure is repeated for an entire year, the total data consists of only 34,944 values. To further reduce the amount of data, progressively older data can be aggregated.

We said that measurement data can be used to compute peak utilization. To be precise, we should say that it is possible to compute the utilization during the 15-minute interval with the most traffic. For capacity planning purposes, such an estimate is quite adequate. If additional accuracy is needed, a manager can reduce the interval size. To summarize:

> *To compute peak and average utilization on a link, a manager measures traffic in fixed intervals. An interval size of 15 minutes is adequate for most capacity planning; smaller intervals can be used to improve accuracy.*

Of course, the computation described above only estimates utilization for data traveling in one direction over a connection (e.g., from the Internet to an enterprise). To understand utilization in both directions, a manager must also measure traffic in the reverse direction. In fact, in a typical enterprise, managers expect traffic traveling between the enterprise and the Internet will be asymmetric, with more data flowing from the Internet to the enterprise than from the enterprise to the Internet.

7.16 Estimated Peak Utilization And 95th Percentile

Once a manager has collected statistics for average and peak utilization in each direction over many weeks, how can the statistics be used to determine when a capacity increase is needed? There is no easy answer. To prevent all packet loss, a manager must track the change in absolute maximum utilization over time, and must upgrade the capacity of the link before peak utilization reaches 100%.

Unfortunately, the absolute maximum utilization can be deceptive because packet traffic tends to be bursty and peak utilization may only occur for a short period. Events such as error conditions or route changes can cause small spikes that are not indicative of normal traffic. In addition, legitimate short-lived traffic bursts can occur. Many sites decide that minor packet loss is tolerable during spikes. To mitigate the effects of short spikes, a manager can follow a statistical approach that smooths measurements and avoids upgrading a link too early: instead of using the absolute maximum, use the 95th percentile of traffic to compute peak utilization. That is, take traffic measurements in 15 minute intervals as usual, but instead of selecting one interval as the peak, sort the list, select intervals at the 95th percentile and higher, and use the selected intervals to compute an estimated peak utilization. To summarize:

> *Because traffic can be bursty, a smoothed estimate for peak utilization avoids reacting to a single interval with unusually high traffic. A manager can obtain a smoothed estimate by averaging over intervals at the 95th percentile and higher.*

7.17 Relationship Between Average And Peak Utilization

Experience has shown that for backbone links, traffic grows and falls fairly steadily over time. A corresponding result holds for traffic on a link connecting a large organization to the rest of the Internet. If similar conditions are observed on a given link and absolute precision is not needed, a manager can simplify the calculation of peak utilization.

One more observation is required for the simplification: traffic on a heavily used link (e.g., a backbone link at a provider) follows a pattern where the ratio between the estimated peak utilization of a link, calculated as a 95th percentile, and the average utilization of the link is almost constant. The constant ratio depends on the organization. According to one Internet backbone provider, the ratio can be approximated by Equation 7.2:

$$\frac{Estimated\ peak\ utilization}{Average\ link\ utilization} \approx 1.3 \tag{7.2}$$

7.18 Consequences For Management And The 50/80 Rule

How does a constant peak-to-average ratio affect managers? For a connection to the Internet that is heavily used, a manager only needs to measure the average utilization, and can use the average to estimate peak utilization and draw conclusions. Figure 7.1 lists examples of average utilization and the meaning.

Average Utilization	Peak Utilization	Interpretation
40%	52%	Link is underutilized
50%	65%	Comfortable operating range
60%	78%	Link is beginning to fill
70%	91%	Link is effectively saturated
80%	100%	Link is completely saturated

Figure 7.1 Interpretation of peak utilization for various values of average utilization assuming a constant ratio. Although utilization is limited to 100%, peak demand can exceed capacity.

As the figure shows, a link with average utilization of 50% is running at approximately two-thirds of capacity during peak times, a comfortable level that allows for unusual circumstances such as a national emergency that creates unexpected load. When the average utilization is less than 50% and extra link capacity is not reserved for backup, the link is underutilized. However, if the average utilization is 70%, only 9% of the link capacity remains available during peak times. Thus, a manager can track changes in average utilization over time, and use the result to determine when to upgrade the link. In particular, by the time the average utilization climbs to 80%, a manager can assume the peak utilization has reached 100% (i.e., the link is saturated). Thus, the goal is to maintain average capacity between 50% and 80%. The bounds are known as the 50/80 Rule:

On a heavily used Internet connection, a manager can use average utilization to determine when to upgrade link capacity. When average utilization is less than 50%, the link is underutilized; when average utilization climbs to 80%, the link is saturated during peak times.

Of course, measurements may reveal that a given Internet connection is sometimes unused. In particular, if an enterprise closes during nights and weekends, the traffic during those periods can fall to almost zero, which will significantly lower average utilization and make the ratio between peak and average utilization high. To handle such cases, a manager can measure average utilization only over in-use periods.

7.19 Capacity Planning For A Complex Topology

Capacity planning for a large network is much more complex than capacity planning for individual elements and links. That is, because links can be added and routes can be changed, capacity planning must consider the performance of the entire network and not just the performance of each individual link or element. The point is:

> *Assessing how to increase the capacity of a network that contains N links and elements requires a manager to perform more work than planning capacity increases for each of the N items individually.*

7.20 A Capacity Planning Process

Capacity planning in a large network requires six steps. Figure 7.2 summarizes the overall planning process by listing the steps a network management team performs. The next sections explain the steps.

1. Use measurement of the current network and forecasting to devise an estimate of the expected load.

2. Translate the expected load into a model that can be used with capacity planning software.

3. Use the load model plus a description of network resources to compute resource utilization estimates and validate the results.

4. Propose modifications to the network topology or routing, and compute new resource utilization estimates.

5. Use resource utilization estimates to derive estimates on the performance needed from network elements and links.

6. Use performance estimates to make recommendations for capacity increases and the resulting costs.

Figure 7.2 An overview of the steps a network management team takes to plan capacity increases in a complex network.

7.20.1 Forecasting Future Load

Forecasting the future load on a network requires a network manager to estimate both growth in existing traffic patterns and potentially new traffic patterns. Estimating growth in a stable business is easiest. On one hand, a manager can track traffic over a long period of time, and can use past growth to estimate future growth. On the other hand, a manager can obtain estimates of new users (either internal users or external customers), and calculate additional increases in load that will result.

Estimating new traffic patterns is difficult, especially in a rapidly expanding provider business. The load introduced by new service offerings may differ from the past load and may grow to dominate quickly. An ISP sets sales targets for both existing and new services, so a manager should be able to use the estimates to calculate the resulting increase in load. Before a manager can do so, however, the manager must translate from the marketing definition of a service to a meaningful statement of network load. In particular, sales quotas cannot be used in capacity planning until the quantity, types, and destinations of the resulting packets can be determined. Thus, when marketing defines and sells a service, a network manager must determine how many new additional packets will be sent from point A to point B in the network.

> *Forecasting future load is especially difficult in cases where a network must support new services because a manager must estimate the quantity, type, and destinations of packets that will be generated.*

7.20.2 Measuring Existing Resource Use

We have already discussed the measurement of existing resources. We have seen that most large network elements, such as routers, contain an API that allows a manager to obtain measurements of performance. We know that the traffic on a link varies over time, that it is possible to measure traffic in intervals, and that a network manager can use the measurements to calculate average and peak utilization. To smooth the estimate of peak utilization, a manager can compute the peak at the 95th percentile and above. Finally, we know that on heavily utilized backbone links the expected load is smooth, with a constant ratio of peak-to-average utilization. When measuring a network, a manager must measure each network element and link.

7.20.3 A Load Model Based On A Traffic Matrix

Effective estimates of resource use rely on an accurate model of network traffic. Once a model has been derived, the model can be used to compute the effect on underlying resources, and can allow managers to test the effect of possible changes.

One technique has emerged as the leader for modeling network load: a *traffic matrix*. Conceptually, a traffic matrix corresponds to connections between the network and outside traffic sources and sinks. That is, a traffic matrix has one row for each network ingress point and one column for each network egress point. In practice, most connections between a network and outside sources are bidirectional, which means a traffic matrix has one row and one column for each external connection. If T is a traffic matrix, T_{ij} gives the rate at which data is expected to arrive on external connection i destined to leave over external connection j. Figure 7.3 illustrates the concept.

A traffic matrix is an especially appropriate starting point for future planning because a matrix specifies an expected external traffic load without making any assumptions about the interior of a network or routing. Thus, planners can build a single traffic matrix, and then run a set of simulations that compare performance of a variety of topologies and routing architectures; the matrix does not need to change for each new simulation.

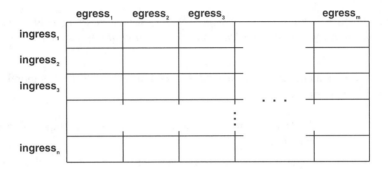

Figure 7.3 The concept of a traffic matrix. Each entry in the matrix stores the rate of traffic from a source (ingress) to a destination (egress). For bidirectional network connections, row i corresponds to the same connection as column i.

A traffic matrix is most useful for modeling the backbone of a large network where aggregate traffic flows can be averaged. It is more difficult to devise a traffic matrix for a network that connects many end-user computers because the individual traffic from each computer must be specified. Thus, for a large service provider, each input or output of the traffic matrix represents a smaller ISP or a peer provider. For an enterprise, a traffic matrix can model the corporate backbone, which means an input or output corresponds to either an external Internet connection or an internal source of traffic, such as a group of offices.

What values should be placed in a traffic matrix? The question arises because traffic varies over time. Should a traffic matrix give the average traffic expected for each pair of external connections, the peak traffic, or some combination? The ultimate goal is to understand how traffic affects individual resources, but peak loads on individual resources do not always occur under the same traffic conditions. As we have seen, for heavily-loaded backbone links, average and peak utilization is related. In other cases, planning is focused on the worst case — a network manager needs to ensure sufficient resources to handle the worst possible combinations of traffic. Thus, the manager uses peak load as the measure stored in the traffic matrix.

Unfortunately, we know that traffic varies over time. Furthermore, peak traffic between a given pair of external connections may occur at a different time than the peak traffic between another pair of connections. The notion of independent temporal variations can impact capacity planning. For example, consider an ISP that serves residential customers and businesses. If business traffic is high during business hours and residential traffic is high in the evening or on weekends, it may be possible to use a single network infrastructure for both types of traffic. However, if a traffic matrix represents the peak traffic for each pair of connections without specifying times, a manager can plan a network with twice the capacity actually required. The point can be summarized:

> *A traffic matrix that stores peak traffic loads without documenting temporal variations can lead to overestimation of needed capacity.*

How can a manager create a load model that accounts for temporal variation? There are two possibilities:

- Use multiple traffic matrices, where each matrix corresponds to a single time slot.
- Use a single matrix, but make each entry correspond to the peak traffic only during the busy time of the network.

To use multiple matrices, a manager divides time into blocks, and specifies a traffic matrix for each block. For example, in the ISP mentioned above, a manager might choose to create a traffic matrix for business hours and a separate traffic matrix for other hours. The chief disadvantage of using multiple matrices is that a manager must spend time creating each.

The single-matrix approach works best for networks in which a manager can easily identify a time slot during which peak demand occurs. For, example, some ISPs experience peak demand when business hours from multiple time zones overlap.

7.20.4 Flows And Aggregates

We said that a traffic matrix can represent the peak traffic from each ingress to each egress. Another complication arises when managers add estimates of future traffic to a traffic matrix: instead of starting with aggregates of traffic for each combination of ingress and egress, a manager may be given estimates of traffic from specific flows. For example, suppose an enterprise plans to install a new application. If a manager can estimate the amount of traffic each user will generate, the estimates must be combined to create aggregates. Similarly, if an ISP plans to sell new services, the traffic resulting from the new service must be aggregated with other traffic.

It may be difficult to generate aggregate estimates from individual flows for two reasons. First, in many cases, the actual destination of a new flow is unknown. For example, if an ISP offers a VPN service that encrypts data and expects to sell N subscriptions to the service, a manager may find it difficult to estimate the locations of the endpoints. Second, peaks from flows may not coincide even if the flows cross the same link. Thus, to build a traffic matrix, a manager must estimate the combined effect of new flows on aggregate traffic without knowing exactly how the peaks will coincide.

7.20.5 Deriving Estimates And Validation

Once a traffic matrix has been produced, a manager can use the matrix plus a description of the network topology and routing architecture to compute peak resource demands for individual links and network elements. In essence, traffic for each *(source, destination)* pair is mapped onto network paths, and the traffic is summed for each link or network element in the path. The capacity needed for a link is given by the total traffic that is assigned to the link. The switching capacity needed for a device such as an IP router can be computed by calculating the number of packets that can arrive per second (i.e., the sum over all inputs).

One of the key ideas underlying the process of capacity planning involves *validation* of the traffic matrix: before adding estimates of new traffic, a manager uses measures of current traffic, maps data from the traffic matrix to individual resources, and compares the calculated load to the actual measured load on the resource. If the estimates for individual resources are close to the measured values, the model is *valid* and a manager can proceed to add estimates for new traffic with some confidence that the results will also be valid.

If a traffic model does not agree with reality, the model must be *tuned*. In addition to checking basic traffic measurements, a manager checks assumptions about the times of peak traffic with peak times for individual links. In each case where an estimate was used, the manager notes the uncertainty of the estimate, and concentrates on improving items that have the greatest uncertainty.

7.20.6 Experimenting With Possible Changes

The chief advantage of a traffic model lies in the ability of managers to investigate possible network enhancements without disrupting the network. That is, a manager postulates a change in the network, and then uses the traffic matrix to see how the change affects behavior. There are three types of changes:

- Change the network topology
- Change routing in the network
- Change assumptions about failure

Changes in topology are the easiest to imagine. For example, a manager can explore the effect of increasing the capacity of one or more links or the effect of adding extra links. If the calculation of resource usage is automated, a manager can experiment with several possibilities easily. The next sections discuss changing the routing architecture and changing assumptions about failure.

7.21 Route Changes And Traffic Engineering

One of the more subtle aspects of capacity planning concerns routing: a change in the Layer 3 routing structure can change resource untilization dramatically. In particular, one alternative to increasing the capacity of a link involves routing some traffic along an alternative path.

Managers who are concerned with routing often follow an approach known as *traffic engineering* in which a manager controls the routing used for individual traffic flows. In particular, a manager can specify that some of the network traffic from a given ingress to a given egress can be forwarded along a different path than other traffic traveling between the same ingress and egress.

The most widely recognized traffic engineering technology is *Multi-Protocol Label Switching (MPLS)*, which allows a manager to establish a path for a specific type of traffic passing from a given ingress to a given egress. Many large ISPs establish a *full mesh* of MPLS paths among routers in the core of their network. That is, each pair of core routers has an MPLS path between them†.

7.22 Failure Scenarios And Availability

Another aspect of capacity planning focuses on planning network resiliency in the face of failure. The idea is straightforward: consider how a network will perform under a set of *failure scenarios*, and plan excess capacity and backup routes that will achieve the required availability. Failure planning is especially critical for service providers because the business depends on being able to guarantee availability; it can also be important for enterprises.

Typically, failure scenarios are chosen to consider *single point failures*. The most obvious cases include the failure of a single link or a single network element. However, many planners focus on failure of a *facility*. For example, a planner might observe that: network elements residing in a physical rack share the same source of power, several logical circuits are multiplexed onto the same underlying fiber, or a set of services are located within a single *Point Of Presence (POP)*. Thus, for planning purposes, a manager can define a facility to be a rack, a cable, or a POP. Once a facility has been defined, a manager can consider how the network will perform if all items in the facility become unavailable. The point is:

---

†A later chapter on tools for network management discusses MPLS traffic engineering.

In addition to planning capacity to handle increases in traffic, network managers consider possible failures and plan capacity sufficient to allow a network to route around problems.

7.23 Summary

Performance measurement and assessment is one of the key parts of network management. There are two aspects. The first focuses on understanding how resources are currently being used and how an existing network is performing. The second focuses on long-term trends and capacity planning.

The primary measures of a network are latency, throughput, packet loss, jitter, and availability. No single measure of performance exists because each application can be sensitive to some of the measures without being sensitive to others. Although measuring individual items in a network is easiest, meaningful assessment requires end-to-end measurement, possibly with active probing.

Measurement is used to find bottlenecks and do capacity planning. Planning the capacity of a single switch is straightforward and involves knowing the number of ports.

Utilization is related to delay. To measure link utilization, a manager makes multiple measurements over time; 15-minute intervals work well for most networks. Peak utilization can be computed from the 95th percentile. In heavily used links, the peak-to-average ratio is almost constant, which allows a manager to measure average utilization and employ the 50/80 Rule.

Managers use a traffic matrix to model network load, where the matrix gives the average or peak data rate from each network ingress to each egress. Given a network topology, a manager can use values from the traffic matrix to determine capacity needed on a given link or network element. To plan capacity, a manager experiments by changing assumptions about network topology or routing and calculating new resource requirements. In addition to planning capacity for normal circumstances, managers consider the excess capacity needed to accommodate failure scenarios.

Chapter Contents

8.1   Introduction, 97
8.2   The Illusion Of A Secure Network, 97
8.3   Security As A Process, 98
8.4   Security Terminology And Concepts, 98
8.5   Management Goals Related To Security, 99
8.6   Risk Assessment, 100
8.7   Security Policies, 101
8.8   Acceptable Use Policy, 102
8.9   Basic Technologies Used For Security, 102
8.10   Management Issues And Security, 105
8.11   Security Architecture: Perimeter Vs. Resources, 105
8.12   Element Coordination And Firewall Unification, 106
8.13   Resource Limits And Denial Of Service, 107
8.14   Management of Authentication, 107
8.15   Access Control And User Authentication, 108
8.16   Management Of Wireless Networks, 109
8.17   Security Of The Network, 110
8.18   Role-Based Access Control, 111
8.19   Audit Trails And Security Logging, 112
8.20   Key Management, 112
8.21   Summary, 113

8

Security

8.1 Introduction

Early chapters provide general background on the topic of network management. Previous chapters each explain one aspect of the FCAPS model.

This chapter concludes the discussion of FCAPS by focusing on the management of network security. Rather than focus on technologies or products for security, the chapter explains security from a management point of view. It examines security risks with which managers must contend, and outlines steps that can be taken to control risks.

8.2 The Illusion Of A Secure Network

Many managers hold a fundamentally flawed view of security: they view a *secure network* as a goal to be achieved. If a secure network is the goal, the management question becomes: "what steps should be taken to make the network secure?" Vendor advertising feeds the misconception by touting products that make a network secure against a particular threat.

When is a computer network totally secure? Unfortunately, absolute security is an illusion — no technology will ever exist that can guarantee a network remains immune to all possible risks. In July, 1999, the New York Times ran a story on computer networking that expresses the idea succinctly:

There is no such thing as a secure computer network.

8.3 Security As A Process

If a network can never be absolutely secure, how should a manager view security? The answer lies in understanding that security is a process of improvement instead of a goal — although a network can never become absolutely secure, managers continually strive to improve security. That is, a manager evaluates potential risks, takes actions to solve or avoid security problems, and reevaluates risks in the resulting network. Figure 8.1 lists the process that a manager performs.

- Assess potential risks
- Establish policies to avoid risk
- Evaluate technologies and mechanisms
- Deploy appropriate procedures and technologies
- Measure effectiveness of solutions

Figure 8.1 Activities that constitute the process a manager performs continually to evaluate and improve network security.

As the above discussion shows, management of security differs fundamentally from other aspects of network management. Security policies have broad impact on all aspects of a network, including the configuration and operation of network elements, protocols, and network services. Security policies affect network managers as well as internal and external users of the network. The point is:

Security differs from other aspects of FCAPS because security is a continual process that has pervasive impact on network elements, services, and users.

8.4 Security Terminology And Concepts

Before continuing a discussion of security management, we need to define basic terminology. Rather than give extended explanations and examples, this section provides brief summaries of the following terms that are adequate for the remainder of the discussion:

- Identity
- Authentication
- Authorization
- Data integrity
- Privacy and confidentiality
- Encryption

Identity. Many security issues involve verifying the identity of an individual, application program, or network element. To permit such verification, an entity must be assigned a unique *identity*, which may be a number, a string of text, or other value. An assignment of identity is typically configured into each element, but can also be permanently fixed (e.g., a serial number burned into the hardware).

Authentication. The term *authentication* refers broadly to verification of the identity of a correspondent. That is, a receiver uses an authentication mechanism to validate the identity of the sender when a message is received. Authentication can be employed when communication is first initiated (i.e., to establish a connection) or with each message exchange.

Authorization. To control access, management systems assign each manager or management application program a set of restrictions and privileges. Whenever it receives a request, a management system first validates the identity of the requester, and then invokes an authorization mechanism to determine whether the request falls within the privileges granted to the requester.

Data Integrity. A data integrity mechanism allows a receiver to test whether the data in a message was changed during transit across a network. Typical data integrity schemes require a sender to include additional information with each message; the additional information allows the receiver to determine whether the contents of a message were altered.

Privacy And Confidentiality. Although security experts draw distinctions, most networking professionals use the terms *privacy* and *data confidentiality* interchangeably. In essence, a mechanism that keeps data confidential encodes each message to prevent eavesdroppers from being able to extract meaning or interpret the message. The resulting communication is ''private'' in the sense that even if a third party makes a copy of messages as they flow across a network, the third party will not be able to decode the message and read the contents.

Encryption. An encryption mechanism arranges for a sender to run a computation that scrambles the bits of a message in such a way that only the intended recipient can unscramble the message. Encryption is the primary mechanism used to achieve authentication and privacy.

8.5 Management Goals Related To Security

A network manager concentrates on three aspects of security:

- Protection of resources
- Control of access
- Guarantee of confidentiality and safety

Protection. A manager tries to protect resources against unauthorized use, sabotage, copying, and theft. A manager must be concerned with attacks on the network itself as well as attacks that use a network to reach end-user systems or other resources. In addition, a manager must establish policies for protection against physical as well as electronic attacks. Finally, managers must extend protection beyond the base infrastructure to include application services.

Control Of Access. One of the most important parts of network security focuses on controlling access to services reachable over a network and the network itself. A manager establishes policies that specify who can access each resource and what that person or computer account may or may not do. Access control applies to network managers as well as to users — a given member of a network management team may have permission to control or modify some parts of the network, but not others†.

Guarantee Of Confidentiality And Safety. A network manager must maintain information as securely as necessary. That is, in consultation with the owner of data, a manager considers the need for confidentiality and takes steps to ensure the need is met. Confidentiality extends to data stored on end-user systems as well as data passing across the network. The confidentiality of both internal data from local users and data from external customers is important.

8.6 Risk Assessment

Assessing risk involves considering a key tradeoff between ease-of-use and risk. On one hand, a network that has no restrictions is easiest to use, which means higher productivity for employees and customers. On the other hand, a network that has no restrictions is most vulnerable to misuse.

Thus, when evaluating risks, a manager must consider the overall goals of the organization, and align network security with security policies for the rest of the organization. For example, a financial institution usually has rigorous constraints on security throughout the organization. Thus, financial institutions usually place tight constraints on the use of their computer networks, even if doing so increases the difficulty of using the network.

A second aspect of risk assessment focuses on financial impact: the potential cost to the organization if a security breach occurs. To estimate the cost, a manager must analyze the probability that a given event will occur and the negative effect on the organization if the event does occur. For example, a manager considers potential losses in terms of: lost revenue, lower employee productivity, loss of intellectual property, and the potential for criminal liability.

Understanding the probability of each risk as well as the potential cost is important because all security work involves tradeoffs between the cost of preventing problems and the cost that results if the problem occurs. Eventually, a manager must use the

---

†We will revisit the topic of limited access by network administrators later in the chapter.

results of risk assessment to make choices about which security problems to solve and which to leave unsolved.

8.7 Security Policies

Before a network manager can make decisions about procedures or technologies for security, the manager must devise and document a security policy for the organization. Security policies can contain sweeping statements about network operations such as:

> No financial data shall pass across the company's network without being encrypted.

A security policy can contain statements that focus on personnel and specify qualifications needed to handle specific items related to security, such as:

> Only a senior security manager may have a written copy of the company's private key.

A security policy can also contain statements about procedures to be followed when a security violation occurs, such as:

> The network management team must report each incident that appears to compromise security to the Chief Security Officer when the incident is first detected.

Finally, a security policy can specify record keeping, such as:

> A log of security incidents must be kept that specifies the time each incident was detected and a report of the action taken.

Policies work best if they specify a desired result instead of specifying exactly how to achieve the result. If a policy specifies details, either the policy must be rewritten to accommodate change or the policy will become out of synch with reality. For example, suppose a policy specifies the use of a specific encryption technology. If the technology becomes obsolete, it is likely that whoever chooses a replacement technology will not understand the criteria used to make the original selection. However, if instead of specifying a technology, the policy states the goal clearly, a manager will understand how to choose a replacement technology that fills the need, and the policy can survive the transition unchanged.

8.8 Acceptable Use Policy

One aspect of network policy stands out as unusual: an *acceptable use policy* (*AUP*). An AUP defines a set of rules regarding the use of a network, including traffic and activities that are allowed or not allowed. Typically, an AUP is written to constrain users. For example, an AUP can specify applications that are prohibited (e.g., users may not run peer-to-peer file sharing programs) or limit interaction (e.g., a user may only run client programs and not server software).

AUPs are unusual because limitations on use can arise from legal, financial, or security considerations. At some universities, for example, an AUP prohibits the use of the university network for profit-making activities. From a security standpoint, a manager must decide which uses of the network jeopardize security policies. For example, an AUP might specify that it is unacceptable to forward packets onto a network from an outside source because doing so allows outsiders to access the network without passing through the organization's firewall and other security mechanisms.

8.9 Basic Technologies Used For Security

The technologies used as the basis for network security can be divided into three broad classes:

- Encryption technologies
- Perimeter control technologies
- Content control technologies

8.9.1 Encryption Technologies

Encryption forms the basis for both confidentiality and authentication. From a network management point of view, encryption can be divided into three types:

- Shared secret key encryption
- Public key encryption
- Session key

Shared Secret Key Encryption. As the name implies, an encryption scheme that uses a shared secret key requires all parties who participate to know a key that is kept secret. The principal management issues focus on policies and procedures for the secret key. For example, which network managers are permitted to know the secret key? If multiple sites are using encryption to send data, how is a copy of the shared key communicated from one site to the other?

Public Key Encryption. The second main form of encryption is known as a *public key* scheme. Unlike a shared key technology, public key encryption requires each party to hold two keys: a *private* key that is kept secret and a *public* key that is widely distributed. Thus, a private key is kept secret within the organization that owns the key, but everyone knows an organization's public key.

Note that although both types of encryption require a manager to keep a secret, the two differ dramatically regarding how many parties keep each secret. In a public key approach the secret information is restricted to one organization — no outside parties need to know an organization's private key. In a shared key approach, all communicating parties need to know the secret key.

Session Key. Encryption technologies such as SSL rely on a mechanism known as a *session key* or *one-time key*. In essence, both ends of the connection negotiate a key to be used to encrypt data during the session (e.g., for one web transfer). Most session keys are generated automatically; a manager does not need to manage the keys or keep them secret.

8.9.2 Perimeter Control Technologies

The *perimeter* of a network can be defined as the set of network elements that can receive packets from an outside network. A manager uses *perimeter control technologies* to give a precise definition of the boundary between an organization's network and outside networks. Perimeter control determines which outsiders have access to the network and what outsiders can do. For example, a manager can use perimeter control to limit the types of packets that outsiders can inject into the network and the set of destinations to which packets can be sent.

Three important mechanisms used for perimeter control are:

- Stateful firewall
- Intrusion Detection System (IDS)
- Virtual Private Network (VPN)

Stateful Firewall. A manager configures a firewall to act as a packet filter. That is, a manager gives a set of rules that specify which packets are allowed to enter the network (i.e., pass through the firewall), and the firewall blocks other packets from entering. Most firewalls allow a manager to create a separate set of rules that specify how to filter outgoing packets†. A firewall is *stateful* if a manager can specify a rule that automatically accepts replies to outgoing communication. Thus, instead of creating a rule for each possible web site, a manager can specify that whenever an internal user opens a connection to a web site, the firewall should permit incoming packets on the connection to pass into the organization's network.

Intrusion Detection System. In principle, an IDS provides passive monitoring. That is, an IDS merely watches traffic pass from an ingress port to an egress port, and informs a manager when unexpected patterns of traffic are detected that indicate a potential security violation. In practice, an IDS may also act as a packet filter — when a potential violation is detected, the IDS automatically establishes a rule that blocks further packets from the source until a manager can examine the situation and choose whether to leave the restriction in place or admit the traffic.

Virtual Private Network. An interesting and special case of perimeter control involves management of VPN technologies. In essence, a VPN can circumvent perimeter restrictions and allow an outsider direct access to the network, or can join two sites of an organization across the public Internet. Although it is useful for employees who work remotely, VPN technology is prone to abuse because almost any computer inside an organization can be configured to operate VPN software that provides access to outsiders. Managers must constantly watch for covert VPN software that employees inadvertently import in the form of a virus.

8.9.3 Content Control Technologies

The third class of technologies used for security focuses on the data being transferred. That is, instead of examining individual packets, a *content control technology* extracts and analyzes a complete data stream. Often a content control system operates as a proxy that performs an operation on behalf of a user, analyzes the data involved, and only allows the operation to complete if the data passes the test.

Three widely-used forms of content control are:

- Spam filter
- Virus scanner
- Pattern matcher

A *spam filter* works in conjunction with an email server to discard incoming email that is classified as spam. An incoming email message is placed in temporary storage, examined by the spam filter, and either discarded as spam or forwarded to the destination mailbox. In some systems, instead of being discarded, the spam is placed in a special mailbox, and the user can choose how to dispose of the spam.

---

†One network manager pointed out to the author that using private IP addresses on an internal network makes firewall rules easier to configure and less prone to human error.

A *virus scanner* spans multiple applications because virus scanning can be applied to incoming email, an incoming data file retrieved by a file transfer application, or an incoming web page. As with a spam filter, the incoming data is accepted and placed in a temporary storage area before a virus scanner is invoked. If a data item is found to be free from any known viruses, the data item is allowed to pass on to its destination.

A *pattern matcher* is a generalization of a virus scanner. Instead of looking for patterns in the data that match a well-known virus, a pattern scanner looks for arbitrary patterns. For example, a pattern scanner can be used to check images to determine whether an image contains an unusually large area of skin tones.

One of the most important management considerations of content control systems arises from the storage and processing time required — a manager must plan sufficient processing power to prevent transfers from becoming unusably slow, and must ensure that sufficient temporary storage is available to hold all data that is being examined. Temporary storage can present a problem because data items can be arbitrarily large. Thus, a manager can limit the size of data items (e.g., bound the size of an email message).

8.10 Management Issues And Security

The next sections consider several important management issues related to security. The descriptions are not meant to serve as a comprehensive list of all security management tasks or problems. Instead, the discussion points out a set of management problems that are particularly significant.

The sections consider a fundamental question about security as well as more mundane issues and day-to-day tasks. In particular, our discussion begins by asking about the overall approach an organization can take regarding security. The answer determines how an organization organizes its network security system and selects which security technologies to use.

8.11 Security Architecture: Perimeter Vs. Resources

We use the term *security architecture* to refer to the overall design of a security system. A fundamental question underlies the choice of a security architecture: at what level should the network be protected? A network manager must answer the question when designing a security architecture. There are two broad approaches that help a manager understand the issue; they can be characterized by the following extremes:

- Focus on the perimeter: erect a security barrier at the perimeter of the network that only gives access to trusted parties, and allow a trusted party to access any resource in the network.

- Focus on resources: ignore the perimeter and allow anyone to access the network, and erect a separate security barrier around each individual resource.

Perimeter Security. Because employees are treated as "insiders" and others are treated as "outsiders", an enterprise tends to favor perimeter security. That is, an enterprise often focuses on enforcing perimeter security, but does not require internal users to cross a security barrier for each resource. In some cases, an enterprise divides the network into *internal* and *external* segments, and limits outsiders to the external segments.

Resource Security. Because they offer transit services, service providers tend to favor resource security. That is, a provider's network does not filter packets or restrict access — an arbitrary user on the Internet can exchange packets with any of the provider's customers. Thus, a provider depends on customers to protect their resources. If the provider itself offers services such as web hosting, each service is protected.

In practice, of course, most networks combine some amount of perimeter security with some amount of resource security. For example, although an enterprise restricts its internal network to employees, the enterprise may still require a user to enter a password before granting access to payroll data. As another example, some networks provide a *quarantine region* (typically a single subnet) to which outside traffic is restricted†. Thus, one of the fundamental questions a manager must ask when designing a security architecture concerns the tradeoffs between trying to restrict the network to trusted users and trying to control security for each resource. To summarize:

> *When creating a security architecture, a manager must consider when to rely on perimeter security and when to require security for each individual resource.*

8.12 Element Coordination And Firewall Unification

Recall from Chapter 3 that network elements are designed to be configured and managed independently. As a result, one of the main problems a network manager faces lies in providing *coordination* among multiple network elements. For example, a network manager must coordinate security mechanisms running on servers in the network with client-side mechanisms that run on users' computers. Although Part 2 of the text discusses tools and platforms that can be used to coordinate devices securely, no coordination scheme is widely accepted. That is:

---

†The existence of portable computers complicates quarantine because an employee can import viruses or other problem software by connecting a computer to the organization's network after the computer has been exposed to an outside network.

> *In many networks, a human is responsible for ensuring that all network elements are configured to enforce the same security policies.*

One case of coordination stands out as particularly important: firewall configuration. The problem is known as the *firewall unification problem*, and is especially significant because misconfiguration can allow intruders to enter the network and access resources.

8.13 Resource Limits And Denial Of Service

We mentioned that content control technologies such as a virus scanner require temporary storage for incoming data. Storage for content control is a specific example of a more general problem with which network managers must contend: protection against resource overrun. There are two issues:

- Protection for a single network element
- Protection for the network at large

Protection for a single element means ensuring that no application running on the element can consume arbitrary resources. For example, if an email server allows incoming messages to be arbitrarily large and stores incoming messages on disk, an attacker can disable the email system by sending a large enough message to fill the disk.

Protection for the network at large is more difficult. The easiest attack, known as a *Denial Of Service attack (DOS attack)*, consists of flooding packets into the network at such a high rate that the network becomes unusable. Of course, if all packets come from a single source, a manager can change the firewall rules to filter traffic from the source. Thus, attackers hijack many computers at various Internet sites, and arrange for the hijacked computers to send packets. The result, known as a *Distributed Denial Of Service attack (DDOS)*, is much more difficult to control.

8.14 Management of Authentication

Authentication refers to validating the source of a communication. A manager can choose to apply authentication at various levels:

- Authentication of a packet
- Authentication of a message
- Authentication of a computer system

Authentication Of A Packet. The IETF has defined a technology known as *IPsec* that allows a receiver to authenticate the source of each incoming IP datagram. Although IPsec is not widely deployed, managers need to be aware that such technologies exist.

Authentication Of A Message. Authentication can be applied to each individual message that is transferred from one computer to another. For example, a mail server can authenticate the source of each incoming email message. Because it has lower overhead, message authentication is often preferred to packet authentication.

Authentication Of A Computer System. When an application communicates with a remote system (e.g., a web site), the application can use an authentication scheme to validate the identity of the remote computer. Authentication helps avoid *spoofing* and other attacks. For example, a browser validates the identity of a web site before indicating to a user that the site can be trusted for e-commerce.

A manager must choose and configure an authentication scheme for each resource (typically for servers). In many cases, authentication relies on a *hash algorithm*. Hash algorithms are built on standard encryption mechanisms. Thus, once a manager has established the keys needed for encryption, no additional facilities are needed for authentication that uses a hash algorithm.

8.15 Access Control And User Authentication

A variety of schemes have been used to validate users' identities. The schemes can be divided into three basic approaches that check:

- What the user knows (e.g., a password)
- What the user has (e.g., a SmartCard or badge)
- What the user "is" (e.g., a fingerprint)

Password management stands out as surprisingly difficult. First, passwords are used for a variety of reasons, including logging onto a specific computer, authenticating oneself to an application, and accessing a web page. Second, password mechanisms are usually managed independently — each application or computer system devises a scheme to accept and validate passwords. To avoid requiring a user to remember dozens of passwords, many managers look for ways to *coordinate* passwords across platforms. Thus, a chief management problem centers on password coordination.

What makes password coordination difficult? The primary difficulty arises because passwords span heterogeneous systems. For example, in addition to web pages that have password access controls, a large network usually includes multiple operating systems. Computers run operating systems such as Linux, Windows, Mac OS, and Solaris. Large mainframe computers introduce additional possibilities. Heterogeneity means that the rules for valid passwords differ. To summarize:

> *The heterogeneity present in a large network makes password coordination difficult. In addition to using independent mechanisms, each system defines rules for valid passwords.*

Password management is also difficult because many security policies specify using *forced password rollover* to prevent users from retaining the same password for an extended time. To implement rollover, the network manager periodically gives users a deadline by which all passwords must be changed. The manager invalidates any account for which the password remains unchanged by the deadline. On systems that do not have an automated mechanism for rollover, managers must handle invalidation manually. Unfortunately, experience has shown that forced rollover can have the opposite effect than is intended: instead of making passwords more secure, rollover can create an unsecure situation. The reason is that if a user must remember many passwords and each password changes frequently, the user is more likely to write the passwords down and keep the written list close to the computer. We can summarize:

> *Forcing password changes to occur at a frequent rate can result in a less secure network.*

A final issue can make password management difficult: risk that arises from the transmission of passwords. When setting a password policy, a manager needs to understand exactly where passwords will be transmitted and how they are represented. In particular, it makes no sense to enforce strict rules on passwords and then use software that sends passwords across networks in *clear text* (i.e., unencrypted). Surprisingly, many applications do transmit unencrypted passwords. In particular, the *Post Office Protocol* (*POP*) used to access email sends passwords in clear text. We can summarize:

> *Password management includes the transmission of passwords; a manager must be aware that applications such as web and email can transmit unencrypted passwords.*

8.16 Management Of Wireless Networks

Wireless networks pose special problems for the management of security. In particular, Wi-Fi networks that allow multiple computers to share bandwidth create potential security risks. A frame transmitted over a Wi-Fi network is subject to eavesdropping — a third party can obtain a copy of all frames traveling over the Wi-Fi network†. An encryption technology named *Wired Equivalent Privacy* (*WEP*) was developed to encrypt Wi-Fi frames, but WEP can be broken given enough time. Thus, even if WEP is used, a third party can capture a copy of a conversation, break the encryption, and

---

†Note that because transmissions can extend beyond the boundary of a building, an eavesdropper can remain outside the physical premises.

read messages. As a result, many managers seek other encryption technologies that can be used with Wi-Fi†.

Other security problems in Wi-Fi arise from the use of a 32-character string called a *Service Set IDentifier* (*SSID*). An SSID is used to identify each wireless LAN — before a computer can become *associated* with a Wi-Fi access point, both the wireless interface in the computer and the access point must be configured to have the same SSID. Unfortunately, SSIDs alone do not provide security because a third party can monitor the network, capture copies of frames, and extract the SSID. Furthermore, the default configuration in many access points is open: the access point broadcasts its SSID. Finally, managers must contend with a subtle detail in some software: when it boots, a computer that has been connected to an access point will try using the same SSID again, which can compromise a company's SSID if a laptop that was used inside the company is booted outside the company. The point is:

> *In addition to allowing eavesdropping, wireless networks that use Wi-Fi technology have an SSID that gives an illusion of security but can be compromised easily.*

8.17 Security Of The Network

In addition to considering security for data and end-user systems, a network manager must establish security policies for the network itself. Of course, the devices and media that constitute the network must be kept physically secure. In addition, security for a network includes technology to protect network elements and links from electronic attack. For example, a manager may need to consider how to secure DNS servers. In addition, procedures and guidelines are needed for the personnel who manage and operate the network.

Establishing guidelines and checks on personnel is especially important, because it is well-known that many security breaches are caused by humans, either through mistakes made when configuring elements or through maliciousness. Thus, some managers require all changes that affect misson-critical aspects of the network to be performed by a team. At least one member of the team is assigned to check the work of others to ensure that no mistakes occur. The point is:

> *In addition to technologies that protect the network itself, a manager needs to find ways to check changes that personnel make because many security problems arise from human error.*

---

†Although alternatives have been proposed, none is a widely accepted standard.

8.18 Role-Based Access Control

One particular aspect of securing network elements stands out: management of passwords. Network elements that offer a command-line interface usually employ a login process that requires a manager to log into the system before entering management commands. Login on a network element resembles login on a conventional computer: an ID and password are required. Thus, a manager must assign and control IDs and passwords for multiple network elements.

As with standard passwords, the question of *coordination* among multiple elements is important: can a network manager use the same ID and password on all switches and routers, or does each element define its own set of IDs? Obviously, a manager will find it much easier to use the same login on all network elements.

Unlike the logins and passwords assigned to users, logins assigned to network elements introduce a further complication: *sharing*. In a shared environment, a single login and password is established on each network element, and the entire network management team uses the shared login.

Sharing a single login has two chief advantages: it makes password administration trivial, and allows a team member to find out the password from another team member. However, sharing also has two significant disadvantages. The first disadvantage arises because a shared account needs maximal privilege — the single login must have sufficient power to permit arbitrary control of a network element. The second disadvantage arises because a shared login does not provide *accountability*. That is, if a network element is changed, the login used to make the change does not identify an individual. We can summarize:

> *Sharing logins and passwords among a management team poses a security weakness in which all team members have maximal privilege, and does not provide accountability among team members.*

How should a set of logins and passwords be organized to accommodate management of a network? The ideal solution, which is known as *Role-Based Access Control* (*RBAC*), allows the assignment of specific privileges to each job classification. For example, a member of the management team who is responsible for routing can be allowed to change IP routes or configure routing protocols without also being allowed to change VLAN assignments.

It may seem that an RBAC system requires each network element to contain complex user interface software that understands authorization and only allows a given individual to enter commands for which the individual is authorized. However, many RBAC systems use a central server to simplify authorization. When a network manager logs into a network element, the network element asks for a login ID and password as usual. When the user enters a command, the network element sends the command and the user's login information to an RBAC server to request authorization. The server decides whether the user is authorized. Thus, RBAC can be applied to each individual command even if the network element does not have the sophisticated software needed to evaluate RBAC. The point is:

> *Role-Based Access Control allows specific privileges to be assigned to each job classification; a network element can use RBAC even if the network element does not have a powerful user interface that can evaluate privileges.*

8.19 Audit Trails And Security Logging

Chapter 5 discusses event logs in the context of fault detection. An event log used for fault detection contains a record of unusual events as well as faults. The point of a fault log is to help a network manager diagnose the cause of a problem that does occur or spot unexpected events that indicate potential trouble and take action to prevent the problem.

Event logs used for security fill a similar role, and may be combined with other logs. On one hand, a log of events that are related to security can help a manager take action to prevent a problem from developing. On the other hand, a log of events can help a manager audit actions that were taken and determine the underlying weakness when a problem does occur.

8.20 Key Management

One of the most significant management issues surrounding the use of encryption is known as *key management*. Encryption technologies that employ a shared secret key are the easiest to manage: a manager must protect the secret key from being compromised. A manager stores a copy of the key securely, and establishes polices that control which personnel have access as well as limits on what they can do with the key. In addition to local control, a manager must communicate the secret key to other parties with whom secure communication is needed. Typically, secret keys are sent out-of-band, meaning that a manager uses the telephone or a postal service to communicate the key.

Key management for public-key encryption is complex. A manager must establish local policies to control access to the organization's secret key. In addition, a manager must distribute the organization's public key. It may seem that almost any distribution mechanism would suffice (e.g., sending the public key in an email message). However, unless a receiver has assurance that a public key does indeed come from the correct organization, the public key cannot be trusted. Thus, a receiver must be able to authenticate the copy of a public key and determine who sent it. The process of sending out public keys is known as *key distribution*. Unfortunately, although several key distribution schemes exist, no single infrastructure for key distribution has emerged as the standard. Thus:

> *When public-key technology is used, a manager must choose a key distribution strategy.*

8.21 Summary

No network is absolutely secure; security is a process of continual assessment and improvement that is concerned with protection of resources, control of access, and guarantees of confidentiality and safety. Network managers devise and implement a security policy.

The three basic technologies managers use for security are: encryption, perimeter control, and content control. A manager must choose a security architecture as a compromise between the extremes of perimeter security and resource security.

Management issues related to security include element coordination, protection of the network, the level of authentication (packets, messages, or computers), password management, wireless network management, and key management. Role-based access control mechanisms provide a way to authorize members of a network management team for specific management tasks and not for others.

Part II

Existing Tools And Platforms For Network Management

Chapter Contents

9.1   Introduction, 117
9.2   The Principle Of Most Recent Change, 117
9.3   The Evolution Of Management Tools, 118
9.4   Management Tools As Applications, 118
9.5   Using A Separate Network For Management, 119
9.6   Types Of Management Tools, 120
9.7   Physical Layer Testing Tools, 121
9.8   Reachability And Connectivity Tools (ping), 122
9.9   Packet Analysis Tools, 123
9.10   Discovery Tools, 124
9.11   Device Interrogation Interfaces And Tools, 126
9.12   Event Monitoring Tools, 127
9.13   Triggers, Urgency Levels, And Granularity, 127
9.14   Events, Urgency Levels, And Traffic, 129
9.15   Performance Monitoring Tools, 129
9.16   Flow Analysis Tools, 132
9.17   Routing And Traffic Engineering Tools, 133
9.18   Configuration Tools, 133
9.19   Security Enforcement Tools, 134
9.20   Network Planning Tools, 134
9.21   Integration Of Management Tools, 135
9.22   NOCs And Remote Monitoring, 136
9.23   Remote CLI Access, 137
9.24   Remote Aggregation Of Management Traffic, 138
9.25   Other Tools, 140
9.26   Scripting, 141
9.27   Summary, 141

9

Management Tools And Technologies

9.1 Introduction

Earlier chapters define the problem of network management and provide general background. The previous five chapters each explain one of the levels of network management that are embodied by the FCAPS model.

This chapter begins a new part of the text that focuses on existing tools and platforms that network managers use to plan, configure, monitor, control, and diagnose networks. Instead of listing specific commercial products, the chapter characterizes tools and describes the range of functionality. Successive chapters each examine a major technology in more detail.

9.2 The Principle Of Most Recent Change

How do network managers solve problems? The manager at one large company wryly observes that his network runs just fine until one of the management team members makes a mistake. Thus, he can solve management problems by discovering who made the most recent change and undoing it. We call the approach the principle of most recent change:

> *Many management problems can be solved by undoing the most recent change made by a member of the management team.*

Many networks follow the principle of most recent change as a strategy to resolve network problems. For a small network, where members of the management team tend to remain in close proximity, personal contact suffices — one team member can easily ask others who made a recent change. For larger networks, where dozens of team members work on many devices, however, documentation of changes and the time at which the change occurs is essential in identifying the cause of problems.

9.3 The Evolution Of Management Tools

The networking industry has traditionally focused marketing on devices that offer higher speed and more features. As a result, engineers have been encouraged to devise faster, more powerful packet switching technologies; the development of mechanisms and tools that configure, monitor, and control networks has been an afterthought.

In the early Internet, management was not an issue. Researchers focused on designing and understanding individual protocols. Tools were built to test or measure one protocol at a time, and the tools were designed to aid research, not to help manage large networks. As we will see, some of the early test tools are still used.

By the 1980s, as the Internet grew, it became apparent that tools would be needed to automate management tasks. Groups of researchers experimented with a variety of mechanisms and approaches. In the 1990s, commercial vendors began offering network management facilities, including software that presented a graphical display of network state and performance. The sections below explain how tools have evolved further.

9.4 Management Tools As Applications

One of the earliest debates in network management focused on the position of management protocols in the protocol stack. Engineers who built the ARPANET argued that management had to be performed at a low layer of the stack. They devised a set of diagnostic and control protocols that operated at Layer 2, and arranged AR-PANET packet switches to give priority to the control protocols. When the ARPANET malfunctioned, managers operating the network used the low-level control protocol to diagnose the problem. A Layer 2 control protocol worked well in the ARPANET because of uniformity: all packet switches were the same.

The advent of internetworking introduced a fundamental change in the form of heterogeneity. Engineers who were familiar with low-level control and diagnostic protocols argued that low-level management protocols were essential and should be standardized. They pointed out that only low-level protocols allowed a manager to bypass normal forwarding. Thus, even when forwarding was broken, management packets could get through.

Meanwhile, researchers began to investigate another approach. They argued that because an internet contains many types of physical networks, attempting to standardize layer 2 protocols across all network hardware is hopeless. In fact, they observed, it may be that the only way to traverse the path between a manager and a managed network element is with IP. Thus, they argued for using IP and standard transport-layer protocols (i.e., TCP and UDP) for management tasks.

While the debate raged, another interesting idea emerged: if standard transport protocols are used, management software can be built as an application and run on an arbitrary computer. Thus, instead of requiring special-purpose computers or operating systems to generate and handle packets for a specialized layer 2 protocol, a manager can use commodity hardware (e.g., a PC). After much debate, the higher-layer approach emerged as the most widely used:

> *A typical network management tool consists of an application program that uses standard transport-layer protocols to communicate and runs on a conventional computer such as a PC.*

Of course, there are exceptions to the rule. For example, tools that monitor and debug optical networks usually consist of specialized hardware devices that contain tunable optical lasers. However, even specialized management tools often consist of two parts: a device that performs low-level functions and an inexpensive commodity computer used to control the low-level device and display results.

9.5 Using A Separate Network For Management

A second major debate pervaded early discussions of how to build network management systems. The debate focused on the importance of having a separate physical network for management traffic. There are two advantages of using a separate physical network:

- Robustness
- Performance

Robustness. Telephone companies pioneered the idea of separating the management infrastructure from the production network. One of the chief arguments in favor of separation arises from the desire for robustness: if the same network is used for data and control packets and a network element fails in such a way that it stops accepting data packets, a manager will not be able to send management commands. Thus, having a separate control path to each network element means that a manager can always use tools to control elements remotely.

Performance. A second motivation for separating the management infrastructure from the production network arises from a desire for increased performance. As we will see, to provide continuous updates, a monitoring tool usually maintains continuous contact with a device. That is, packets flow from the device to the monitor in a steady stream. If a manager monitors a single device, the extra traffic is minor. However, in a large network where a manager may monitor hundreds or thousands of devices, the monitoring traffic can become significant. Thus, segregating management traffic onto a separate network can improve overall performance of the data network.

The chief disadvantage of using a separate network is cost. Of course, if all network elements are in close proximity and each element has a separate management Ethernet interface, creating a separate management network is inexpensive. An additional Ethernet switch is installed, the management interface from each element is connected to the switch, and the manager's workstation (i.e., the computer that runs the management applications) is connected to the switch. In the general case, however, where network elements are geographically distributed and the types of management interfaces on some elements differ from the types on others, a separate network is expensive or infeasible. Consequently:

> *Although a separate management network can improve robustness and performance, most sites choose a low-cost option of running management traffic over the same network that carries data.*

9.6 Types Of Management Tools

Network management tools can be grouped into twelve basic types:

- Physical layer testing
- Reachability and connectivity
- Packet analysis
- Discovery
- Device interrogation
- Event monitoring
- Performance monitoring
- Flow analysis
- Routing and traffic engineering
- Configuration
- Security enforcement
- Network planning

The next sections each explain one of the basic types and give examples of the functionality of available tools.

9.7 Physical Layer Testing Tools

Although managers seldom test physical layer properties of wired networks, it is important to understand tools that exist because they can be a shortcut to diagnosing a problem. We will briefly review three tools:

- Carrier sensor
- Time-domain reflectometer
- Wireless strength and quality tester

Carrier Sensor. A carrier sensor is a trivial device. A sensor usually consists of an LED that lights when a carrier is present. Thus, a carrier sensor can be used to determine whether a connection has been wired correctly. For example, most devices that have Ethernet ports include a carrier sensor on each port.

Time-Domain Reflectometer (TDR). A TDR is usually a small, hand-held device that can measure the length of a cable by sending a signal down the cable and waiting for the electrical reflection to return. Thus, when a copper cable has been cut, a TDR can compute the distance to the break.

Wireless Strength And Quality Tester. A strength and quality tester is a useful tool for diagnosing interference problems in wireless networks, especially in a Wi-Fi network where computers can move easily. Typically, a wireless tester operates as an application that uses conventional network interface hardware.

Although it is possible for a wireless tester to display results numerically (e.g., strength 93%, quality 89%), a visual display can also be used. Figure 9.1 illustrates one possible display.

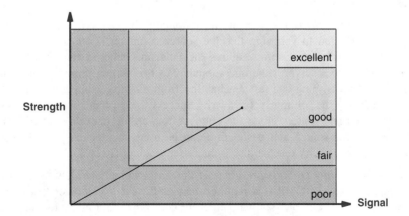

Figure 9.1 Illustration of a two-dimensional display produced by a wireless testing tool. The example signal and strength are in the *good* range.

9.8 Reachability And Connectivity Tools (ping)

Tools that test *reachability* and *connectivity* are among the oldest and most widely used management tools. The purpose of such tools is straightforward: verify that it is possible to communicate from one point in the network to another. Although tools exist to test other layers, reachability is almost always tested at Layer 3 by sending IP datagrams across the network and verifying that they arrive.

One particular reachability tool dominates all others: an application program known as *ping*†. Ping employs the *echo* facility in the *Internet Control Message Protocol (ICMP)*. When a manager runs ping, the application generates and sends an ICMP *Echo Request* message to a specified destination. When an Echo Request arrives at a destination, ICMP software sends an *ICMP Echo Reply* back to the source. Thus if an echo reply arrives that matches the request sent, ping announces success; if no matching reply arrives after a few seconds, ping announces failure.

It may seem that ping is too trivial to be useful. However, there are five reasons for ping's popularity:

- Intuitive appeal and ease of use
- End-to-end verification
- Wide availability of software
- Usefulness in scripting
- Options for advanced testing

Intuitive Appeal And Ease Of Use. Ping is so trivial that in its basic form, ping can be used without training by almost anyone. Furthermore, ping is intuitively appealing because the underlying approach of sending a test probe and receiving a reply makes sense to humans.

End-To-End Verification. Despite its simplicity, ping exercises many aspects of a network. In addition to verifying that the source computer is connected to a physical network, successful use of ping requires the Domain Name System to be configured correctly and a DNS server to be operational. Most important, ping verifies a network *end-to-end*. That is, ping can test reachability from a source computer to a destination computer that can be arbitrarily far away. Success means that routing is in place (in both directions) and routers along the path are forwarding packets correctly. Furthermore, because the source and destination can be users' computers instead of network elements, ping can verify reachability from a user's point of view‡.

Wide Availability Of Software. One of the reasons ping is widely used arises from its ubiquity. Because ICMP is a required part of IP, every computer that connects to the Internet includes ICMP software that answers ping. Furthermore, ping software comes with every computer and most network elements. Thus, a manager can choose an arbitrary system as a source and another arbitrary system as a destination.

---

†The term *ping* originally expanded to *Packet InterNet Groper*.

‡Some sites choose to block incoming ping traffic. Thus, it may not be possible to reach some destinations (e.g., an arbitrary web server).

Usefulness In Scripting. We will learn that automated scripts are often used to manage large sites. Ping is an essential part of many scripts, and has been used in scripts for many years. Indeed, an early version of ping that was developed for the Unix operating system was one of the first management tools to be invoked in a script.

Options For Advanced Testing. Despite its simplicity, ping does provide advanced features. Ping reports the time that expires between transmission of a probe and reception of a response, which allows a manager to assess the current performance of a network. In addition, most versions of ping offer an option that can be used to set the packet size. Managers can use the option to determine whether large packets are causing problems in a network. Another option allows ping to emit a steady stream of requests, usually one per second. A stream of packets allows a manager to probe the network for a period of time and then receive a report on total packets sent, average and maximum round trip times, and packet loss rate.

We can summarize:

> *Although it is deceptively simple and easy to run, the ping program is the most widely used tool to test end-to-end reachability. In addition to humans invoking it directly, ping is used by automated management scripts.*

9.9 Packet Analysis Tools

A *packet analyzer*, also called a *protocol analyzer*, is a tool that can capture copies of packets, display information in packet headers, and accumulate statistics, such as the number of IP datagrams that have arrived. Packet analyzers were first invented as a tool to aid in protocol implementation and testing, but are now primarily used by network managers to diagnose problems or understand the set of protocols that contribute to traffic on a network.

A wide range of packet analyzers exists. To handle the highest-speed networks, a packet analyzer requires special-purpose hardware. Thus, a high-speed analyzer usually consists of a stand-alone device. However, a conventional computer has sufficient power to capture and analyze packets from a slower network. Thus, a low-speed analyzer usually consists of software that runs on a commodity computer. An analyzer that runs on a laptop computer is especially convenient because the laptop can be moved easily.

A typical packet analyzer has options that allow a manager to control the operation and display. For example, a manager can select to accumulate statistics or capture copies of packets for later processing. Once packets have been captured, a typical analyzer allows a manager to step through the captured packets and view the headers and contents of each packet. Some analyzers allow a manager to specify a *packet filter*. That is, a manager can instruct the analyzer to ignore all packets except those in which header fields contain specific values. Thus, a manager might choose to restrict the display to: a specific transport protocol (e.g., TCP), a specific host (e.g., traffic from or to host X), or a specific application (e.g., VoIP traffic). Filtering is particularly helpful when diagnosing a problem.

Many commercial and shareware packet analyzers exist. Some are packaged with operating systems such as Solaris and Linux, and others are sold as stand-alone devices. One of the most popular analyzers is a program named *Ethereal* that is available from:

http://www.ethereal.com/

Part of Ethereal's popularity arises because versions are available for multiple platforms, including Windows and Linux. Ethereal uses conventional network interface hardware, but changes the hardware configuration to make the interface accept all packets instead of just packets destined for the computer. Thus, if a computer running Ethereal is connected to a hub or has a wireless LAN interface, Ethereal can capture each packet that traverses the corresponding network.

To summarize:

> *One of the most popular packet analyzers is an open source application program named Ethereal. Versions are available for a variety of platforms, including Windows and Linux.*

Interestingly, Ethereal's license allows users to modify the program and add their own features. Of course, such modifications require extensive programming expertise that is beyond the scope of most network managers. However, sites that have in-house expertise can tailor Ethereal for specific needs.

9.10 Discovery Tools

As the name implies, discovery tools can be used to learn about a network. There are two primary categories:

- Route discovery
- Topology discovery

Route Discovery. We said that managers use the ping program to test end-to-end reachability. If ping fails, however, the tool does not provide a manager with the location of the problem. It could be that the failure occurs near the source computer, near the destination computer, or somewhere in between. Therefore, to debug a reachability problem, a manager must discover the path from the source to the destination.

Of course, a manager can learn a route by manually examining the IP routing table in each network element along the path. Unfortunately, a manual process is both time-consuming and error prone. Thus, instead of a manual process, most managers use a *route discovery tool* to trace paths automatically. A typical route discovery tool is an application program that runs on a host or router, and uses probes to discover the path to a specified destination.

One of the most popular route discovery tools is an application program known as *traceroute* that uses a series of probes with successively higher hop counts to find and list all the routers along a path to a destination†. Although traceroute was originally built to work with Unix, versions are now available for most operating systems. For example, the Windows operating system uses command name *tracert*. Traceroute can be obtained from:

http://traceroute.org/

To summarize:

> *A route discovery tool, such as the* traceroute *application, produces a list of the network elements along a path from a source to a destination.*

Topology Discovery. An interesting management problem arises because Internet technology makes extending a network easy. For example, consider a small enterprise that provides an Ethernet connection to each office. If a user connects an inexpensive hub to the Ethernet, the user can connect additional computers and printers. In a large enterprise, the situation is worse: because the IT staff is large and the network contains many subnets, additions or changes to the network that are not documented can be overlooked.

A *topology discovery tool* helps managers learn about undocumented parts of an enterprise network. Topology discovery tools are automated, and do not require the manager to enter a description of the network. Instead, a topology discovery tool proceeds by sending probe packets, usually to all possible addresses on one of the subnets‡. Once it has collected responses, the discovery tool further probes each responding device to determine whether the device is a host computer or a router.

Topology discovery tools use a variety of output formats. In the simplest case, a tool merely lists the IP addresses of computers in use on a given subnet. Some discovery tools draw a picture to illustrate a network, with boxes representing network elements and lines showing connections between elements and subnets. A picture that represents a network with many interconnections can become too dense to read easily. Thus, tools that have a pictorial display often allow a manager to zoom in on a single subnet. The point is:

---

†To hide their internal network architecture, some ISPs configure routers to ignore traceroute probes. Thus, traceroute may not be able to discover the addresses of some routers along a path.

‡Some discovery tools send ICMP Echo Requests. Cisco Systems has defined a *Cisco Discovery Protocol* (*CDP*).

> *Although pictorial output works well to display the topology of a*
> *small network, a tool that displays the topology of a large network*
> *works best if a manager can select a subset of items to view.*

9.11 Device Interrogation Interfaces And Tools

How does a manager learn the status of a given network element? Three basic interfaces are used:

- Command line interface
- Web interface
- Programmatic interface

Command Line Interface (CLI). Most network elements support a CLI that allows
a manager to examine (or change) management data. For example, a manager can use a
CLI to ask whether a specific interface is *up* or *down* or to ask for the IP address assigned to an interface. Because they are designed for humans, CLIs are usually incon-
venient for programs to use directly.

Web Interface. Some network elements use a *web interface*. That is, the network
element runs a web server, and a manager can uses a browser to contact and interrogate
the network element. Web interfaces require network connectivity between the
manager's computer and the network element, and are even less convenient for programs to use than a CLI.

Programmatic Interface. Unlike a CLI or web interface, a *programmatic interface*
is not intended for humans to use directly. Instead, a human runs a tool, usually an application program, that communicates with a network element. The tool sends requests
over the network to a network element, and displays responses in a form suitable for a
human manager. The most common programmatic interface currently uses the *Simple*
Network Management Protocol (SNMP†), a vendor-independent standard from the
IETF; other programmatic interfaces are also available (e.g., CMIP and XML). The important point is:

> *Because it decouples the tool a manager uses from the underlying net-*
> *work elements, a programmatic interface allows a manager to choose*
> *a vendor-independent tool as the mechanism used to interact with net-*
> *work elements.*

---

†The next chapter describes SNMP in more detail.

9.12 Event Monitoring Tools

One of the key ideas in network management focuses on the concept of *event monitoring*. An event can correspond to a hardware failure, an alarm generated by software, a change in the state of a network element, or a change in traffic load. Managers choose a set of events to monitor and configure an *event monitoring tool* to check the events. That is, the tool monitors each of the possible events continuously, and notifies the manager when an event occurs (e.g., by flashing a red symbol on the manager's screen). A manager uses the notification as an indication of a problem.

The interaction between an event monitoring tool and a set of network elements can follow one of two paradigms:

- Polling
- Asynchronous notification

Polling. In a system that uses *polling*, the event monitoring tool controls all interaction. The monitor continuously contacts each network element, interrogates the current status, and displays the results for a manager. To control the rate of polling, a manager configures the monitoring tool.

Asynchronous Notification. In a system that uses *asynchronous notification*, individual network elements are configured to watch for specified events and send reports to the monitoring tool when they occur. The monitoring tool waits passively for reports to arrive, and then updates the display for a manager. For example, the next chapter describes the asynchronous notification facility in SNMP (the same vendor-independent standard used for device interrogation). To summarize:

> *An event monitoring tool can use polling or asynchronous notification to collect data. When an important event occurs, the monitoring tool changes the display to notify a manager.*

9.13 Triggers, Urgency Levels, And Granularity

In either the polling or asynchronous approach to data collection, each event is assigned a *trigger level* at which a manager should be notified. For example, consider a carrier loss event. If a particular connection is important (e.g., the line that connects an organization to the Internet), a manager might associate an event with carrier detection and set the trigger level for carrier loss to the highest priority. However, not all carrier loss needs to be reported with the same urgency. If a particular cable is used for testing and is often unplugged for a few seconds, a manager might choose to set the trigger for carrier loss to a lower priority.

In an ideal event management system, the software allows a manager to give a precise definition for each event along with the notification details. For example, a manager should be able to specify that on an important connection, the system must report carrier loss immediately with a bright red icon that flashes; while on another connection, carrier loss is reported using a small yellow icon that does not flash and the notification only appears after the cable remains unplugged for three or more minutes. Thus, the monitor will alert a manager immediately when an important cable is disconnected, but will only inform a manager after an unimportant cable is left unplugged for an extended period. To summarize:

> *Ideally, event monitoring software allows a manager to set both a trigger level at which an event will occur and the notification details for the event.*

In practice, few event monitoring tools provide the ideal environment described above. Instead, typical software specifies a few basic *levels of urgency*, and requires a manager to associate each event with one of the predefined levels. Each level corresponds to a display (e.g., a color). For example, Figure 9.2 lists a set of urgency levels.

Level	Display	Meaning
Emergency	Red	Immediate attention required
Problem	Yellow	Corrective action needed
Warning	Orange	Action may be needed
Notification	Green	No action required

Figure 9.2 Illustration of basic levels of urgency provided by event monitoring software. A manager associates each event with one level.

Some tools also provide for *escalation* of events — an event can start at one level of urgency and move up over time. For example, when an event first occurs the software reports it as a *problem*. However, if the problem is not resolved after ten minutes, the software raises the urgency level to *emergency*.

We can summarize:

> *To help focus a manager's attention on important events, a monitoring tool can allow a manager to assign levels of urgency to each event and use colors to distinguish levels of urgency when displaying a report.*

9.14 Events, Urgency Levels, And Traffic

In addition to allowing a manager to classify the urgency level of each event, many monitoring tools also allow a manager to control the urgency levels displayed. For example, a manager can specify that all events are to be displayed or limit the display to emergency-level events only.

In a system that uses polling, limiting the display usually has no effect on the traffic between the event monitor and the network being monitored. To make a decision about which events to display, the monitoring tool must continuously check all possible events. In a system that uses asynchronous notification, however, the choice of display has a direct effect on traffic because software running on individual network elements can make a decision about which events to report. Thus, the volume of traffic decreases dramatically when a manager limits the display†.

One aspect of traffic from asynchronous monitoring is related to the granularity of control offered by some monitoring tools. Instead of allowing a manager to control asynchronous events for individual items, the monitoring tool only allows a manager to specify an urgency level (e.g., red, yellow, or green), which means that a network element will report all events at the specified level or higher. Thus, it is not possible to request events for one interface without receiving equivalent events for all interfaces.

In terms of traffic and display, having only a few levels of urgency means that a device is often at one of two extremes: either the device is too quiet (the information a manager needs is not reported) or the device is too chatty (a manager is inundated with extraneous information). The point is:

> *The volume of traffic generated in an asynchronous monitoring system depends on the level of detail that a manager examines. A monitor that uses levels of urgency to control devices provides little differentiation, which means a manager may receive too much information or too little.*

9.15 Performance Monitoring Tools

Monitoring performance is closely related to event monitoring. Like an event monitoring tool, a *performance monitoring tool* interacts with network elements and displays information for a manager. Also like an event monitor, a performance monitor can either use a polling or asynchronous notification paradigm.

The chief difference between event and performance monitoring arises from the types of display. In the case of event monitoring, the display is intended to report discrete conditions such as whether a link is up or down. In the case of performance

---

†Traffic does not cease completely because even if no events need to be reported, the monitoring tool continuously checks to ensure that the network element is online and operational.

monitoring, the display is intended to report a continuously changing value such as the load average of a CPU or the response time of a server.

> *Unlike event monitoring, which focuses on discrete values and thresholds, performance monitoring provides continual assessment that shows a manager changes over time.*

The most common measures of performance correspond to an assessment of the traffic. For example, Figure 9.3 lists several measures of traffic that a performance monitor can report.

Measure	Value Reported
Link utilization	Percentage of capacity
Packet rate	Packets per second
Data rate	Bits per second
Connection rate	Connections per second

Figure 9.3 An illustration of items related to traffic load that a performance monitor can report.

As the figure shows, a variety of traffic measures can be reported. Because a performance monitor reports changing values, a question arises: how should the data be displayed for a manager? There are two common ways to display performance data:

- Time progression graph
- Dynamic histogram

Time Progression Graph. A time progression graph consists of a two-dimensional plot where the x-axis corresponds to time and the y-axis corresponds to performance. Either the display shows an extended time period (e.g., an entire week), or the display constantly shifts to show the most recent window (e.g., the display always corresponds to the most recent five minutes). The chief advantage of a time progression graph arises from a manager's ability to see a trend — a manager can easily tell whether performance is improving or becoming worse.

Dynamic Histogram. Unlike a time progression that includes history, a dynamic histogram only shows the current state. That is, the display contains a set of columns that each correspond to an item being measured, and the height of a column corresponds to the performance. The chief advantage of a dynamic histogram arises from the simultaneous display of many measurements — a manager can easily judge the performance of multiple network elements or links.

Using an application program to generate a display means that a manager is not restricted to one format. For example, a manager can begin with a screen that shows histograms for multiple links. If the performance for a particular link appears to be outside expected parameters, the manager can select the individual link and view a time progression graph. Similarly, a manager can dynamically vary the time interval over which a time progression is displayed to zoom in on the period during which trouble started to occur. Finally, once a problem has been resolved, a manager can return to a histogram that displays multiple measurements.

To help a manager assess performance, a display can be marked with boundaries that delineate acceptable and unacceptable performance. Possibilities for boundaries include fixed limits, a baseline measure, or an extreme for the previous N time units (e.g., the minimum and/or maximum over the previous week). For example, Figure 9.4 illustrates a histogram of link utilization with boundaries marked for the 50/80 Rule†.

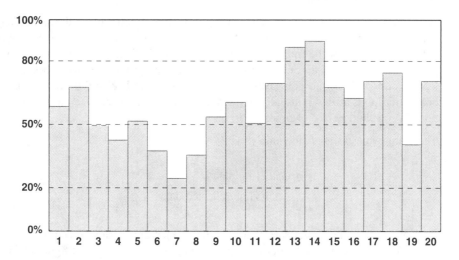

Figure 9.4 Illustration of a display with histograms showing the current utilization on twenty separate links. Boundaries allow a manager to tell which links are operating within target bounds.

On a computer display, vivid colors can be used to make performance problems stand out. For example, links over 50% can be shown in yellow, and links over 80% can be shown in red. The point is:

---

†The 50/80 Rule is described on page 88.

*A performance monitoring tool can use a graph to show how the per-
formance of a resource varies over time or can use a histogram format to display the performance of many resources. Boundaries or
colors on the display make it easy for a manager to spot performance
that falls outside expected bounds.*

9.16 Flow Analysis Tools

Most performance tools provide a measure of *aggregate traffic* on a link or
through a network element. For example, a performance tool might show the total
number of bits that cross a link in a given time period or might report the link utilization. Although they can help a manager assess the total load, reports of aggregate performance do not provide details about the traffic.

A *flow analysis tool* assists a manager by providing details about the individual
flows that make up a traffic aggregate. We define an individual *flow* to be the communication between a pair of endpoints, usually a pair of application programs. A flow
is easiest to understand if a connection-oriented transport protocol is used because a
flow corresponds to one transport-layer connection (i.e., a TCP connection). For connectionless transport, a flow is usually defined as a set of packets between a pair of applications over a short period of time.

There are two aspects of flow analysis:

- Gathering data
- Analyzing collected data

Gathering Data. For a network that operates at medium or slow speed, gathering
data about flows is not difficult. For example a Linux system can be configured to in-
tercept packets and keep a record of flows on an Ethernet. For high-speed networks,
however, special-purpose hardware is required to capture flow data.

Chapter 11 describes one of the most well-known mechanisms used to gather flow
data. The mechanism, named *NetFlow*, was developed by Cisco Systems, and has become a de facto standard that is supported by other vendors.

Analyzing Collected Data. Usually, the analysis of flow data is conducted offline.
That is, after information about flows has been gathered, the data is passed to an application program that performs analysis and presents the results for a manager. Chapter
11 explains flow analysis further.

Flow analysis is helpful for two reasons. First, analysis can help a manager understand the nature of traffic (e.g., whether the traffic on a link corresponds to a few long-
lived connections that each transfer large volumes of data or to many short-lived con-

nections that each transfer a small amount of data). Second, analysis can help a manager isolate the source of problems (e.g., identify the flows responsible when a link becomes overloaded). For now, it is sufficient to understand:

> *Flow analysis helps a manager examine the constituent components of the traffic at a given point in a network. The analysis identifies individual flows that correspond to communication between a pair of endpoints.*

9.17 Routing And Traffic Engineering Tools

Although routing is among the most automated of management tasks, a set of management tools exist that allow managers to control routes. In particular, *routing and traffic engineering tools* allow a manager to specify the route that specific flows will follow. In addition, such tools allow a manager to control the resources allocated to a specific flow and select a backup route for the flow in case the primary route fails. Chapter 12 discusses routing and traffic management in more detail, and explains how managers engineer traffic.

9.18 Configuration Tools

A wide variety of *configuration tools* exist to help managers configure sets of network elements. Some tools are designed for a specific vendor's products, and others are designed to handle elements from multiple vendors. Some tools offer a convenient interface for a manager, independent of the interface used with the underlying network elements. Some tools merely provide remote access. That is, although a manager can access a network element from a remote location, a remote access tool requires a manager to enter commands exactly as if the commands were being typed on the element's console.

Configuration tools can use a variety of interfaces to interact with network elements. For example, some tools use the device's command-line interface. Other tools use a programmatic interface (e.g., SNMP). Finally, in cases where an underlying device only offers a web interface, some tools use the web interface. That is, the tool acts like a web browser by sending requests to a device in HTML format and receiving HTML responses. The tool then examines the HTML to extract pertinent information, a process known as *screen scraping*.

Because they are designed for human interaction, most command-line interfaces do not work well with a program. The syntax is often verbose, with error messages and instructions presented as text with no special punctuation or other means to delineate a message from other data. More important, many CLIs use context to eliminate repetitious typing. Thus, after a human enters a command such as *using interface 2*, all successive configuration commands apply to interface 2. A CLI that offers context-dependent commands needs a mechanism that allows a human to determine the context. For example, when asked about context, a network element might respond:

You are currently configuring interface 2.

Although such output can be easy for humans to understand, a program must parse the sentence and extract information.

Some vendors of network elements attempt to accommodate both a human operator and a computer program. For example, Juniper builds routers that start with a programmatic configuration interface. Then, Juniper adds a CLI interpreter suitable for humans. The advantage is that an automated configuration tool can use the programmatic interface without losing functionality. The point is:

> *The interface a network element provides determines whether building software to configure the element will be easy or difficult and whether all functionality available to human operators is also available to software.*

9.19 Security Enforcement Tools

A variety of tools exist that help a manager enforce security policies. For example, tools exist that unify an organization's firewall policy. The tool accepts a policy statement plus a list of firewall devices, and configures each device to enforce the policy.

In some cases, separate security tools are not needed because security enforcement is an integral part of other tools. For example, a traffic engineering tool that establishes an MPLS tunnel; may have an option to use encryption for data passing through the tunnel.

9.20 Network Planning Tools

A final category, *network planning tools*, covers application programs that managers use to plan networks and configurations. Network planning tools exist that help managers plan a variety of network functions, including future *capacity* needs, *security* architectures, and *failover* strategies.

As we have discussed, capacity planning and routing are intrinsically linked. As a result, capacity planning tools are closely related to tools that plan routes. The point is:

Although vendors sell tools that managers use to plan network capacity and architecture, such plans cannot be made without considering the effect on routing and traffic engineering.

9.21 Integration Of Management Tools

The previous sections describe a set of tools that managers can use to configure a network element, monitor a set of events, and monitor performance. That is, we have focused on element management systems and described a set of independent tools. A significant question remains unanswered: to what extent have vendors integrated individual management tools into a coordinated system?

The question about integration is especially meaningful because many of the tools are related. For example, when an event occurs, a manager may need to interrogate network elements, examine routes, and check traffic on a particular link. Thus, it makes sense to combine management tools to produce a single, unified management system. In addition to combining multiple tools, a unified system could make it possible to coordinate configuration across multiple network elements. Thus, instead of requiring a manager to configure one network element at a time, a unified system could configure a set of network elements.

Standards bodies and vendors have attempted to unify network management tools either by providing a way to manage multiple network elements or providing a uniform interface that a manager can use to access multiple tools. For example, the *netconf* working group of the IETF has been chartered to produce a standard protocol for network configuration:

http://www.ietf.org/html.charters/netconf-charter.html/

The Free Software Foundation has developed a high-level language for expressing configuration policy known as the *GNU configuration engine* (*cfengine*):

http://ftp.gnu.org/gnu/cfengine/

In addition, vendors offer products that provide a unified management interface. For example, Cisco Systems offers a family of management products that focus on security under the name *CiscoWorks*:

http://www.cisco.com/en/US/products/sw/cscowork/ps4565/index.html

Hewlett Packard offers a product named *OpenView*:

> http://www.managementsoftware.hp.com/

The IBM management products are marketed under the name *Tivoli*:

> http://www.ibm.com/software/tivoli/

Computer Associates offers multiple network management products:

> http://www3.ca.com/products/

OPNET Technologies offers integrated products, such as *IT Guru*:

> http://www.opnet.com/products/itguru/

To summarize:

> *In addition to tools that each handle one aspect of network manage-*
> *ment, vendors offer integrated tools that provide a uniform interface a*
> *manager can use to handle multiple management tasks.*

9.22 NOCs And Remote Monitoring

As the discussions above imply, many management tools consist of application programs that run on a conventional computer. For a small site, all tools can run on a single management computer. We use the term *management workstation* to refer to a computer on which managers run management tools. Large sites use multiple management workstations, each with its own display. Often, a large site collects the management workstations into a single physical location, which is known as a *Network Operation Center* (*NOC*).

Collecting management stations into a NOC is convenient because doing so allows managers to monitor and control an entire network from one location. However, centralizing management workstations has consequences for network design for two reasons:

- Connectivity to remote devices
- Management traffic

Connectivity To Remote Devices. It may seem that the issue of providing connectivity to remote devices is moot — after all, management packets can pass over a network between a NOC and an arbitrary device as easily as other data. Thus, the NOC can use SNMP to access any network element.

Unfortunately, SNMP requires three conditions to hold. First, SNMP requires a network to provide connectivity and routing to remote devices. Second, SNMP requires each managed device to include an SNMP agent; some small, special-purpose devices do not offer SNMP access. Third, the same functionality must be offered through SNMP as through the command-line interface (many network elements offer a richer set of options through a CLI than through the SNMP interface). The point is:

> *Even if a network element runs SNMP software, the configuration and control functionality available via SNMP may differ from the functionality available via a CLI.*

Management Traffic. Although we think of network management as consuming few resources, the use of polling or asynchronous event notification generates continuous background traffic. In particular, instead of generating notifications at a fixed rate, flow monitoring generates traffic proportional to the number of flows on a network. Thus, if a NOC monitors many links and network elements, the traffic can become significant. The situation is exacerbated if an organization has multiple NOCs (e.g., a primary and a backup), each monitoring the same set of links and elements. As a result, the management data transferred across a network can interfere with other data traffic.

One particular case of traffic stands out as especially troublesome: ping traffic. Of course, running ping manually does not generate much traffic. However, a NOC uses automated software that can be configured to ping a set of interfaces continuously. In many cases, a manager configures the software to check each interface on each device in the network. A large network element can have hundreds of interfaces, which means that ping traffic can become significant. The point is:

> *Although we think of management traffic as insignificant compared to data traffic, automated tools that check events, report on flows, or test reachability can generate large volumes of traffic.*

9.23 Remote CLI Access

We said that some network elements provide richer functionality through CLI than through SNMP. There are two ways a manager can access an element's CLI remotely:

- Remote terminal software

- Inverse serial multiplexor

Remote Terminal Software. Software running on a manager's station acts as a client that uses the network to communicate with a remote terminal server on a network element. In essence, the remote terminal software creates a window on the manager's workstation that appears to connect to the console of the remote network element. That is, keystrokes entered while in the window are sent to the network element, and output from the network element appears in the window.

Two remote terminal technologies are popular: *telnet* and *ssh*, and each uses TCP to carry data (i.e., the software forms a TCP connection between a manager's workstation and a remote network element). To a manager, either telnet or ssh provides the same essential service of allowing one to interact with a remote device. The difference between the two technologies arises from the level of security each provides. Telnet sends keystrokes and responses in clear text; ssh encrypts all data before transmission. Thus, ssh prevents eavesdropping from occurring between the manager's station and the managed device. The point is:

> *Some network elements use remote terminal facilities such as telnet or ssh to provide a manager access to an element's CLI from a remote location. Ssh encrypts all communication.*

Inverse Serial Multiplexor. Although it provides CLI access, the remote terminal approach relies on a network to remain operational along the path between the manager and the managed entity. An alternative approach uses serial hardware to avoid relying on the data network. That is, a manager runs serial cables from each network element back to a centralized control point.

Rather than use an ASCII terminal to interact with a given serial cable, a manager can employ a device known as an *inverse serial multiplexor* and use remote terminal software to access the multiplexor. Figure 9.5 illustrates the architecture.

9.24 Remote Aggregation Of Management Traffic

We said that although it makes management tasks easier, a centralized NOC can impose a significant traffic load on a network. As a managed network grows, management traffic between the NOC and managed entities increases. Eventually, a network can reach a size where the overhead incurred by communication between the NOC and network elements cannot be tolerated.

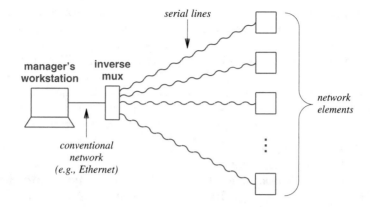

Figure 9.5 Illustration of an inverse serial multiplexor (mux) used to provide
remote access to network element consoles. Remote terminal
software is used on the connection between a manager's workstation and the inverse multiplexor.

To manage a large network from a central location without causing undue traffic, a
manager can install a set of *remote aggregation points*. Each aggregation point interacts with a set of nearby network elements to obtain management data. The aggregation point filters and analyzes the raw data to consolidate pertinent information into a
short summary that can be communicated back to the NOC. As a result, the amount of
traffic transferred between a NOC and a remote aggregation point is much less than the
traffic required for a NOC to communicate directly with each network element. Figure
9.6 illustrates the concept.

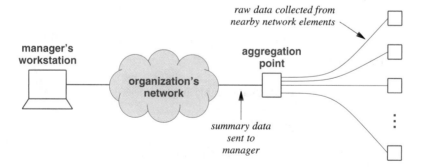

Figure 9.6 Illustration of an aggregation point used to reduce management
traffic. The aggregation point gathers data from nearby network
elements and sends a summary to a management station in the
NOC.

Remote aggregation works well for a variety of management activities. For example, a remote system can receive and filter asynchronous notifications and alarms (e.g., SNMP traps) and decide when to alert a manager. Similarly, a remote system can collect and consolidate performance data from a set of systems. When polling is used, a remote system can handle the polling locally, without continuously sending data between a NOC and remote network elements. In each case, the amount of data sent between a NOC and remote network elements is substantially reduced. The point is:

> *Remote aggregation can be used to reduce the amount of management traffic that passes between a NOC and a set of remote network elements. The remote aggregation system captures and consolidates management data; only a summary is sent to a manager.*

9.25 Other Tools

Our description of management tools has focused on the major categories of tools available to a manager. Other tools exist, including commercial products, open source management platforms, and specialized tools that each solve a small problem. For example, Cisco Systems sells an *ISC* tool that can be used to configure a VPN, the *openNMS* project is creating an open source management platform, and the *dig* program provides a way to explore the Domain Name System.

Many management tools and prototypes available from the research and open source communities can be found on the web. Examples include *Cricket, Cacti, ntop, OSSIM, FlowScan, RRDTool, DAGs, DShield, Honeynets,* the *NETwork DOcumentation Tool* from the University of Oregon, *AANTS* from the University of Wisconsin, and *RANCID*, which can be obtained from:

http://www.shrubbery.net

Tools can also be found at:

http:/www.caida.org/tools

and

slac.stanford.edu/xorg/nmtf

Finally, additional technologies are available that provide the support system needed for management tools. For example, the Free Software Foundation has produced the *Radius* system that can be used for authentication.

9.26 Scripting

Although the descriptions above mention the need for automated interfaces, much of the chapter focuses on tools that interact with a network manager. Chapter 13 explores an important idea that allows all tools to scale: scripting. We will see that scripts can allow a manager to automate repetitive tasks and tailor a management environment to accommodate the needs of a given organization.

9.27 Summary

A wide variety of management tools have been created, including tools that test the physical layer, discover topology or routes, analyze packets, test reachability, interrogate and configure network elements, monitor events or performance, handle security, and help a manager plan network capacity. The interface between tools and network elements can consist of command-line interaction, a web interface, or a programmatic interface such as SNMP.

A centralized Network Operations Center (NOC) has the advantage of focusing all management activities in a single location. However, a centralized NOC has the disadvantage of forcing all management traffic to flow to a single point. As an alternative, remote aggregation can be used to reduce NOC traffic.

Chapter Contents

10.1   Introduction, 143

10.2   The Remote Management Paradigm And Applications, 143

10.3   Management Functions And Protocol Definition, 144

10.4   The Read-Write Paradigm, 145

10.5   Arbitrary Operations And Virtual Items, 146

10.6   Standards For Network Management Protocols, 146

10.7   SNMP Scope And Paradigm, 147

10.8   Basic SNMP Commands And Optimizations, 148

10.9   Asynchronous Traps And Event Monitoring, 148

10.10 Traps, Polling, Bandwidth, And CPU Cycles, 149

10.11 Management Information Base (MIB) And Variables, 150

10.12 A Hierarchy Of MIB Variable Names, 151

10.13 Advantages And Disadvantages Of A Hierarchy, 153

10.14 Complex Data Aggregates And MIB Tables, 154

10.15 Granularity Of Aggregate Access, 155

10.16 Transport Protocols And Interaction, 155

10.17 Updates, Messages, And Atomicity, 156

10.18 The Remote Monitoring MIB (RMON), 157

10.19 A Manager's View Of MIB Variables, 158

10.20 Security And The Community String, 159

10.21 Summary, 160

10

Simple Network Management Protocol (SNMP)

10.1 Introduction

Chapters in the first part of the text provide general background and define network management. The previous chapter contains an overview of tools and technologies that are available to manage networks. The chapter also explains that many tools consist of application programs that run on a manager's workstation.

This chapter continues the discussion of existing network management platforms by describing a technology that is widely deployed. Instead of giving details and message formats, the chapter focuses on the underlying paradigm and the use of a hierarchical namespace. In later chapters, we will see that both concepts are fundamental when we consider how the approach can be extended to create a more powerful network management system.

10.2 The Remote Management Paradigm And Applications

By the late 1980s, various groups had explored network management. Most of the work concentrated on element management systems. One of the ideas that emerged during the early work was a *remote management paradigm* in which software running on a manager's workstation allowed a manager to interact with a set of network elements without physical contact. That is, management software could be used to configure, interrogate, monitor or control an arbitrary network element or service.

Once the remote management paradigm became an accepted goal, a question arose: exactly how should remote access be provided? As Chapter 9 discusses, one approach employs an inverse multiplexor to provide access to an element's serial console connection. Researchers also considered a more general approach: using an application-layer protocol running over TCP/IP to permit a management application to interact with a network element.

Using an application-layer protocol has three distinct advantages. First, no additional wiring or devices are needed. Second, because TCP/IP provides universal connectivity, a manager can access an arbitrary network element. Third, an application protocol can provide complex functionality and transfer larger volumes of data than a command-line interface that operates over a serial line. We can summarize:

> *Building an element management system as an application that runs over TCP/IP lowers cost, permits universal accessibility, and allows more complex functionality than a traditional CLI.*

10.3 Management Functions And Protocol Definition

The principle of using an application-layer for element management provides an overall architecture for software, but does not specify details about the interaction between the management application and the managed element. Before software can be built, the exact format of messages must be defined, the rules for exchanging messages must be specified, and meaning must be assigned to each item in the messages. In short:

> *Before element management software can be built, all details of a protocol must be specified, including the exact syntax and semantics of messages that can be exchanged.*

One of the primary issues that arises when designing a management protocol concerns the set of functions that will be included in the protocol. From earlier chapters, we know that a manager needs to configure, interrogate, and monitor network elements. In addition, a manager may need to perform tasks such as installing new versions of software, resetting hardware devices, or rebooting a network element. Consequently, early work on management protocols focused on compiling a list of operations that can be used to perform all management tasks.

Unfortunately, as new technologies arise, the list of management functions continues to change. For example, when firewalls appeared, managers needed to create and

examine firewall rules. Similarly, when Wi-Fi networks were invented, managers needed to control the SSID in each access point. It became apparent to researchers that:

> *It is impossible to create a comprehensive list of element management*
> *operations that will remain sufficient because new technologies intro-*
> *duce new needs.*

10.4 The Read-Write Paradigm

By the mid 1980s, an interesting proposal arose for element management protocols: instead of attempting to create a fixed list of all possible operations, make a protocol *extensible*. Furthermore, to avoid having many, incompatible versions of a protocol,
do not allow additional operations to be added to the protocol. Instead, keep the message format fixed, and limit extensions to semantics. That is, keep the protocol for
communication between a management station and a network element fixed, but allow
messages to encode arbitrary operations.

One particular approach to building extensible management protocols gained wide
acceptance: limit a protocol to two basic commands and allow parameters to specify all
the details. In particular, researchers proposed that a protocol be defined from the
management station's point of view and that the two operations correspond to *read* and
write (i.e., transfer data *from* the managed entity to the manager's workstation, or
transfer data from the manager's workstation *to* the managed entity). The idea is known
as the *read-write paradigm*.

As examples of the read-write paradigm, consider device interrogation and configuration. To interrogate a device, a manager's workstation sends the device a message
that specifies a *read* operation. In addition to the *read* operation, the message contains
information that specifies exactly which item is being requested. To change the configuration in a device, the manager's workstation sends a *write* request; further information in the message specifies the item to be changed and a new value to be assigned.
Thus, the protocol only needs two message forms to handle requests:

$$read\,(\,ItemToBeRead\,)$$

$$write\,(\,ItemToBeChanged,\ NewValue\,)$$

Of course, a protocol will need additional message types to carry responses back to
the manager's workstation. However, the set of operations remains small. We can
summarize:

A protocol that uses the read-write paradigm is extended by specifying new parameters; the set of operations remains small and fixed.

10.5 Arbitrary Operations And Virtual Items

Although it works well for device interrogation and configuration, the read-write paradigm does not appear to accommodate arbitrary operations. For example, consider rebooting a device. A traditional management protocol includes an explicit *reboot* operation — when a manager sends a message that specifies the reboot operation, the device reboots itself.

If a management protocol follows the read-write paradigm, all operations, including reboot, must be cast as a *read* or *write* operation. Doing so is straightforward: a new, *virtual* item is defined. The protocol designer imagines a new item (i.e., an item that does not correspond to a value stored in the network element), chooses a name for the item, and specifies how the name should be interpreted. Software on both sides must agree to recognize the name and perform the specified action. For example, a protocol designer can choose the name *Reboot* to correspond to a reboot operation, and can specify that a network element must agree to reboot itself when a message arrives that specifies writing a value to the *Reboot* item. Thus, to reboot a device, a manager can send:

write (Reboot, 1)

To cast additional management operations into the read-write paradigm, a protocol designer merely specifies additional virtual items and gives the semantics for each. We can summarize:

An arbitrary set of operations can be cast into the read-write paradigm by creating virtual items and specifying semantics for each.

We will understand the significance of virtual items in Part 3 of the text when we consider architectures for network management.

10.6 Standards For Network Management Protocols

By the late 1980s, several groups started work on management protocols that followed the read-write paradigm. Eventually, the *Open Systems Interconnection (OSI)* effort produced a pair of interlinked standards known as the *Common Management Information Protocol / Common Management Information Service (CMIP/CMIS)*. The IETF produced the *Simple Network Management Protocol (SNMP)*. SNMP is widely accepted among vendors, and has become the de facto industry standard.

10.7 SNMP Scope And Paradigm

Informally, managers use the term *SNMP* to refer to all aspects of SNMP technology, including software that implements SNMP as well as the protocols. To be accurate and precise, we need to understand that SNMP technology includes five major pieces:

- Message format and message exchange
- Message encoding
- Specification of items that can be accessed
- Software that runs on a network element
- Software that runs on a manager's workstation

Message Format And Message Exchange. The technology is built around the SNMP protocol. The protocol specifies communication between a manager's workstation and a managed entity by giving the details of message format and the rules for message exchange. The protocol does not include a large set of commands, nor does it change frequently. Instead, SNMP follows the read-write paradigm described above, which means that the basic protocol remains fixed; when the need for new functionality arises, new items are created.

Message Encoding. In addition to the message format, the SNMP technology includes a set of *Basic Encoding Rules* (*BER*) that specify how messages are encoded in binary for transmission across a network.

Specification Of Items That Can Be Accessed. To foster extensibility, the specification of items that can be accessed is independent of message format and encoding. SNMP uses the term *Management Information Base* (*MIB*) to denote the set of items that can be managed, and keeps the MIB definition separate from the message protocol.

Software That Runs On A Network Element. SNMP uses the term *agent* to refer to the software that runs on a network element, and uses the SNMP protocol to communicate with a manager's workstation. An SNMP agent responds to requests the manager sends by returning the requested information or performing the action associated with the item being changed.

Software That Runs On A Manager's Workstation. Client software that runs on a manager's workstation provides a link between a manager and the SNMP protocol — the software accepts requests from a manager, forms SNMP requests and sends them to the appropriate network element, and receives responses from the network element and displays results for the manager. As we will see, much of SNMP technology is focused on details that a manager does not need to understand. As a result, managers usually prefer a user interface that hides the details of SNMP and presents information in a form suitable for humans.

> The term SNMP *is used loosely to refer to the communication protocol, encoding rules, definition of managed items, and software.*

10.8 Basic SNMP Commands And Optimizations

Although it follows the read-write paradigm, SNMP uses the terms *Get* and *Set* instead of *read* and *write*. Even though managers seldom encounter the terminology directly, the human interface on some SNMP software refers to *Get* and *Set* operations.

In addition to the two basic operations, SNMP includes commands that are intended to optimize interaction with a network element. Optimization is especially helpful when automated software uses SNMP to perform management tasks. For example, consider a program requesting a large set of related items from a given network element. To follow the read-write paradigm, the program must send a *Get* request for each item. To optimize the interaction, SNMP provides a *Get-Bulk* command that can be used to obtain a set of items with a single request.

SNMP's *Get-Next* command provides another optimization by allowing an application to step through the entire set of items in a given network element one at a time. Each time a network element returns a response, the application extracts the name of the item and uses a *Get-Next* to request the "next" item beyond the one that was returned. Because it allows an application to retrieve the entire set of items from a network element without knowing a priori which items are present, the *Get-Next* command increases the functionality of SNMP.

To summarize:

> *In addition to* Get *and* Set, *SNMP includes* Get-Bulk *and* Get-Next *commands that are especially useful when an automated management application uses SNMP.*

10.9 Asynchronous Traps And Event Monitoring

SNMP includes one additional command that increases SNMP's functionality substantially: a *Trap* command. Trap differs from other commands in two significant ways:

- Agent software generates traps
- Traps are asynchronous

Recall that SNMP agent software runs in network elements. Thus, a *Trap* message originates in a network element. The *asynchronous* property of *Traps* means that a network element can generate and send a *Trap* message without waiting for an explicit *Get* message from the manager's workstation. That is, a *Trap* message is unprompted.

When does a network element send a *Trap* message and to which destination is the message sent? Because a *Trap* message is unprompted, an agent cannot use an incoming message to trigger a *Trap*, nor can an agent extract the workstation's address from an incoming message. The answer lies in configuration: a network element will not generate SNMP *Trap* messages unless a manager configures the agent software.

Typically, a manager uses SNMP *Traps* for event monitoring. That is, a manager specifies conditions under which a trap should be generated (e.g., a link becomes saturated or a large number of arriving packets have an invalid checksum) and the address of a management workstation to which a *Trap* message should be sent. Agent software in the network element tests each of the conditions continuously, and generates a *Trap* when it finds that a condition has been met†.

We can summarize:

> SNMP Trap *messages provide the basis for automated event monitoring; a manager configures a network element to generate SNMP Trap messages by specifying a set of conditions and the address of a management workstation.*

10.10 Traps, Polling, Bandwidth, And CPU Cycles

In theory, the inclusion of *Trap* messages in SNMP can be viewed as another form of optimization rather than as an extension. A *Trap* does not increase functionality because it is possible to achieve the same results by polling: software running on a management station can continuously send *Get* messages to request information from a network element, analyze the values that are returned, and alert a manager if any of the conditions are met.

In practice, polling is only feasible in the simplest of cases for two reasons. First, polling generates excessive network traffic. Polling traffic is proportional to the number of network elements and the number of items that must be examined in each. The number of items to be examined is important because a single condition can refer to multiple values. Second, a manager's workstation has limited CPU cycles. In addition to generating polling requests and analyzing the results, the CPU is used to run a protocol stack and update the display. Thus, lower overhead means an asynchronous *Trap* can handle situations where polling is too expensive. For example, asynchronous *Traps* work best if a network contains many network elements and a manager specifies conditions that involve many data items or chooses to request frequent updates.

The point is:

> The inclusion of an asynchronous Trap *message allows SNMP to be used for event monitoring in situations where polling is impractical.*

---

†A later section discusses an RMON MIB, which allows a manager to control the rate at which *Traps* are generated for events that can reoccur.

10.11 Management Information Base (MIB) And Variables

We said that SNMP technology separates the definition of the communication protocol and encoding from the set of items that can be accessed, and uses the term
Management Information Base (MIB) to describe the set of items.

A MIB defines a set of *variables*, where each variable corresponds to an item that
can be managed. A MIB document defines a *name* for each variable and defines the semantics of a variable precisely, including the range of values and a precise specification
of how a network element responds to a *Get* or *Set* command. For example, one MIB
variable corresponds to a count of packets that have arrived on an interface. The definition specifies that: the counter must have a range equal to a 32-bit integer, *Get* returns
the current value of the counter, and *Set* assigns a new value to the counter. A MIB
also defines a variable for each virtual item that a manager can control (e.g., the *reboot*
item described above). The point is:

> *An SNMP MIB defines a* variable *for each item that can be managed.*
> *The definition gives a name along with the exact semantics that in-*
> *clude the range of values and the meaning of* Get *and* Set *operations.*

Early MIB standardization efforts attempted to collect the definitions of all possible variables into a single document. After a few years, however, the popularity of
SNMP meant that the document was continually being revised to accommodate new
variables. Consequently, the IETF decided to divide the MIB standard into multiple
documents and allow each to be changed independently. Thus, if a group, such as a
standards organization or a consortium of vendors, creates a new technology, the group
can define a set of MIB variables for the technology without revising other MIB standards. Similarly, if a vendor creates a new network element with specialized features,
the vendor can define a set of MIB variables and publish the specification in a separate
document.

The next sections explain why it is possible to partition the MIB standards into
separate, independent documents. For now, it is sufficient to understand that partitioning is needed to handle additions and changes. That is:

> *To accommodate new networking technologies and implementations,*
> *MIB standards are partitioned into a set of independent documents; a*
> *new document can be added or an existing document can be changed*
> *without affecting other MIB standards.*

From a manager's point of view, the presence of multiple MIB standards documents means that a manager must acquire modules that correspond to the MIBs being
used in a network. For example, most SNMP software includes standard MIBs for
basic protocols such as TCP and IP. However, if a manager installs a new type of net-

work, existing SNMP software may not include the MIB definitions for the new technology. Thus, before SNMP can be used to monitor or control new types of network devices, a manager must acquire and install appropriate MIB definitions. To summarize:

> *A manager may need to acquire and install new MIB definitions before SNMP can be used to manage a new type of network or network element.*

10.12 A Hierarchy Of MIB Variable Names

How can separate organizations define MIB standards without creating conflicts or inconsistencies? The key lies in the use of a *hierarchical namespace*. A hierarchy makes it possible to assign authority for names so that each group owns part of the namespace. Thus, a group can assign variable names and meaning within its part of the hierarchy without causing interference with names assigned by other groups.

In fact, the idea of a naming hierarchy did not originate with SNMP or MIBs. Instead, MIB variable names are assigned from the *object identifier* namespace, a global naming hierarchy administered jointly by the *International Organization for Standardization (ISO)* and the *International Telecommunications Union (ITU)*. Figure 10.1 illustrates the position of MIB variable names in the global hierarchy by showing the portion of the hierarchy relevant to MIB variables.

As the figure shows, each node in the naming hierarchy is assigned both an alphabetic and a numeric label. The name of a node is given by the path through the hierarchy, and is written using dots to separate labels along the path†. Humans prefer to use alphabetic labels when writing a name; numeric values are preferred when sending messages because numeric encoding requires fewer bits.

MIB variables names are located under the node with label *mib*, which is located under *mgmt* (management). The *mgmt* node is located under *internet*, the portion of the hierarchy that has been assigned to the U.S. Department Of Defense (*dod*). Thus, the full name of the node with label *mib* is:

$$iso.org.dod.internet.mgmt.mib$$

When the same path is expressed using numeric labels, the resulting string is:

$$1.3.6.1.2.1$$

---

†The format is specified by a standard known as *Abstract Syntax Notation.1 (ASN.1)*.

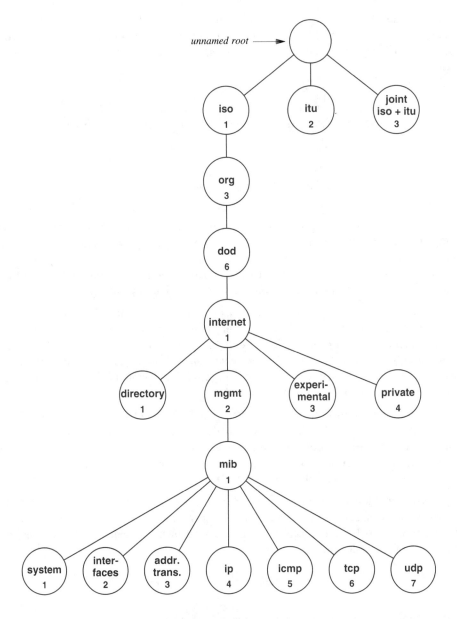

Figure 10.1 The object namespace hierarchy used for MIB variable names. Each node has both an alphabetic and numeric label, and the name of a node corresponds to the labels along a path from the root.

Individual MIB variables are assigned under the lowest levels of the hierarchy shown in the figure. All MIB variables that pertain to the Internet Protocol are assigned under the node labeled *ip*, MIB variables that pertain to TCP are assigned under the node labeled *tcp*, and so on. For example, a MIB variable that contains a count of all IP datagrams that a network element has received is given the label *ipInReceives*, and is assigned under node *ip*. Thus, the full name of the variable is:

$$iso\,.\,org\,.\,dod\,.\,internet\,.\,mgmt\,.\,mib\,.\,ip\,.\,ipInReceives$$

Observe that although MIB variables are divided into separate protocols, all MIB variables are located in the same subtree of the global naming hierarchy. Thus, each MIB variable name includes the portion of the lengthy path from the root to the MIB subtree, and has additional labels that specify an item. We can summarize:

> *The name of a MIB variable corresponds to a path in the object namespace hierarchy. Because they are located in the same part of the hierarchy, MIB variables share a common prefix:*
> $iso\,.\,org\,.\,dod\,.\,internet\,.\,mgmt\,.\,mib.$

10.13 Advantages And Disadvantages Of A Hierarchy

As we have seen, SNMP uses a standardized, hierarchical namespace for MIB variables. The namespace is *global* in the sense that a single hierarchy encompasses objects other than MIB variables. The names are *absolute* in the sense that each name specifies a complete path through the hierarchy.

The use of a standardized, global hierarchy with absolute names represents a trade-off. The chief advantage of a global hierarchy lies in the guarantee that MIB variable names will not conflict with other identifiers. Furthermore, because names are absolute, no context is needed to interpret a name, and no ambiguity can arise about whether a name refers to a MIB variable or another item.

The chief disadvantage of an absolute naming scheme arises from the length of variable names. Each name must contain a long prefix, even if all software using the name understands that only MIB variables are being referenced. In particular, because SNMP software only uses MIB variable names, the prefix carries no useful information (i.e., information that identifies a variable is carried in the final few labels).

Long prefixes are especially important when we consider that variable names must be transferred in SNMP messages. For example, consider a message that contains many *Get* requests. Each *Get* specifies a variable name, and each name repeats the same prefix. Thus, redundant prefixes mean that the amount of data being sent is larger than necessary, which wastes bandwidth. When SNMP is transferred over UDP, large requests must be divided into multiple messages. We can summarize:

> *Although SNMP follows a fundamental design principle of using global absolute object names with long prefixes to distinguish MIB names from other types of names, no other types of object names are used. As a result, SNMP MIB names are longer than necessary.*

10.14 Complex Data Aggregates And MIB Tables

The description of MIB variables given above is adequate for individual values, such as an integer value that stores a count of packets received. However, many items that must be managed consist of complex *data aggregates* that contain multiple values.

An an example, consider an IP *routing table*, also known as an IP *forwarding table* or a *Layer 3 forwarding table*. A manager thinks of a routing table as a series of entries that each specify multiple values. Figure 10.2 lists items that can appear in an IP routing table entry along with their size and meaning.

Item	Size	Meaning
Destination address	32 bits	IP address of a destination
Address mask	32 bits	Bit mask for the above
Next-hop IP address	32 bits	Address of the next router
Interface number	16 bits	Outgoing interface
Route origin	8 bits	Source of the entry
Time to live	32 bits	Time the entry expires

Figure 10.2 Examples of items that can be present in a single entry of an IP routing table.

To accommodate data aggregation, the MIB naming scheme includes a *table* construct. A table is a generalization that is used for both *homogeneous* and *heterogeneous* data aggregates. That is, a table can correspond to a data aggregate in which all items are the same or an aggregate in which items differ. Using programming language terminology, we say that a table can correspond to an *array* in which each entry has the same type as other entries or a *structure*† in which each entry has a type that can differ from the types of other entries.

The SNMP MIB defines tables for data structures and facilities in a network element. For example, one table corresponds to an ARP cache (i.e., the table has one entry for each item in the cache). In addition, the MIB defines a table that corresponds to the physical interfaces in a network element (i.e., the table has one entry for each interface).

As in programming languages, tables can be nested to an arbitrary depth. Thus, it is possible to define a MIB table in which each entry is a table, and so on. The items in the tables at each level of nesting can differ.

---

†Some programming languages use the terminology *record* instead of *structure*.

An IP routing table provides an excellent example. In a conventional programming language, an IP routing table corresponds to an array, where each entry of the array consists of a structure that defines a set of fields (e.g., the items listed in Figure 10.2). In terms of MIB variables, the entire routing table is defined as a homogeneous MIB table, each entry of which is a heterogeneous MIB table.

We can summarize:

> *To accommodate data aggregates, the MIB naming scheme uses a* table *construct. Each table can correspond to a homogeneous or heterogeneous aggregate, and tables can be nested to arbitrary depth.*

10.15 Granularity Of Aggregate Access

One issue surrounding aggregate data items concerns the granularity of access. Consider IP routing, for instance. A routing table contains multiple entries, each of which can contain the items listed in Figure 10.2. Sometimes, a manager needs to treat an entire entry as a single unit, and other times, a manager needs to refer to individual items. For example, when removing an entry from a routing table, a manager needs to refer to the entire entry. However, when changing the value of a *next hop*, a manager only needs to refer to one value and leave others intact.

Fortunately, the MIB naming scheme provides for both types of access. That is, the naming scheme assigns a name to an entire table as well as a name to each individual item. Consequently, an SNMP message can specify that an operation be performed on an entire data aggregate or on a single item in the aggregate. To summarize:

> *Because the MIB naming scheme includes a unique name for each table as well as names for items within a table, an SNMP message can specify an operation on a complete data aggregate or on one item within an aggregate.*

10.16 Transport Protocols And Interaction

Recall that one of the fundamental distinctions among network management technologies arises from the scope of control: a technology that can only manage a single device at a time is classified as an element management technology. In that sense, SNMP is an element management technology. SNMP uses a request-response interaction in which management software sends a message to a network element and the network element sends a response indicating whether the request was honored. That is:

> *SNMP is inherently an element management technology because SNMP allows a manager's workstation to interact with one network element at a time.*

Interestingly, confusion arises because SNMP allows the use of either *connectionless* or *connection-oriented* transport protocols (i.e., *UDP* or *TCP*). That is, when it uses SNMP to communicate with an agent, management software can either send each message in a separate UDP packet or can open a TCP connection to the agent and send a series of messages across the connection. If it receives a request via UDP, an agent will use UDP to return a response; if it receives a request via TCP, an agent will return a response over the same TCP connection used for the request.

The important idea is that a TCP connection can persist across multiple SNMP messages — once a connection is opened, the connection can remain open for subsequent message exchanges. However, the persistence of a TCP connection does not change the underlying interaction: even if management software opens TCP connections to a set of multiple network elements and leaves the connections open, each request sent across a connection is handled independent of other requests.

To summarize:

> *Although SNMP can use either UDP or TCP for transport and can allow a TCP connection to persist, the choice does not affect the underlying interaction because agent software handles each message independently.*

10.17 Updates, Messages, And Atomicity

Conceptually, a single key aspect determines whether a technology provides element management or network-wide management. The key aspect is the *atomicity* that the system provides when updating information. An atomic update means that the system guarantees all-or-nothing — if any part of the update fails, nothing is changed. Thus, the distinction between element management and network management arises from the granularity over which an atomic update can be performed. An element management system can only guarantee to update a single network element at a time, whereas a network-wide management system can guarantee to update many elements at the same time. The independence of SNMP messages means that if management software sends *Set* requests to multiple elements, some of them can succeed and others can fail. To summarize:

An element management system only guarantees atomicity for a single element; a network-wide management system guarantees atomicity across multiple elements.

Interestingly, although it can only update a single element at a time, the SNMP protocol does specify strict rules for atomicity: all commands in a given message must be applied or none are applied. We say that SNMP guarantees *per-message atomicity*. Thus, if a manager sends a single SNMP message that changes three routes, either all three routes will be changed or none will (the response indicates whether all changes were successful).

To summarize:

Although it does not handle atomic update across multiple network elements, SNMP guarantees that either all Set *commands in a given message must succeed or none of them should be performed.*

The requirement for atomicity within a given message has two consequences for management software. First, it allows management software that uses connectionless transport to avoid problems that can occur if messages are reordered. Second, it allows management software to avoid inconsistent states that can occur if one small change is made at a time. Of course, if the interface provided to human managers does not allow a manager to specify how commands are grouped into messages, a manager may not be able to control atomicity or simultaneous update.

10.18 The Remote Monitoring MIB (RMON)

One aspect of MIB variables is especially important because it adds new functionality to SNMP. As we have seen, the original definition of an SNMP MIB focuses on an interaction paradigm in which software on a manager's workstation interacts with a set of network elements. The software initiates interaction, receives responses, and selects items to display. When used to monitor many network elements, the approach produces a large volume of network traffic and requires a manager's workstation to spend CPU cycles to process and analyze responses. Even if Trap commands are used to reduce the load, a manager must control the generation of Traps.

It became obvious that although basic MIB variables adequately describe data structures, the variables do not allow a manager to specify details of how and when to generate Traps and manage interaction. Several vendors invented software to control interactions, but each vendor produced a proprietary solution. To standardize control functions, the IETF followed an interesting approach: instead of creating another application-layer protocol, the IETF defined an additional set of MIB definitions that allow a manager to control interactions with a remote device.

The IETF standard is known as the *Remote MONitoring* (*RMON*) MIB. In essence, RMON defines a large set of virtual items that a manager can *Set* to control how a device gathers, stores, and communicates management information. For example, a manager can specify that a device should keep statistics about packets, store a log of events, and generate an alarm if a specified condition is met. In addition, RMON specifies a set of variables that a manager can *Get* to interrogate the stored values.

Because RMON uses many variables to define control functions, the standard divides variables into separate *groups*. Each group corresponds to a broad management function or protocol. Figure 10.3 lists examples of groups in an RMON MIB along with the purpose of each†.

Group	Controls Details Of
statistics	Statistics about packets and counters
history	Periodic packet sampling
alarm	Statistical samples and thresholds for notification
host	Record of hosts from which packets arrive
hostTopN	Statistics about hosts that send packets
matrix	Statistics about communication between host pairs
filter	Specification of packets for events and alarms
packet capture	Copies of packets captured and stored for analysis
event	Generation of outgoing notifications

Figure 10.3 Example groups in an RMON MIB and their purpose.

To summarize:

> An RMON MIB defines variables that allow a manager to control the collection of statistics and generation of alarm Traps without using an additional protocol.

10.19 A Manager's View Of MIB Variables

Two types of tools are available that use SNMP. Most managers prefer tools that provide a high-level interface. Such tools hide the details of MIB variables and SNMP messages. Instead of requiring managers to understand MIB names, high-level tools use a language related to the task at hand and use graphical output to display results in a form that is easy to understand.

Tools also exist that provide managers with a low-level interface to SNMP. A low-level tool allows a manager to form and send a message, including the details of

---

†Technically, the groups illustrated in the figure are from RMON 1; RMON 2 defines additional groups, including groups for higher-layer protocols.

Get and *Set* commands as well as a specification of a MIB variable name for each command. Low-level SNMP tools may be needed when a new device or service is added to a network before high-level management tools are installed.

> *Managers usually prefer tools that hide the details of SNMP and MIB variables, but can use low-level tools to handle cases where it is necessary to specify the exact details of a message or MIB variable names.*

10.20 Security And The Community String

Versions 1 and 2 of the SNMP protocol provide little security: message contents are not encrypted, and the authentication scheme is weak. Authentication is handled by requiring each SNMP message to carry a *community string* that a receiver uses to authenticate the message. For example, consider a network element that receives an SNMP request. When the message arrives, the element must verify that the value of the community string in the message matches the value that has been configured into the network element. If the two do not match, the network element rejects the message. Separate community strings are used for three levels of access: *read*, *write*, and *write-all*.

Many early SNMP products supplied a default value for a community string. Interestingly, the default value was *public*. Many managers installed SNMP software without changing the default, which weakened security because the community password was easy for an attacker to guess.

Version 3 of SNMP improved security substantially. The standard requires three types of security:

- Authentication
- Privacy
- View-based access control

Version 3 messages are *authenticated*, which means a network element can guarantee that a message is from a valid manager. To prevent messages from being read as they pass between a manager's workstation and a managed element, version 3 includes *privacy* through encryption.

Perhaps the most interesting aspect of SNMP version 3 arises from its use of a *Role-Based Access Control (RBAC)* mechanism. SNMP uses the term *view-based access control*, which means that the items a manager can read or change in a network element depends on the authorization that a manager uses. Thus, it is possible to configure the version 3 software in a network element so that one manager is only permitted to change a routing table and another manager is permitted to interrogate and reset packet counters.

10.21 Summary

SNMP is a popular management technology that provides communication between a manager's workstation and a managed entity. SNMP casts operations into a read-write paradigm using *Get* and *Set* commands; variables in the Management Information Base (MIB) are assigned names from a standardized hierarchical namespace. Two additional commands, *Get-Bulk* and *Get-Next*, are included to optimize interaction. In addition to variables for basic data items and variables for virtual items, a MIB includes tables that correspond to data aggregates. An asynchronous Trap command extends SNMP functionality to permit event monitoring. Traps make event monitoring practical in cases where polling is infeasible.

Although it provides per-message atomicity, SNMP does not provide synchronization among multiple network elements. As a consequence, SNMP is an element management technology.

The RMON MIB specifies variables that allow a manager to control interaction with a remote network element. For example, a manager can specify the conditions under which an element generates Traps, statistical packet sampling, and the accumulation of data in a traffic matrix.

Versions 1 and 2 of the SNMP protocol lack security. Version 3, the current version, offers authentication, privacy and view-based access control.

Chapter Contents

11.1   Introduction, 163
11.2   Basic Traffic Analysis, 163
11.3   The Flow Abstraction, 164
11.4   The Two Types Of Flows, 165
11.5   The Purpose Of Flow Analysis, 166
11.6   Levels Of Flow Aggregation, 167
11.7   Online And Offline Flow Analysis, 168
11.8   Examples Of Flow Data Analysis, 169
11.9   Flow Data Capture And Filtering, 171
11.10 Packet Inspection And Classification, 173
11.11 Capture For Online And Offline Analysis, 174
11.12 Flows Using Packet Content, 175
11.13 Flows And Optimized Forwarding, 175
11.14 Flow Data Export, 177
11.15 Origin Of NetFlow Technology, 178
11.16 Basic NetFlow Characteristics, 178
11.17 Extensibility And Templates, 179
11.18 NetFlow Message Transport And Consequences, 180
11.19 Effect Of Configuration Choices, 181
11.20 Summary, 182

11

Flow Data And Flow Analysis (NetFlow)

11.1 Introduction

Chapters in this part of the text discuss tools and technologies that are used to manage networks. The previous chapter examines the SNMP technology used to communicate between a manager's workstation and managed elements or services. This chapter continues the discussion by examining technologies that managers use to analyze the data that flows across a network.

The chapter presents the underlying motivation and purpose, shows how managers can use the results, explains the architecture needed to collect and assess data, and considers NetFlow, which has become a de facto standard. The next chapter continues to explore management technologies by focusing on routing and traffic management.

11.2 Basic Traffic Analysis

We use the term *traffic analysis* to describe a process of measuring network traffic, assessing the constituent parts, and understanding the purpose of traffic being carried on a network. Chapter 7 documents one use of traffic analysis: building a traffic matrix for use in capacity planning and network optimization. The results of traffic analysis can also be used for anomaly detection and fault diagnosis because understanding normal traffic patterns can help a manager spot unusual conditions.

As we have seen, a variety of tools exist to help managers analyze traffic. For example, a manager can use a packet analyzer to examine the packets on a given link. Alternatively, a manager can use an RMON MIB and SNMP to collect statistics for a set of links.

Because it analyzes one packet at a time, a packet analyzer or RMON client cannot look at relationships among packets. That is, an analyzer repeatedly reads a packet, examines packet headers, updates statistical information and counters, and moves to the next packet. As a result, an analyzer cannot determine whether an individual packet is traveling to the same destination as a previous or subsequent packet, nor can an analyzer report whether a sequence of packets is part of a single conversation. In essence, focusing inspection on individual packets limits analyzers to collecting basic statistics. For example, a packet analyzer can tell a manager what percentage of the measured traffic consists of email, but cannot tell how many separate email messages were sent. The point is:

> *Because it evaluates individual packets, a packet analyzer or RMON MIB can only provide aggregate statistics.*

11.3 The Flow Abstraction

To gain deeper insight into network traffic, a manager must be able to assess communication that involves a sequence of packets. A manager also needs to assess traffic origins and destinations, how protocols are used, and the details of communication between individual application programs. For example, a manager might ask about the average, median, and maximum sizes of email messages transferred across a network or the average duration of a VoIP phone call, or a manager might ask about the maximum number of simultaneous TCP connections that appear on a given link.

To capture the idea of communication that involves multiple packets, we define an abstraction known as a *flow*. We adopt the view that all traffic on a network can be divided into a set of disjoint flows and can be assessed in terms of the underlying flows.

To keep the notion of flows flexible enough to allow arbitrary communication, the abstraction is not defined precisely. Instead, a manager can apply the concept in many ways. For example, a manager might choose to define each communication between a pair of application programs to be a flow. Alternatively, a manager might choose a coarse granularity in which all packets traveling to a specific web server are considered to be part of a single flow. The point is:

> *Intuitively, each flow corresponds to a sequence of related packets; the definition of flow is sufficiently general to permit a manager to apply the concept in a variety of ways.*

11.4 The Two Types Of Flows

Flows can be categorized into two basic types:

- Unidirectional flows
- Bidirectional flows

Unidirectional Flows. As the name implies, a *unidirectional flow* corresponds to traffic flowing in a single direction (e.g., one way across a link). It may seem that a unidirectional flow is useless because computer communication is bidirectional — even if data is being transferred in a single direction, protocols send requests and acknowledgements in the reverse direction. Ironically, unidirectional flows are the most popular. To understand why, observe that many links in a network are *full duplex*, which means that traffic in the two directions proceeds independently. Thus, when a manager analyzes traffic on a full duplex link, it makes sense to think of two separate links that each carry traffic in one direction. Using a unidirectional flow abstraction also allows a manager to consider asymmetric routing in which traffic moving in one direction is forwarded along a different path than traffic moving in the opposite direction.

Bidirectional Flows. A bidirectional flow captures the complete interaction between two communicating entities, including packets moving in both directions. Bidirectional flows are most useful for assessing environments in which applications send approximately the same amount of data in each direction and packets sent between the two applications follow a single path, independent of the direction. Unfortunately, few protocols send equal amounts of data in each direction. As a consequence, bidirectional flows are less popular than unidirectional flows.

To summarize:

> *Although most computer communication involves a two-way packet exchange, a unidirectional flow abstraction is often preferred because unidirectional flows provide more generality and flexibility than a bidirectional flow abstraction.*

Of course, a given tool that uses the flow abstraction may limit a manager to one type of flow or the other. We will see, for example, that one popular flow technology only permits a manager to define and analyze unidirectional flows. More important, even if a tool permits a manager to define bidirectional flows, it may be impossible to collect information about such flows unless the data traveling in both directions passes through a common point.

11.5 The Purpose Of Flow Analysis

We use the term *flow analysis* to refer to the process of analyzing data about flows. A variety of tools are available to analyze flow data and display information for a manager. Typically, flow analyzers produce graphical output, using colors to distinguish among various pieces of information.

A few examples will illustrate why flow analysis is an important technology. The examples listed are not meant to be exhaustive; they merely demonstrate the range of possible ways managers can use flow analysis.

- *Traffic Characterization.* Managers use flow analysis to understand the composition of network traffic. For example, a manager can display traffic by protocol type, by application, or by destination.

- *Throughput Estimation.* As we will see, flow data can be used to estimate throughput.

- *Accounting And Billing.* Flow data can be used to calculate charges for services.

- *Ingress/Egress Traffic Comparison.* One of the interesting ways managers use flow analysis is to compare traffic flowing into a site with traffic flowing out.

- *Confirming Quality Of Service.* Flow analysis can be used to determine whether QoS goals are being achieved.

- *Anomaly Detection.* A manager can use flow analysis to spot unusual events or changes in traffic.

- *Security Analysis.* Flow analysis can help identify denial of service attacks and the spread of a virus or worm.

- *Real-time Troubleshooting And Diagnostics.* Real-time flow analysis can help a manager determine the cause of a problem while the problem is occurring.

- *After-The-Fact Forensics.* Historical flow data can be used to evaluate the root cause and identify earlier events that led to a problem.

- *Capacity Planning.* As Chapter 7 points out, a traffic matrix is fundamental to capacity planning; flow analysis can be used to build such a matrix.

- *Application Measurement And Planning.* In addition to global planning, managers can also use flow analysis to track individual applications. For example, a manager can use flow analysis to monitor the sources of traffic arriving for a particular server.

11.6 Levels Of Flow Aggregation

Intuitively, an individual flow corresponds to a single communication between a pair of endpoints. We said, however, that the flow abstraction is sufficiently flexible to allow a manager to choose a granularity at which to apply the definition. Of course, specific tools impose restrictions on the choice. In practice, most tools permit a manager to compose a flow definition by specifying packet header fields; some tools also include temporal specifications (e.g., packets that have the same header fields must occur less than thirty seconds apart to be considered part of the same flow).

We use the term *flow aggregation* to refer to a definition that collects many individual communications into a single measurement, and use the term *level of aggregation* to refer to the granularity. A few examples will clarify the concept by showing possibilities for aggregation. A manager can choose to aggregate flows by:

- IP address
- Network element interface
- Transport protocol type
- Application type
- Content reference
- Application endpoint

IP Address. When using an IP address for aggregation, a flow analyzer groups all packets that have the same IP address into a flow. For example, if a manager specifies aggregation by source IP address, all packets from a given computer form a single flow, which allows a manager to understand the number of computers contributing to a traffic stream. Aggregating by destination IP address allows a manager to count the number of destinations. Using both source and destination address in the aggregation creates one flow for each pair of communicating computers.

Network Element Interface. In many cases, a manager is more concerned with local traffic behavior than with the ultimate source or destination. To understand local behavior, a manager can use the *ingress* or *egress* interface on a network element for aggregation. Thus, to analyze the traffic leaving each interface on a router, a manager can use the egress interfaces to aggregate. Similarly, to determine a traffic matrix for a given network element, a manager can use the ingress and egress interfaces for aggregation.

Transport Protocol Type. Basic protocol analysis is a special case of flow analysis. To examine the protocol composition of traffic (e.g., UDP, TCP, ICMP), a manager can define one flow aggregate per *protocol type*.

Application Type. Flow analysis can help managers understand how network traffic is divided among applications (e.g., the percentage of traffic that carries email and web browsing). To separate traffic by application, a manager specifies aggregation by destination *protocol port number*. Because each application has been assigned a specific port, each flow will correspond to one application†.

Content Reference. Some flow analysis tools provide *deep packet inspection*, which means a manager can include arbitrary items from the packet in the flow definition. If a deep packet inspection facility is available, a manager can define flows to correspond to individual requests. For example, a manager can define one flow for each web page, and use a flow analyzer to examine web requests.

Application Endpoint. To study the details of communication, a manager can define a flow to correspond to communication between a pair of endpoints, where an endpoint is identified by a combination of IP source and destination addresses, source and destination protocol port numbers, and protocol type.

11.7 Online And Offline Flow Analysis

As the description above implies, there are two broad classes of flow analysis tools that perform:

- Online analysis
- Offline analysis

Online Analysis. The term *online* refers to tools that analyze flows in real time. That is, data about flows is sent to the analysis program as soon as data has been collected. Furthermore, online analysis implies continual update in which a manager's display continues to change over time.

Managers generally think of online tools as displaying changes immediately, and use online tools for diagnosing a problem as it occurs. In a practical sense, a small delay occurs between the time traffic changes and the time a manager's display is updated to reflect the change. The lag between occurrence and display depends on many factors, including the speed of a manager's workstation, the level of aggregation, the complexity of the analysis being performed, and the delay introduced by transporting data from the point at which measurements are taken to the point at which analysis is computed. Thus, to reduce delays, a manager can use a higher-speed computer, move a computer (e.g., a laptop) closer to the source of flow data, increase the level of aggregation, or specify a less complex computation or display.

Offline Analysis. The term *offline* refers to analysis performed after flow data has been collected and stored. For example, offline analysis can be performed once per night, and can process all flow data collected over a twenty-four hour period.

Offline analysis is important for after-the-fact situations such as forensics or cases where the exact items to be examined are not known in advance. The chief advantage

---

†In practice, the definition is more complex because a protocol type must be specified and packets traveling from a server back to a client have the well-known port in the source port field.

of offline analysis arises because computation is not constrained by time. Thus, instead of forcing a manager to aggregate traffic, offline analysis can compute data for fine-grained flows (e.g., each flow corresponds to an application endpoint). Furthermore, offline analysis can involve arbitrary computation that generates complex displays.

11.8 Examples Of Flow Data Analysis

A wide variety of tools are available to analyze flow data and display results. For example, tools exist that display:

- Percentage of traffic from/to each autonomous system
- Comparison of ingress and egress traffic by protocol
- Hosts probing a large number of protocol ports
- Percentage of traffic by protocol
- Number of active IP addresses
- Percentage of traffic by device interface
- Rate at which new flows appear

One of the most interesting aspects of flow analysis tools arises from their use of graphical output and color. For example, tools that display traffic by percentage often use a dynamic pie chart format, where the size of each piece varies as new flow data arrives. A pie chart provides an easy way to assess the composition of traffic at a given time. Figure 11.1 illustrates a pie chart that divides traffic according to the protocol used.

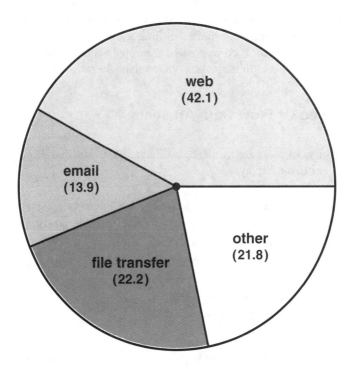

Figure 11.1 A pie chart that shows the percentage of traffic for each protocol
type. On a computer display, a pie chart changes continuously
to reflect the most recent flow data that has been received.

To spot trends and understand how data traffic changes over time, a manager can
use a time-progression graph that shows a history of traffic composition. A typical
time-progression graph uses colors to show the contribution of each traffic type. For
example, the y-axis can show the percentage of each type, and the x-axis can show
changes over time. Figure 11.2 illustrates a time-progression graph that plots the percentage of traffic carrying data for web, email, file transfer, and other applications.

As the name implies, a time-progression graph is updated continuously. In the figure, new measurements are introduced on the right, and older measurements are shifted
to the left. Thus, with the settings shown, a manager can visualize trends over the past
ten hours.

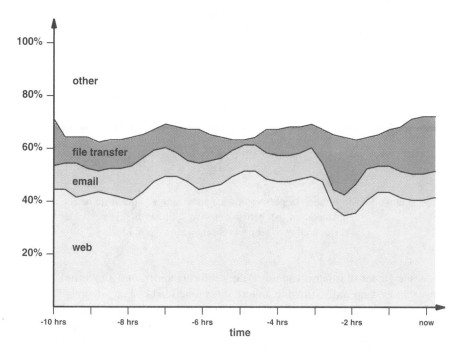

Figure 11.2 Illustration of a time-progression graph showing the percentage
of three key applications. New data appears on the right, and
existing data shifts left continuously. On a computer display,
colors can be used to identify the traffic types.

11.9 Flow Data Capture And Filtering

Before flow analysis can be performed, data about flows must be *captured*. Two
approaches are used:

- Passive flow capture
- Active flow capture

Passive Flow Capture. In *passive* flow capture, hardware used to collect information about flows is separate from hardware used to forward or process packets. For example, inserting an Ethernet hub between two devices makes it possible for a passive
monitoring device to obtain a copy of each packet by listening to the hub in promiscu-
ous mode. Alternatively, some VLAN switches offer a *mirror port* that can be configured to receive a copy of all packets that traverse a specified VLAN. An optical splitter
can be used to enable passive capture from an optical fiber: the splitter creates a copy of
the light being transmitted on the fiber, and the copy can be sent to a passive monitor-

ing device. In each case, packet capture does not affect the underlying network, nor does it affect packet transmission. Figure 11.3 illustrates a flow collector inserted on the link between two network elements.

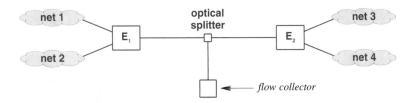

Figure 11.3 Illustration of passive flow capture using an optical splitter on the link between two network elements, E_1 and E_2. The collector receives a copy of all packets sent across the link.

As the figure illustrates, capturing flow information from a single link can help a manager understand traffic flowing among several networks. For example, flows across the center link in the figure include traffic between networks on the left and networks on the right. The link between an organization and the Internet is a special case because capturing flows on the link helps a manager understand traffic between the site and the Internet.

Active Flow Capture. In *active* flow capture, a conventional network element is enhanced with additional hardware and/or software that enables the element to capture flow information. For example, a router that consists of blades plugged into a chassis can have an extra blade that monitors the backplane and extracts flow information. Alternatively, a network element can have special hardware for flow capture integrated with normal packet processing modules. Figure 11.4 illustrates a flow connector attached to a router.

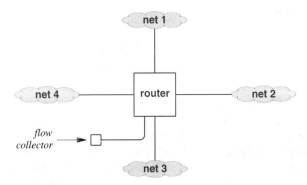

Figure 11.4 Illustration of active flow capture handled by a router. The router can report traffic that travels from any of the four networks through the router to another network.

Active and passive approaches to flow capture each have advantages and disadvantages. The chief advantage of passive capture lies in its unobtrusive nature — a passive system can collect information without slowing or changing network traffic. However, most passive technologies can only capture information from a single VLAN or link.

The chief advantage of an active capture system arises from its ability to extract information for all packets that pass through a given network element. Thus, an active capture mechanism that runs in a router can report packets flowing across any pair of interfaces; a large router can connect to many networks. In addition, a router may be able to use flow information to improve forwarding performance. However, an active capture mechanism requires additional hardware and software in a network element.

11.10 Packet Inspection And Classification

To understand how flow capture works and how it can be configured, it is necessary to know basics about packet layout and processing. Rather than review protocol details, we give an example to explain the concept. To simplify the presentation, the example considers an Ethernet packet that carries a request to a web server. The packet contains an *Ethernet header*, *IP header*, and *TCP header*, which precede an HTTP request. Figure 11.5 illustrates how protocol headers are arranged in such a packet.

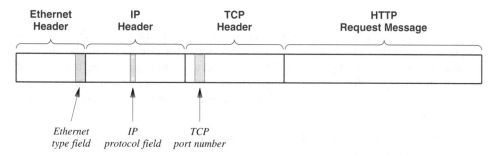

Figure 11.5 The conceptual arrangement of headers in a packet that contains a web request. Each header contains a field that specifies the type of the next header.

As the figure indicates, each header contains a field that specifies the type of the following header. The *type* field in the Ethernet header contains hexadecimal *0800* to specify that the packet contains an IP datagram. The *protocol* field in the IP datagram header contains *6* to specify that the datagram contains a TCP segment. The *destination port number* in the TCP header is set to *80* to specify that the packet is destined for a web server. Note that a flow collector does not need to examine a complete packet to decide whether the packet is destined for a web server. Instead, the collector only needs to check the Ethernet type field, IP protocol field, and the TCP destination port number. If all three fields contain the correct values, the packet is destined for a web server†.

---

†In practice, a classifier must also check for the presence of options in the IP header because options change the location of successive headers.

We use the term *classification* to describe the process of checking selected fields in packet headers, and say that a network element *classifies* the packet. Classification is faster than full packet processing, and can be further optimized by using special-purpose classification hardware. More important, hardware can be designed to extract values from specified fields and check whether the same combination has been encountered previously. The point is:

> *A flow collector examines selected header fields in each packet, and uses the results to classify the packet. Hardware exists to optimize classification.*

Knowing that the underlying system can use classification to process packets helps us understand flow configuration. We see, for example, that the computation required during capture is proportional to the number of header fields examined. Thus, flow aggregation can be efficient if the aggregation only uses a few header fields. For example, to aggregate by transport protocol, a flow collector only needs to examine two fields: the Ethernet type field (to verify that the packet contains an IP datagram) and the protocol field in the IP header (to determine the type of protocol being carried).

11.11 Capture For Online And Offline Analysis

A previous section discusses online and offline flow analysis. The distinction has important consequences for flow capture. Following a strictly *online* paradigm means a flow collector must classify each packet as the packet arrives. Following a strictly *offline* paradigm means that although classification is not needed as packets arrive, a flow collector must store full information about each packet and allow analysis software to classify packets into flows later.

The distinction between the online and offline approaches is important for managers for two reasons.

- Generality
- Resource requirements

Generality. Because it stores raw data, an offline system can give a manager more information. In particular, the offline paradigm allows a manager to run an analysis tool multiple times, using a different aggregation each time. Thus, a manager might choose to aggregate flows by protocol and later examine the same data with flows aggregated by IP destination address.

Resource Requirements. The chief disadvantage of an offline system arises from the amount of storage required. To avoid using arbitrary amounts of disk space, an offline system must either limit the duration of information capture to a short time or use statistical sampling (e.g., process one packet out of one thousand) to reduce the quantity of data. Neither approach is optimal for all purposes: a short duration may not give a manager an accurate picture of traffic, and sampling can skew the results. More important, if a manager is only interested in one particular flow aggregate, classifying packets early can reduce the data size and allow for a longer duration measurement.

11.12 Flows Using Packet Content

The preceding discussion of packet headers and flow classification omits one important issue: using packet content to identify flows. As an example, consider what happens if a manager uses URLs to divide web server traffic into flows. That is, suppose a manager at Example Corporation manages a web server for *example.com*. The manager might choose to define one flow for all traffic that requests URL:

www.example.com

The manager might define another flow for all traffic that requests URL

www.example.com/products

and so on for each possible URL the server offers. From a manager's point of view, defining one flow per URL seems as straightforward as defining one flow per protocol. From the point of view of a flow collector, however, using a URL differs dramatically from using a protocol because a URL is not located in a fixed header field. Thus, a flow collector must examine the contents of the packet (i.e., parse an HTTP message and extract the URL). Such processing, known as *deep packet inspection*, requires significantly more computational resources than extracting fixed fields from protocol headers. Thus, an analyzer that inspects content operates slower than an analyzer that inspects fixed fields in headers. We can summarize:

> *A flow definition that depends on deep packet inspection to assess content incurs more overhead, and cannot process as many packets per second as a flow definition that uses fixed header fields.*

11.13 Flows And Optimized Forwarding

Although flow capture and packet forwarding seem unrelated, they are not — the same data that managers use for flow analysis can be used to optimize packet forwarding. To understand why, consider packet forwarding in a high-speed IP router. Recall that when a packet arrives, the router examines the packet type field to verify the packet contains an IP datagram, extracts the IP destination address, and uses the destination address as a lookup key for the IP routing table. Each routing table entry specifies a next-hop address and an interface over which the packet should be forwarded.

To optimize forwarding, a router can combine flow classification with a *forwarding cache*. The use of flow technology is straightforward: a router uses classification hardware to extract fields from a packet that identify a flow. Mathematically, classification provides a mapping from a packet to a flow:

$$classification: \ packet \ \rightarrow \ flow$$

Typically, each flow is assigned an integer *flow identifier* (*flow ID*), and classification maps a packet to a particular flow ID.

Assuming the definition of a flow is chosen such that all packets in a flow are forwarded to the same next hop, forwarding can use a flow identifier without examining the packet headers again. That is, a separate mapping can be maintained to translate a flow ID to next-hop information:

$$forwarding: \ flow \ ID \ \rightarrow \ next\text{-}hop \ information$$

Typically, the mapping is implemented as a table in memory, and the flow ID is used as an index into the table.

The purpose of a cache can now be explained: a forwarding cache is a high-speed hardware mechanism that accelerates the mapping from a flow ID to next-hop information. A cache, which operates much faster than memory, holds a recent set of flow mappings. After a packet is classified to produce a flow ID, f, hardware checks the forwarding cache. If the cache contains a mapping for f, the router extracts the next-hop information from the cache, and forwards the packet. Otherwise, the router extracts the forwarding information from the table in memory, saves a copy in the cache for subsequent packets, and proceeds to forward the current packet.

Caching optimizes performance in situations where the probability of encountering multiple packets from a flow is high — although a table lookup is performed for the first packet in a flow, forwarding information for subsequent packets can be extracted from the cache. The term *temporal locality of reference* refers to the probability of repetition. Fortunately, experience has shown that many networks exhibit a high degree of temporal locality of reference. Thus, a forwarding caching can improve router performance significantly. In a later section, we will learn that performance enhancement provides a major motivation for capturing data about flows, and that a device uses a separate cache to hold flow information.

To summarize:

Although flow analysis may seem unrelated to packet forwarding, temporal locality means that router hardware can achieve higher forwarding performance by combining flow classification hardware with a forwarding cache.

11.14 Flow Data Export

We use the term *flow data export* to refer to the communication of flow data from its point of origin to another device. Often, the source of flow data is a router, and the destination of exported flow data is a flow analysis application running on a manager's workstation. Two questions arise:

- What format should be used to represent exported data?

- What protocols should be used to transport exported data?

Format. The question about format focuses on how flow data should be represented. The tradeoff lies between the amount of information and efficiency. On one hand, sending the maximum amount of data allows a receiver to decide what is important and discard the rest. On the other hand, because the transmission of flow data takes network bandwidth, transmitting unneeded information wastes resources such as bandwidth and storage.

One of the primary choices surrounding format concerns metadata (i.e., information about the data being collected). For example, flow export systems usually include a time stamp that allows a receiver to save exported information for later analysis without introducing ambiguity about the exact time each message was generated. In addition, metadata can include an ID for the device that captured the data.

Protocols. The question about protocols revolves around the scope and generality of the transfer system. On one hand, if the transport mechanism uses a Layer 2 protocol, flow data can only be sent across a single network and the receiving system must be able to receive the Layer 2 protocol. On the other hand, using a standard transport protocol to transfer flow data allows complete generality to send the data across an internet, but requires both the sending and receiving system to be assigned an IP address and to run a TCP/IP stack.

As the next section explains, the industry has adopted one particular flow export technology as a de facto standard. The technology defines a representation for flow data and uses UDP to transport messages. The use of UDP means that a manager can choose to transfer flow information to an arbitrary location because messages carrying flow data can cross an arbitrary number of intermediate networks from a point of origin to a final destination. We can summarize:

> *The most popular flow export technology uses UDP. As a result, flow data can travel across multiple networks from its source to the final destination.*

11.15 Origin Of NetFlow Technology

The most widely-used flow technology, *NetFlow*, was invented by Cisco Systems. In addition to Cisco, network vendors such as Juniper Networks follow the NetFlow format when exporting flow data, which means that flow analysis tools work across multiple vendors. The protocol that NetFlow uses to export flow data has been published as RFC 3954. The IETF used version 9 of NetFlow as the basis for *IPFIX*, a flow export technology that adds security and allows transfer of flow data across a congestion-sensitive transport mechanism.

Interestingly, engineers who designed NetFlow did not originally intend to devise a system that exported flow data for analysis. Instead, NetFlow was designed to be an optimization that improves the forwarding speed of an IP router, as Section 11.13 describes. To allow managers to monitor performance, NetFlow exported information about flows and the performance of the forwarding cache. When customers realized that flow data was being exported, the customers asked for details about the format, and began to create tools for flow analysis.

11.16 Basic NetFlow Characteristics

NetFlow uses an active flow capture paradigm in which a router or switch records information about each flow and exports the resulting flow data to an external collector. Because it originated as a forwarding optimization, NetFlow uses a unidirectional flow definition. NetFlow allows a manager to control data collection, including the ability to specify packet sampling. Finally, NetFlow uses a *fine-grained* definition of flows in which the exported information includes many details about a flow as well as metadata such as time stamps. Figure 11.6 lists example items that NetFlow exports.

- Source and destination IP address
- Source and destination protocol port numbers
- IP Type of Service field
- Start and end time stamps
- Ingress and egress interface numbers
- Packet size in octets
- Routing information (e.g., next hop address)

Figure 11.6 Examples of items that NetFlow exports for each flow.

Early versions of NetFlow defined a set of *fixed fields*. That is, NetFlow kept a cache for internal packet forwarding, and only exported information from the cache. Version 9 of NetFlow (the version used by the IETF) extends the basic paradigm: instead of specifying fixed fields, version 9 allows a manager to control exported data by choosing the set of fields that are used to define flows. The remainder of this chapter describes version 9 of NetFlow†. We can summarize:

> *NetFlow defines a flow to be unidirectional, and exports fine-grained information. Version 9 of NetFlow allows a manager to control the set of fields that are exported for each flow.*

11.17 Extensibility And Templates

If a manager can control the set of fields that NetFlow exports, how can a flow collector parse and understand the exported message? Rather than require a manager to enter the same configuration in both the exporting and collecting devices, NetFlow solves the problem by sending descriptive information along with the data. The descriptive information identifies the sending device, and specifies the set of fields that occur in data records by giving the type and length of each field. Thus, a receiver can use the descriptive information to interpret the data that arrives. More important, even if a receiver does not understand all the items in a NetFlow message, the descriptive information provides sufficient detail to permit the receiver to skip items that cannot be interpreted.

We can summarize:

> *Because NetFlow sends additional information that describes the message contents, a manager only configures a NetFlow exporter; a NetFlow collector can use the descriptive information to parse NetFlow messages.*

NetFlow uses the term *template* for the descriptive information. A device that exports NetFlow data sends a template followed by data. In fact, each template is assigned an ID, which means that an exporter can send multiple types of NetFlow data by assigning a unique ID to each type. For example, if a router has four interfaces, a manager can select a set of fields to export for each interface. The router is configured with a template ID for each set of fields, and a collector uses the ID in a data record to associate the record with a particular template. The point is:

> *Because each template is assigned a unique ID, a given device can export multiple, independent sets of NetFlow data, and a collector can parse incoming data without ambiguity.*

---

†The chapter describes export by a router; Cisco switches use a slightly modified export paradigm in which the initial packet of a flow is exported using NetFlow version 5, and version 9 is used for the flow summary.

11.18 NetFlow Message Transport And Consequences

The exact details of message transport are unimportant to network managers. However, knowledge of the conceptual transport mechanism will help us understand the traffic that NetFlow generates and a consequence for managers. In particular, we will see why NetFlow works best when the exporter and collector are close together and connected by a private network.

NetFlow is designed to use UDP for transport. That is, an exporter places each outgoing NetFlow message in a UDP datagram and sends the datagram to the collector. There are two important consequences:

- NetFlow messages can be lost or reordered
- NetFlow traffic can cause congestion

Message Loss And Reordering. The NetFlow protocol is designed to accommodate message loss and reordering. During startup, for example, if data arrives at a collector before a template, the collector stores the data. Once a template arrives, the collector can parse and process the stored data.

The protocol uses two techniques to accommodate reordering and packet loss. First, NetFlow assigns a sequence number to each message, which allows a receiver to place incoming packets in order. Second, the protocol requires a sender to transmit a copy of the template information periodically. Thus, if the initial copy of a template is lost, another will arrive.

Congestion From NetFlow Traffic. Because UDP does not provide a congestion control mechanism, NetFlow traffic is injected into the network without regard to other traffic. Consequently, a manager who chooses to use NetFlow must take steps to avoid situations where NetFlow traffic swamps an intermediate network element or link. In a typical case, a site avoids congestion problems by placing NetFlow traffic on a separate network (e.g., a private VLAN connecting a router's management port to a NetFlow collector). As an alternative, a manager can insert a traffic scheduling device that limits the amount of bandwidth NetFlow can consume, or otherwise can ensure that the exporting device does not transmit large volumes of data (e.g., restrict NetFlow to a template that has few fields).

We can summarize:

> *Although the NetFlow protocol contains mechanisms to compensate for UDP packet loss and reordering, a manager is responsible for avoiding congestion. A manager can relegate NetFlow data to a private network, restrict the bandwidth NetFlow uses, or restrict the amount of data that NetFlow sends.*

11.19 Effect Of Configuration Choices

As we have seen, when a manager configures a NetFlow exporter, the choice of fields to include in a template affects the volume of data that is exported. In addition, other parameters affect the operation of NetFlow:

- Packet sampling rate
- Cache size
- Flow timeout

Packet Sampling Rate. When capturing data from a high-speed link that handles many flows per second (e.g., a backbone link), NetFlow produces a large volume of flow data. To reduce the data rate, a manager can configure an exporter to use *packet sampling.* In essence, sampling specifies that only one packet out of N should be examined when capturing flow data. For example, configuring N to be 1000 means that the capture step will ignore 999 of every 1000 packets, and the rate at which NetFlow data is emitted will be reduced by three orders of magnitude†. Of course, sampling reduces accuracy of the results. Thus, sampling introduces a tradeoff: a manager can choose to increase accuracy or reduce the amount of NetFlow data.

Cache Size. Before data about a flow can be exported, the device performing capture must detect the beginning and end of the flow. Thus, information about a flow must be kept until all packets in the flow have been observed. Once a flow completes, data about the flow is exported. The mechanism used to hold information about flows is known as a *flow cache.* The name arises because a flow cache only retains data for the most recent flows.

Some systems allow a manager to control the size of the flow cache. Making the cache smaller lowers the number of simultaneous flows that the system can track, and thereby lowers the volume of traffic. Of course, making the cache size too small results in inaccurate analysis.

Flow Timeout. Flow capture is straightforward for protocols that use a connection-oriented paradigm. For example, TCP exchanges *SYN* packets to set up a connection, and uses *FIN* or *RST* packets to terminate a connection. Thus, to capture flow information about a TCP connection, a device merely needs to watch for the appropriate SYN, FIN, and RST packets.

For protocols like IP and UDP that follow a connectionless paradigm, capturing flow data is more difficult because there are no special packets to mark the beginning and end of a flow. In such cases, a flow exporter uses a *cache timeout* to control when data is emitted — after an entry remains idle for K seconds, the entry is exported and removed from the flow cache.

---

†In practice, a sampling mechanism can include a slight amount of randomness to prevent examining every N^{th} packet.

A manager can configure the timeout value for a flow cache. However, extremes do not work well. Choosing a value that is too large will allow an idle flow to remain in the flow cache, taking space that could be used to track another flow. Choosing a value that is too small can cause a flow to be exported before all packets have been observed (i.e., subsequent packets will be viewed as a new flow).

We can summarize:

> *In addition to selecting a set of fields to export, a manager may be able to configure the packet sampling rate, the size of the flow cache, and the cache timeout used to remove old entries.*

11.20 Summary

Flow analysis divides traffic into a set of flows, where each flow represents a sequence of related packets. Flow analysis is used for a variety of purposes, including traffic characterization, accounting and billing, and anomaly detection.

The definition of a flow is flexible. A manager can define an aggregate flow to consist of packets to the same destination, packets carrying the same protocol, packets on the same TCP connection, or packets from a given ingress.

Flow analysis can be conducted online (as the data is collected) or offline (after data has been collected and stored). Online analysis is helpful in diagnosing problems; offline analysis allows a manager to view the same data multiple ways.

Flow data can be captured by a passive probe or by an active network element that is forwarding packets. The chief advantage of active capture lies in the ability to track traffic from one interface to another. To achieve high-speed capture, a network element can use classification hardware; early classification reduces the volume of data collected, but does not retain all details.

Many flow analysis tools exist, and most use a graphical display. Two popular display formats are a dynamic pie chart and a time-progression graph.

The most popular flow technology, NetFlow, was invented by Cisco Systems, but is now used by other vendors. NetFlow specifies unidirectional flows with a fine-grained definition. To keep export general, NetFlow sends a template that describes data plus data records; a receiver can use the template to parse NetFlow packets even if the receiver does not understand all fields.

NetFlow uses UDP for transport. The protocol accommodates packet reordering and loss of templates; to control congestion, a manager must either configure NetFlow to send low volumes of data or plan a network path where congestion is not a problem (e.g., a private network connection).

Many flow analysis tools exist. For example, a set of open source tools that use NetFlow data are available at:

http://www.splintered.net/sw/flow-tools/

Cisco Systems provides support for capturing NetFlow data as well as tools that analyze the data. An introduction can be found at:

http://www.cisco.com/warp/public/732/netflow/index.html

Information about the IETF *Internet Protocol Flow Information eXport* (*IPFIX*) can be found at:

http://net.doit.wisc.edu/ipfix/

Chapter Contents

12.1   Introduction, 185
12.2   Definitions Of Forwarding And Routing, 185
12.3   Automation And Routing Update Protocols, 186
12.4   Routing Basics And Route Metrics, 186
12.5   Example Routing Update Protocols, 188
12.6   Management Of Routes, 189
12.7   The Difficulty Of Route Management, 189
12.8   Use Of Routing Metrics To Enforce Policy, 190
12.9   Overcoming Automation, 191
12.10 Routing And Management Of Quality-of-Service, 192
12.11 Traffic Engineering And MPLS Tunnels, 193
12.12 Precomputation Of Backup Paths, 193
12.13 Combinatorial Optimization And Infeasibility, 195
12.14 Precomputation And Fast Convergence For IP Routing, 196
12.15 Traffic Engineering, Security, And Load Balancing, 196
12.16 Overhead, Convergence, And Routing Protocol Choices, 197
12.17 OSPF Areas And The Principle Of Hierarchical Routing, 198
12.18 Management Of Routing And Hidden Problems, 199
12.19 The Global Nature Of Routing, 200
12.20 Summary, 201

12

Routing And Traffic Engineering

12.1 Introduction

Chapters in this part of the text explore tools and technologies used for network management. The previous chapter focuses on flow analysis, one of the key technologies that managers use to understand and assess traffic.

This chapter continues the discussion of management technologies by focusing on the management of routing. We will see that although basic routing is straightforward, many issues and subtleties complicate the management of route propagation.

12.2 Definitions Of Forwarding And Routing

Recall the distinction between *forwarding* and *routing*. Forwarding refers to the action an IP router takes when it receives a packet, chooses a next hop along the path to the packet's destination, and sends the packet to the next hop. Routing refers broadly to the process of establishing the information that routers use when making forwarding decisions. From a manager's point of view, routing is a tool to control forwarding. That is:

> *A manager uses routing mechanisms to establish and control the path
> that a given packet will follow through a network.*

12.3 Automation And Routing Update Protocols

It may seem that the management of routing has been completely automated: a
manager only needs to select and run appropriate routing software, and allow the
software to handle the problem. In fact, many *routing update protocols* exist; each allows routers to exchange messages and propagate routing information across an entire
network. In theory, if a manager chooses a routing protocol and configures a copy of
the software on each router, a set of routers can automatically establish and maintain the
internal tables that make forwarding correct and efficient.

Despite a plethora of protocols and software, network routing is not automated —
establishing and maintaining routes remains one of the most difficult aspects of network
management. In fact, automated routing protocols, which handle trivial cases well, can
present obstacles when a manager needs to override the choices a protocol makes. The
point is:

> *Although automated routing protocols handle small cases well, rout-
> ing remains one of the most difficult aspects of management in a large
> network.*

After a review of basics, remaining sections consider management of routing. We
examine the interaction between routing and policy, consider constraints that make routing difficult to manage, and give examples of routing problems that can remain hidden.

12.4 Routing Basics And Route Metrics

To understand the management aspects of routing, one must understand a few
basic concepts, including

- Shortest paths and route metrics
- Types and scope of routing mechanisms

The next sections define each of these topics. Later sections expand the discussion by
considering the management of routes.

12.4.1 Shortest Paths And Route Metrics

A routing protocol attempts to find the best path through a network, where the definition of *best* depends on the network and routing protocols being used. Typically, the best path is defined to be a *shortest path*, where the length of a path is measured according to a routing protocol metric. Popular metrics include:

- Hops
- Latency
- Jitter
- Throughput
- Redundancy

Hops. A hop metric is the most popular for automated routing update protocols. The number of hops along a path is defined to be the number of routers along the path†. When using hops, a routing protocol chooses to route traffic over a path with fewest hops.

Latency. For applications such as real-time audio or video, the number of hops along a path is less important than the overall delay across the path. In such cases, a manager can choose to send traffic across a path that has minimum latency.

Jitter. Jitter is related to latency because both metrics are important for real-time applications. To give high-quality output for real-time data, routes must be selected that minimize jitter as well as latency.

Throughput. In situations such as file system backups, where bulk traffic will be transferred, neither hops nor delay provide an optimal way to assess paths. Instead, a path should be chosen to maximize throughput.

Redundancy. In situations where availability is more important than other aspects of performance, a manager can use redundancy as the metric and select routes that provide a maximum number of redundant paths.

Unfortunately, no single metric is ideal for all situations. Most networks support a variety of applications, including real-time voice or video as well as data.

> When choosing a routing strategy, a manager must consider the metrics by which routes are measured.

---

†Some protocols define a hop to be a link instead of a router; the difference in definitions amounts to choosing the origin to be one instead of zero.

12.4.2 Types And Scope Of Routing

Unicast vs. Multicast Routing. The primary focus of routing and this chapter is *unicast* traffic. That is, most routing concentrates on routes for packets that are each traveling to a single destination. A secondary set of technologies provides routing for *multicast* traffic. Multicast routing is more complex than unicast routing, and multicast technologies are less mature than unicast technologies. In particular, multicast systems often require substantial effort to configure, monitor, and maintain. Thus, many sites avoid general multicast routing by using unicast tunnels to transport multicast traffic; multicast is only used for final delivery across a local network.

IPv4 vs. IPv6 Routing. Although versions 4 and 6 of the Internet Protocol are conceptually the same, IPv6 changes several fundamental assumptions about addresses (e.g., each link can be assigned more than one prefix at a given time). Consequently, management of IPv6 routing differs from management of IPv4 routing. At present, however, only IPv4 technology is mature; the accumulated knowledge about management of IPv6 is insufficient to draw conclusions.

Interior And Exterior Routing. Traditionally, routing is divided into two broad categories depending on the scope of the underlying infrastructure. *Interior routing* refers to routing within an organization (e.g., within an enterprise), and *exterior routing* refers to routing between two separate organizations. Technically, interior routing is defined to be within a single *autonomous system*, and exterior routing is between autonomous systems. To follow the distinction, a routing update protocol is classified as either an *Interior Gateway Protocol* (*IGP*) or an *Exterior Gateway Protocol* (*EGP*).

Although it seems straightforward, the distinction between exterior and interior routing becomes blurred in large networks. For example, a large enterprise can choose to divide the enterprise network into separate pieces, and manage routing separately within each piece. In practice, one of the chief differences between interior and exterior routing involves the criteria used to select paths: interior routes usually follow shortest paths, while exterior routes are often selected on the basis of contractual or financial requirements. The point is:

> *Although routing is classified as interior or exterior, the distinctions can become blurred in large networks that are managed as multiple, independent pieces.*

12.5 Example Routing Update Protocols

Many protocols have been created to exchange routing information. A single protocol has emerged as the de facto standard for exterior routing in the Internet. Standardized by the IETF, the protocol is known as the *Border Gateway Protocol* (*BGP*). Two popular IGPs are also derived from IETF standards: the *Routing Information Protocol* (*RIP*) and the *Open Shortest Path First* (*OSPF*) protocol. In addition, vendors have defined proprietary IGPs. For example, Cisco Systems sells software for *Interior Gateway Routing Protocol (IGRP)* and an extended version known as *EIGRP*. Finally, a remnant of the Open System Interconnection protocols has recently reappeared: the *Interior System to Interior System* protocol *(IS-IS)*.

12.6 Management Of Routes

Two aspects of routing are important to a network manager:

- Route planning and selection of paths
- Route configuration

Route Planning And Selection Of Paths. Before a routing architecture can be deployed, a manager must understand the overall goals and choose technologies that achieve the goals. Most important, planning involves assessing needs, establishing polices that specify paths over which traffic should be sent, and ensuring that the underlying network can support the resulting traffic. Assessment can be difficult, especially when financial issues are involved. For example, if a large ISP routes traffic through another ISP, the cost depends on the SLA between the two organizations.

Route Configuration. The second aspect of routing focuses on deployment of a routing architecture. Once a routing architecture has been designed, each router must be configured either manually or by using routing update protocols. Configuration may also need to reserve bandwidth (e.g., to ensure that normal data traffic does not interfere with real-time voice traffic).

12.7 The Difficulty Of Route Management

Routing is both important and challenging. On one hand, optimal routing is important because the routes that packets follow affect overall network performance, resilience, and adaptability to failure, as well as the service each application receives. On the other hand, routing is challenging because the choices made when devising a routing architecture are often dictated by external requirements. For example, routing can be constrained by corporate policies or the capabilities of the update protocols being used. In addition, routing can be constrained by contractual obligations (especially for providers) or financial costs. Thus, instead of merely following the shortest path, traffic may follow a route that satisfies an external constraint. The point is:

> *Many factors contribute to make routing management difficult; policies can dictate the use of nonoptimal paths for some traffic.*

As an example of how policy can affect routing, consider Figure 12.1 which shows connections among five sites.

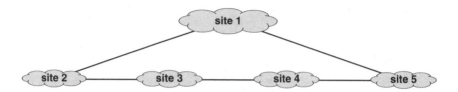

Figure 12.1 Illustration of five sites with connections among them. If sites 2 through 5 are the same size, the shortest path from site 1 to site 3 goes through site 2, but policy may dictate using a longer route.

Figure 12.1 can depict a set of five autonomous systems or a single enterprise with multiple sites. In either case, a policy can lead to nonoptimal routing. For example, if site 1 consists of an ISP and site 2 is one of its customers, the contractual agreement between the two may prevent the ISP from using site 2 for *transit traffic* (i.e., traffic passing through to another site). If the figure depicts an enterprise, a heavy load on the link from site 1 to site 2 may lead the enterprise to prohibit other traffic on the link. Thus, to adhere to policy, a manager at site 1 must configure nonoptimal routes for destinations in site 3.

12.8 Use Of Routing Metrics To Enforce Policy

A manager can manually configure forwarding tables to handle arbitrary policy. However, doing so is tedious and prone to error. Furthermore, manual configuration prevents automatic recovery during failures. Consequently, the question arises: can routing update protocols be used in the presence of policies?

It may seem that routing protocols will override policy because the metrics that protocols use when computing shortest paths are derived from properties of the underlying network rather than from policies. In many cases, however, routing software allows a manager to control routing. There are three general approaches:

- Manual override
- Control of routing exchange
- Control of metrics

Manual Override. The most straightforward mechanism used to control policy allows a manager to insert or change specific entries in a forwarding table. Such entries are permanent in the sense that a routing protocol cannot remove or replace them.

Control of Routing Exchange. Some routing software allows a manager to configure each router with a set of *constraints* that control the transfer of routing information. The constraints specify the information that can be exported to other routers and routing information that can be accepted from other routers. Thus, to enforce policy, a manager can use constraints to prevent a site from learning a shorter route.

Control Of Metrics. Although a constraint system handles some policies, a more flexible approach allows a manager to control the values that a routing protocol sends. For example, consider a protocol, such as RIP, that uses a *hop-count* metric. Some implementations allow a manager to configure the metric RIP uses. Thus, a manager can artificially set the ''distance'' to a given network, and RIP will use the value when it transmits routing information to other routers.

Control of metrics is more powerful than a constraint mechanism. If a manager can control metrics, the manager can choose to discourage or encourage the use of a given route, but still rely on automated routing in cases of failure. In Figure 12.1, for example, a manager can set metrics in site 2 so it advertises a high-cost path to destinations in site 3, and set metrics in site 4 so it advertises a low-cost route to destinations in site 3. When routing information reaches site 1, the path through sites 5 and 4 will appear less expensive than the path through site 2. However, the routing system will still provide backup: if a failure occurs (e.g., the link between sites 4 and 5 disappears), a protocol will automatically detect the failure and use the high-cost route through site 2. The point is:

> *To control path selection, a manager can configure routing metrics to have higher or lower values than the actual cost. If metrics are chosen carefully, routing protocols will select a backup route when a failure occurs.*

12.9 Overcoming Automation

Routing illustrates an important principle in network management: when an automated subsystem does not handle a situation, a manager must resort to devising tricks that will cause the system to produce a desired outcome. In essence, instead of directly specifying the desired outcome, a manager must deduce a set of parameters or inputs that will cause the automation system to achieve the outcome. In the case of routing protocols, for example, a manager must select metrics that will achieve the desired forwarding, and must be careful to calculate the effect that artificial metrics have on routing during failures. The point is:

When controlling the actions of an automated management subsystem, such as a routing protocol, a manager proceeds indirectly by manipulating parameters to achieve a desired outcome. Indirect control can be complex, and can have unintended consequences.

12.10 Routing And Management Of Quality-of-Service

Recall from Chapter 7 that routing is important to overall network performance and forms an integral role in capacity planning. In addition, routing plays a key role in managing the *Quality of Service* (*QoS*) that a network offers. There are three aspects:

- Characteristics of paths
- Anticipation of congestion
- Effect of route changes

Characteristics Of Paths. Each path through a network has characteristics such as latency and jitter that determine the QoS available over the path. The shortest path through a network may not give the best QoS. For example, a path that consists of one satellite link will have much higher delay than a path with two Ethernets. Thus, in cases where QoS guarantees are essential, a manager may need to ensure that the routing protocols do not override QoS considerations.

Anticipation Of Congestion. Recall from Chapter 7 that congestion can cause delay. Thus, when low delay is needed, a manager must route traffic over paths where congestion is minimized. In other words, a manager must carefully control routing to ensure traffic that requires low delay is not routed over links that can become congested, even if such links form part of a shortest path.

Effect Of Route Changes. Interestingly, because route changes increase jitter, routing update protocols can introduce QoS problems by automatically changing to a better path. The problem is especially severe in cases where a routing protocol oscillates between two paths. Thus, to minimize jitter, a manager must prevent continual route changes. The point is:

Routing is inherently linked to QoS management. Because the shortest path through a network does not always meet QoS requirements and route changes introduce jitter, QoS can require a manager to override routing protocols.

Note that management of QoS can be especially challenging in a converged environment where voice, video, and data applications share a network facility and the network uses a conventional forwarding system that does not distinguish among types of traffic. In such cases, a router forwards all traffic that is traveling to a given destination along the same path. Thus, it may be impossible for a manager to select a path that meets the QoS requirements of some traffic (e.g., voice) without forwarding all traffic along the same path. As a consequence, a manager may face a paradox in which a path that satisfies the QoS requirements for one type of traffic cannot be used because forwarding all traffic along the path will increase congestion and violate QoS requirements.

12.11 Traffic Engineering And MPLS Tunnels

Because IP forwarding uses the destination to choose a next hop, Internet forwarding can be viewed as imposing a set of directed graphs, with one graph for each destination. The chief alternative to destination-based forwarding is *traffic engineering*, and the most popular technology is *Multi-Protocol Label Switching* (*MPLS*). MPLS allows a manager to map traffic into a set of flows and specify a path through the network for each flow. Furthermore, a mapping can be specified to start and terminate at any two points in a network, which means a manager can use traffic engineering at some points in the network and use conventional IP forwarding at other points.

Informally, we call an MPLS path a *tunnel*. In essence, once a packet enters an MPLS tunnel, the packet follows a predetermined path to the end of the tunnel without regard to the IP forwarding that has been established. By allowing a manager to separate traffic into flows, MPLS can overcome one of the fundamental limitations of IP forwarding: some types of traffic for a given destination can travel along one path and other types can travel along a different path. Thus, a manager can send VoIP traffic along a path that has low jitter and low congestion, while email and web traffic travel along a path that has high throughput. The point is:

> *Traffic engineering technologies offer an alternative to IP forwarding. Instead of specifying a route for each destination, traffic engineering allows a manager to control forwarding for each flow independently.*

12.12 Precomputation Of Backup Paths

Conventional IP routing protocols are designed to detect and accommodate link failures and other changes in network topology. Once a failure has been detected, routing protocols choose an alternative path to reroute traffic around the failure. The question arises: how does traffic engineering handle such situations?

Technologies exist that provide automated recovery for traffic engineered networks. Unlike conventional routing protocols, the recovery systems designed for a traffic engineered network use *precomputation*. That is, before any failure occurs, a manager specifies a set of potential failures and requests the software to compute and store a backup path for each potential failure. When a failure does occur, the software can switch to a backup path quickly. Some vendors use the term *path protection* to emphasize that the software provides backup and automated recovery for a traffic engineered path analogous to the automated recovery that routing protocols provide for traditional forwarding. The point is:

> *Although traffic engineering assigns each flow to a fixed path, technologies exist that can switch a flow to a precomputed backup path when a failure occurs. Vendors describe such software as providing* path protection.

Of course, QoS requirements can make the computation of alternate paths difficult. To see why, consider Figure 12.2 which illustrates a graph that corresponds to a network that has flows assigned to links.

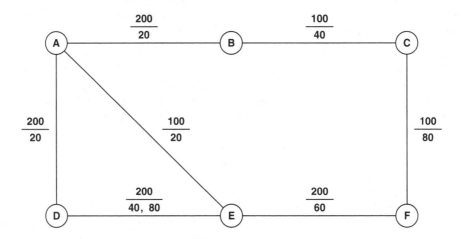

Figure 12.2 A graph depicting six routers with labels on each link showing the link capacity over the allocated flow capacity. Link (D, E) has two flows of 40 and 80 mbps.

In Figure 12.2, the label on a link lists the total link capacity and the amount of capacity that has been assigned to existing flows. To simplify the discussion, assume that each flow listed in the figure is point-to-point between two routers. For example, the link between A and D has a capacity of 200 mbps, and only one 20 mbps flow has been assigned to the link, which means 180 mbps of the capacity is unassigned (i.e., available for best-effort traffic).

To understand the difficulty of precomputing backup paths, consider computing alternative paths for a hypothetical case where the link between D and E fails. Two flows of 40 and 80 mbps are currently assigned to the link; a backup plan must provide an alternative path for each. Because link (B, C) only has 60 mbps of capacity remaining, the only viable backup for the 80 mbps flow is the path:

$$D \rightarrow A \rightarrow E$$

Furthermore, when the backup is needed, adding the 80 mbps flow to link (A, E) means that less than 40 mbps remain. Thus, the only viable backup for the 40 mbps flow is the path:

$$D \rightarrow A \rightarrow B \rightarrow C \rightarrow F \rightarrow E$$

Do the above paths constitute a viable backup plan? Unfortunately, the plan has two potential problems. First, because the backup plan assigns the entire capacity of link (A, E) to flows, no spare capacity remains to carry best-effort traffic. Second, our simplistic example uses point-to-point flows and only considers throughput requirements. In addition to reserving bandwidth for a flow, traffic engineering usually provides a bound on the delay or jitter. In the example backup plan, assigning the full capacity of link (A, E) means that utilization on the link will approach 100%, which will result in arbitrarily high delay and jitter. Thus, computation of backup paths is a multivariate optimization problem. The point is:

> *Precomputing backup paths in a traffic engineered network is complex because in addition to throughput, QoS usually imposes other requirements such as bounds on delay and jitter; a backup plan must accommodate all aspects of QoS.*

12.13 Combinatorial Optimization And Infeasibility

As with many combinatorial optimization problems, one possible outcome of backup route computation is that no solution is feasible. That is, given a network topology, a set of flows, and a potential failure mode, it may be that no set of backup paths can satisfy the QoS constraints. We say that the problem is *overconstrained* and that backup is infeasible.

Of course, deciding that a problem is infeasible can require substantial amounts of computation, especially if the network is large, many flows exist, or each flow has many QoS constraints. To reduce the computation time, typical software does not attempt to enumerate all possible ways to map flows onto the network. Instead, the software uses optimizations related to the well-known *Min-Cut Max-Flow Theorem*†.

---

†The Min-Cut Max-Flow Theorem was originally applied to the flow of commodity goods (e.g., shipping routes).

Even with optimizations, precomputation is usually an offline procedure — rather than waiting for results to be displayed immediately, a manager runs the precomputation in background.

It may seem that a manager would only be interested in viable backup solutions and that infeasibility is unimportant. However, knowing that a backup is infeasible helps managers in two ways. First, it helps managers avoid wasting time attempting to remap flows when a failure occurs. Second, it helps with capacity planning: if a subset of flows is critical, a manager must increase capacity to ensure that the critical flows are protected during failure. The point is:

> *Knowing that a backup is infeasible helps managers plan increased capacity for critical flows, and avoids wasting time searching for a nonexistent backup solution.*

12.14 Precomputation And Fast Convergence For IP Routing

Interestingly, precomputation of backup paths has also been applied to IP routing. The motivation is to provide more rapid convergence than conventional protocols. Vendors use the terms *fast recovery* and *fast failover* to describe the optimization.

To understand why fast recovery is significant, observe that a conventional routing protocol can take several update cycles to converge following a change, and for some protocols a cycle takes tens of seconds. Thus, routing can remain disabled for minutes after a failure while waiting for a routing protocol to converge on a new scheme. With fast recovery, a backup route is precomputed and ready to be installed immediately. Thus, instead of an outage lasting minutes, fast recovery restores forwarding as soon as a failure is detected.

12.15 Traffic Engineering, Security, And Load Balancing

The use of traffic engineering has an effect on many aspects of network management, including security and load balancing. Traffic engineering is sometimes cited as more secure than conventional IP routing because a manager can control the exact path a packet follows through a network. Thus, a manager can ensure that packets will never travel outside a specified area, even if a failure occurs and routing protocols automatically reroute other traffic. Furthermore, traffic traveling through an MPLS tunnel can be encrypted — a packet is encrypted before entering the tunnel, and decrypted on exit.

Interestingly, although it can increase security in some ways, the use of traffic engineering imposes constraints on the overall security architecture. For example, the packet classification needed when a packet is assigned to a path assumes that pertinent fields in the packet are unencrypted. If tunnels use encryption, an unencrypted packet that arrives at a traffic engineered part of a network can be mapped onto the appropriate flow and then encrypted. However, if applications employ end-to-end encryption and packets arrive encrypted, it may be difficult or impossible to map the packet to the correct path. Thus, an architecture that employs encrypted tunnels imposes constraints on the use of end-to-end encryption.

Traffic engineering also impacts *load balancing*. In a conventional routing system, a dynamic load balancing mechanism can be used to divide traffic among two or more parallel paths. More important, the assignment of packets to paths can adapt to conditions — a load balancer continually measures the traffic on each path and divides packets accordingly. As a result, a load balancer can help avoid high utilization, which means lower delay and less jitter. Traffic engineering can conflict with load balancing because traffic engineering takes a static approach in which each flow is preassigned a specific path through the network. If the traffic on every flow is constant and known in advance, the load can be balanced when flows are assigned to paths. However, if the traffic on each flow varies, the lack of dynamic load balancing can result in large delay and increased jitter.

To summarize:

> *Traffic engineering can impact both security and load balancing.*

12.16 Overhead, Convergence, And Routing Protocol Choices

The use of automated routing protocols represents a tradeoff among increased functionality, packet overhead, and configuration complexity. For the smallest networks and simplest topologies, routing protocols are unnecessary because only one path exists. In such cases, a routing protocol adds overhead without giving any benefit. For larger, more complex topologies, routing protocols can detect failures and send traffic along alternative paths, keeping a network operating until the problem can be repaired.

When no failure occurs, packets that carry routing information merely add overhead to a network. Thus, a manager must select a protocol that achieves the needed failure detection with minimum packet overhead. For example, in a topology that has a single connection to the Internet, choosing a protocol that summarizes arbitrary destinations into a single *default* route lowers overhead by reducing the size of update messages. A manager must also choose between two broad types of routing protocols: *distance-vector* and *link-status*. The number and size of messages sent by the two can differ dramatically.

Another management issue involves the time required for *convergence*. After a change in topology or a failure, an automated routing protocol requires time to detect the change and react by changing routes; we say that the system *converges* to a new routing state. The time required for convergence depends on the protocol being used, the network topology, and the location of a failure; convergence times can differ dramatically among protocols. For example, a protocol such as RIP that uses a distance-vector approach can require minutes to converge. Thus, in situations where rapid recovery from failure is required, a manager must select a protocol that converges quickly (e.g., OSPF can converge more rapidly than RIP).

In addition to considering the traffic that routing protocols generate and the convergence times, a manager must be aware of the relative difficulty of configuring and operating a protocol. For example, a protocol such as RIP is easier to install and configure than a protocol such as OSPF. However, RIP cannot be used in a large, complex network, nor does RIP suffice for exterior routing.

We can summarize the points about selection of routing protocols:

> *Choosing a routing protocol can be difficult because a manager must consider packet overhead that a protocol generates, the network size and complexity, the time required for convergence following a change or failure, and the cost to configure and operate the protocol.*

12.17 OSPF Areas And The Principle Of Hierarchical Routing

OSPF presents a particularly important management challenge: the design of a *routing hierarchy*. OSPF uses the term *area* to denote a set of routers that exchange routing messages. When configuring OSPF, a manager divides a network into one or more OSPF areas. The purpose of areas is to lower overhead — routing information is exchanged among routers within an area, but is summarized before being transmitted between areas. Thus, the traffic between areas is much lower than the traffic within an area. The challenge arises because no formula exists to determine the size or composition of an area.

For a network that comprises multiple sites, a manager can use a separate area for each site. More important, a manager can arrange the areas into a routing hierarchy, where traffic follows paths in the hierarchy. A routing hierarchy provides a compromise between a flat routing architecture in which routing protocols can use arbitrary links when computing shortest paths and a traffic engineering architecture in which a manager specifies the path for each flow. We can summarize:

> *A routing hierarchy provides managers with a compromise between flat IP routing and traffic engineering. When moving from one area to another, traffic follows paths along the hierarchy instead of following arbitrary paths through the network.*

12.18 Management Of Routing And Hidden Problems

Management of routing presents an unusual challenge. To increase robustness, some applications contain mechanisms that use an alternate point of contact when the primary contact is unavailable. In addition, many routing technologies provide automated mechanisms that can detect and adapt to failures. Thus, both network applications and the routing infrastructure can compensate for routing problems without alerting a manager or requiring manual intervention.

Examples of routing problems that can remain hidden from managers clarify the concept. We will consider:

- Asymmetric routes
- Nonoptimal routes
- Routing loops
- Dark addresses and black holes
- Subnet ambiguity
- Slow convergence
- Route flapping
- Redundant path failure
- BGP Wedgies

Asymmetric Routes. Routing *asymmetry* refers to a situation in which packets flowing in one direction traverse a different set of links and/or routers than packets flowing in the reverse direction. Although asymmetry is useful in special cases, asymmetric routes are often unintentional (i.e., arise accidentally). Asymmetric routes can lower overall throughput and make troubleshooting difficult (e.g., tracing the route from one side does not identify all routers involved in a two-way communication). Because communication continues, asymmetry can remain undetected.

Nonoptimal Routes. Routing is *nonoptimal* if for some source and destination, a shorter path exists that satisfies all routing constraints. A classic example of nonoptimal routing is known as the *extra hop problem* in which an incorrect route causes a packet to traverse the same network twice before being delivered. Nonoptimal routing can remain hidden because the network continues to operate (perhaps with somewhat degraded performance).

Routing Loops. The term *routing loop* refers to a set of routes that form a cycle. To see how a routing loop can remain undetected, observe that a routing loop may only involve a small set of addresses. If a user can communicate over the network, but cannot reach one site, the user is likely to assume the site is down.

Dark Addresses And Black Holes. The terms *dark address* and *black hole* are used to refer to a situation in which a network does not have a route to all addresses. Typically, black holes are caused by a misconfigured router. If only rarely accessed addresses are affected, the problem may not be apparent to users.

Subnet Ambiguity. When using variable-length subnet addresses, a manager can inadvertently assign subnet numbers such that a subset of host addresses cannot be reached from all parts of the network. Because only specific combinations of source and destination are affected, the problem can remain undetected until a user attempts to communicate between an affected pair of endpoints.

Slow Convergence. Routing protocols can take a long time to converge following a change in routing. One particular convergence problem, known as *count-to-infinity*, can form temporary routing loops that last for minutes. Because routing protocols eventually converge, slow convergence may go undetected and be allowed to reoccur.

Route Flapping. One of the most significant hidden problems arises from continual changes in routing that is known informally as *route flapping*. Changes in routes are undesirable because a change usually increases jitter and can cause packet reordering. Routing continues to operate, but the changes cause lower performance in transport protocols and real-time applications.

Redundant Path Failure. One subtle routing problem concerns backup routes that are used during a failure: if a backup path is inoperable for any reason, the problem may not become apparent until the primary path fails. Similarly, if load balancing is in use, failure of a parallel path may not be apparent because network operation continues.

BGP Wedgies. The use of BGP in a policy-constrained environment can introduce a subtle and unexpected routing problem. The situation occurs if routes have been established with separate *primary* and *backup* paths from an autonomous system to another autonomous system, the primary path fails, and the primary path is later repaired. A consequence of the way BGP operates can leave the backup path in use, even though the primary path is preferred.

We can summarize:

> *Management of routing is particularly difficult because subtle routing problems may not create apparent symptoms.*

12.19 The Global Nature Of Routing

Interestingly, the aspect of routing that introduces the most significant management problems has been implicit throughout the entire discussion: routing and traffic engineering span multiple network elements. Consequently, management of routes and traffic management requires coordination across a set of elements.

Management of routes can be divided into two distinct phases: initial configuration and continuous operation. To ensure that basic IP routing is configured correctly, a manager only needs to establish two basic properties:

- Routing protocols are configured consistently across the entire network.

- Initial routes are sufficient to permit routing protocols to interoperate.

Under the first item, consistency requires that each node on a given link be able to understand the routing protocol used on the link. Thus, routers sharing a link must be configured to run the same routing protocol across the link, which means that correct configuration requires coordination between pairs of routers. Under the second item, a router must be configured with an initial set of routes that enable routing protocols to reach other routers. Thus, correct initial routes can only be determined if the paths to other routers are known.

More explicit coordination of multiple elements is needed for management of traffic engineering. In particular, each pair of routers along a label switched path must agree on the label to be used between the pair. Thus, establishing a label switched path requires stepping through a series of routers and choosing a label to be used across each hop.

Coordinating multiple elements makes routing more complex than other management tasks:

Unlike management tasks that can be performed on one element at a time, management of routing and traffic engineering requires coordination across multiple elements. Coordinating multiple elements adds to the complexity, and helps explain why routing exhibits subtle problems that can remain hidden.

12.20 Summary

Routing is complex. Most networks use automated protocols to exchange routing information and find optimal routes; a variety of metrics exist. Routing can be divided into interior and exterior, but the distinctions blur in large networks.

Routing protocols include BGP, RIP, OSPF, IGRP, and EIGRP. Policies may override the selection of optimum paths; to set policy, a manager can control routing and the metrics used. Management of routing is linked to management of QoS; the path taken through a network determines the service received.

The chief alternative to conventional routing is traffic engineering that uses preassigned paths known as tunnels. MPLS is the most popular technology. Although they do not mandate failure detection and recovery, traffic engineering technologies have been extended to precompute alternative paths; analogous forms of precomputation have been used to provide fast failover for conventional IP routing. QoS considerations make precomputation of backup paths a complex combinatorial problem. Traffic engineering impacts security and load balancing.

Because routing protocols and network applications are designed to circumvent errors, management of routing is difficult and subtle routing problems can remain hidden.

FOR FURTHER STUDY

Griffin and Huston [RFC 4264] describes BGP wedgies, and gives an example topology that illustrates the problem. Norton [2002] presents a fascinating study of techniques that major ISPs use to control routing at peering points. Of particular note are the techniques that optimize revenue by inserting additional items in a BGP path to force traffic along an otherwise nonoptimal route.

Chapter Contents

13.1   Introduction, 205

13.2   Limits Of Configuration, 205

13.3   Iterative Improvement Using The Upgrade Paradigm, 206

13.4   Extending Functionality Without An Upgrade Cycle, 207

13.5   The Traditional Concept Of Scripting, 207

13.6   Scripts And Programs, 208

13.7   Stand-Alone Management Scripts, 209

13.8   CLI, The Unix Expect Program, And Expect Scripts, 210

13.9   Example Expect Script, 211

13.10   Management Scripts, Homogeneity, And Expect, 212

13.11   An Example Stand-Alone Script With Graphical Output, 214

13.12   Using Scripts As An Extension Mechanism, 223

13.13   Example Server With Scripting Extensions, 223

13.14   Example Of Server Extension Points, 225

13.15   Script Interface Functionality, 226

13.16   Example Server Extension Script, 227

13.17   Example Script That Manipulates A Reply, 230

13.18   Handling Multiple Tasks With A Single Script, 232

13.19   Script Timing, External Access, And Overhead, 233

13.20   Summary, 234

13

Management Scripting

13.1 Introduction

This part of the text focuses on facilities and platforms currently available to network managers. After a chapter that surveys management tools, each chapter considers an individual technology. In addition to a chapter on SNMP, chapters cover flow analysis and routing.

This chapter concludes the discussion of technologies, and provides a segue into the next part of the text. The chapter describes the interesting concept of scripting, and explains how scripting can be viewed as a first step in automating network management tasks. The chapter illustrates how a scripting capability can increase the generality of a network management product and enhance the functionality that the product supplies. Chapters in the third part of the text expand the discussion of automation, and consider the future of network management.

13.2 Limits Of Configuration

An intuitive definition characterizes *configuration* as a set of choices a manager makes to control the operation of a device or software system†. A key observation about configuration is that the functionality cannot be extended easily: the set of configuration parameters and the possible values for each parameter are determined when a system is designed. That is, when creating a network element or a service, a designer anticipates ways that the resulting system will be used and chooses parameters that allow a manager to distinguish among modes of use. The point is:

---

†Figure 4.1 on page 40 lists general properties associated with configuration.

> *Although configuration parameters give a manager flexibility within the bounds of the original design, the set of choices is fixed when a system is designed.*

Anticipating the needs of users can be difficult for a system designer. In the case of a system that forms part of a network, the situation is especially complex because users have freedom to choose a network topology and a set of network services. Furthermore, users can place a network system in environments that were not envisioned when the system was designed, and can invent novel ways to deploy a network system in a conventional environment. Consequently, it may be impossible for a designer to foresee all possibilities or define a set of configuration parameters that will suffice for all circumstances.

The point is:

> *The scope and generality of a system or service that relies on configuration is limited by the designer's ability to anticipate future network environments and ways the product will be used.*

13.3 Iterative Improvement Using The Upgrade Paradigm

A single paradigm dominates the production of configurable network systems: each successive release contains new functionality with additional configuration commands and parameters to enable and control new features. To access the new functionality, an existing customer *upgrades* their system to the new release. In addition to commercial products, in-house systems often follow an upgrade paradigm. The chief advantage of using configuration to select new features lies in backward compatibility: if a new feature is not needed for a given situation, the feature can be ignored.

From a vendor's point of view, creating a product that offers optional features can increase the potential uses and, consequently, the potential market. However, each additional feature raises the costs of designing, building, and testing a product. Therefore, before adding a feature to a release, a vendor is likely to assess the potential market and only incorporate features that will yield the highest profit with the least effort.

From a manager's point of view, a product upgrade cycle has several disadvantages:

- A site must pay for an entire upgraded product, even if the site only needs a few of the new features.
- A manager must wait for an upgrade cycle before any of the new features become available.
- A new version of the product must be thoroughly tested before installation in a production network.
- Because a vendor chooses features that maximize profit, a vendor may not include all new features that a given site desires.

The last point is especially important because requirements vary widely among sites. For example, although some sites have strict security requirements and concentrate on limiting access, other sites provide open access. Similarly, some sites need to create detailed accounting records, and others do not.

13.4 Extending Functionality Without An Upgrade Cycle

Can a network product be designed that allows the functionality to be extended without requiring an upgrade to a new version? In some cases, the answer is yes. That is, instead of anticipating all possible uses, a product can be created with extensibility as a fundamental part of the design (i.e., the product contains a mechanism that allows the owner to add new functionality without purchasing an upgrade).

Of course, extensibility is not adequate to handle significant modifications to a product's core functionality. Furthermore, extensibility may not be practical. One drawback arises from the in-house expertise that is required to create extensions: most technologies require programming expertise. Thus, before a site can use such technologies, the site must employ a computer programmer.

One of the most important limitations of extensibility arises from decreased performance: extensions do not execute as fast as built-in mechanisms. Thus, vendors seldom provide extensibility for the forwarding path in high-performance routers or switches. Instead, extensibility usually focuses on low-speed devices or control mechanisms. In fact, the products that are most amenable to extension mechanisms consist of services implemented with application software. We can summarize:

> *Because they result in decreased performance, extension mechanisms are usually associated with low-speed software systems rather than high-speed hardware systems.*

13.5 The Traditional Concept Of Scripting

To understand how management technologies provide extensions, we will review the concept of scripting. Traditionally, the term *script* refers to a computer program with the following properties:

- Concise

- Written in an interpretive language

- Designed to handle one small task

- Invoked on demand

Concise. Compared to large application programs that can consist of millions of lines of code, a script is small. Some scripts are expressed in a few lines of code; many scripts are under one hundred lines of code.

Written In An Interpretive Language. Scripts are distinguished from conventional computer programs because scripts are *interpreted.* That is, instead of being compiled into binary instructions that are executed directly by a CPU, a script is stored in source form and executed by a computer program known as an *interpreter.* Examples of interpretive languages used for scripts include: *awk, Perl, Tcl/Tk,* the *Unix shell,* and *Visual Basic.*

Designed To Handle One Small Task. Unlike a large application that includes code for input, basic computation, and display (output), a script usually handles one aspect of processing. For example, a script might be used to filter the input before processing.

Invoked On Demand. Because it is interpreted, a script can be invoked at any time. For example, a script can be invoked from a command line interface. More important, a script can invoke other scripts to handle part of the processing.

The above description gives a general characterization of scripts; exceptions exist. For example, long scripts have been created that occupy thousands of lines of code, compilers have been developed to provide higher-speed execution of scripts, and scripts have been created that handle all aspects of input, processing, and display. We can summarize:

> *Although exceptions exist, a traditional script consists of a small computer program written in an interpretive language that handles one small task and can be invoked on demand.*

13.6 Scripts And Programs

It may seem that the distinction between a script and an application program arises mainly from its purpose and role in an overall system. Indeed, because most scripting languages are *Turing complete†*, a script can be used to perform arbitrary computation. However, important differences exist that affect the overall costs of writing and using software. In general, scripting is a tradeoff between lower programming costs and slower execution times. Scripts are usually:

- Easier to create and modify
- Faster to debug and test
- Slower to execute

---

†A language that is Turing complete has sufficient power to compute any computable function.

Easier To Create And Modify. Scripting languages are designed to make software creation easier and faster. Thus, a scripting language provides high-level facilities for common tasks. In fact, one of the reasons scripts are typically shorter than application programs arises from the level of the language — a single line of code in a script can perform computation that requires many lines of code in a conventional language. An important consequence of higher-level facilities is that programmers do not need as much training or expertise.

Faster To Debug And Test. Because scripting languages are interpreted, a programmer can debug problems without waiting to compile and link a program. Thus, to test changes, a programmer can alter a script and run the resulting code immediately.

Slower To Execute. Although they reduce the overall cost of producing, modifying, and testing software, scripts execute slower than conventional programs.

The point is:

> *Scripting represents a tradeoff between program development costs and execution speed: a script costs less to develop than a conventional program, but runs slower.*

13.7 Stand-Alone Management Scripts

How can scripts be used to enhance network management? There are two broad ways that scripts help with management: as stand-alone applications and as an extension mechanism. We will consider stand-alone scripts first, and postpone the discussion of scripts as an extension mechanism until later sections.

To a manager, a stand-alone script operates like an application program. The difference between a script and an application lies in adaptability — a script can be altered easily and quickly. Thus, a manager can ask programmers to create or adapt scripts to suit local needs (e.g., tailor the format of the output). Furthermore, the low cost of alteration makes it possible to create multiple versions that differ in minor ways. For example, if a site has multiple managers, programmers can create a version of a script for each manager.

A stand-alone script is especially useful for automating a repetitive management task. For example, suppose a manager needs to make the same change in configuration on thirty routers. Instead of entering the changes manually, it may be possible to create a script that reads a list of router addresses and automatically issues a command to each router on the list. The point is:

> *Scripting provides an especially useful way to eliminate repetitive management tasks; a stand-alone script can be created that automatically propagates a management command to each network element in a set.*

13.8 CLI, The Unix Expect Program, And Expect Scripts

Recall that network elements often offer management access via a *Command Line Interface (CLI)*. Also recall that in some cases, a network element may offer a richer set of functions through its CLI than through other interfaces (e.g., SNMP). Thus, many management tools focus on CLI interaction.

One particular technology has become especially popular for building stand-alone management scripts that use CLI to interact with network elements. The technology centers on an application program known as *expect*. Expect is written in the *Tool Command Language (Tcl)*, and was originally designed to run under the Linux operating system; versions are now available for other systems, including Windows.

The idea behind expect is straightforward: instead of manually entering commands to control or configure a network element, save the set of commands in a file and allow expect to enter them automatically. Thus, the main input to expect consists of a *command file* (i.e., a text file that contains a series of commands). The term *expect script* is commonly used to refer to a command file.

Of course, blindly entering a series of commands is not sufficient — if a problem arises or an error occurs, continuing to enter commands may not have the intended effect. Thus, expect provides mechanisms that a script can use to detect and handle unusual conditions.

We can summarize:

> *A popular technology used for CLI interaction is known as* expect; *the steps to be taken and conditions to be tested are specified in a command file that is popularly known as an* expect script.

In essence, an expect script acts like a miniature computer program. That is, instead of merely containing text to be sent to a remote system, the command file specifies a series of steps that expect should perform during the interaction. One possible step consists of sending a text string to the system, and another consists of waiting for the system to respond. In addition, an expect script can interact with a user. Thus, an expect script can report progress to a manager, display output, or inform a manager if an error occurs.

One of the most important features of expect is the ability to handle conditional execution. Thus, a manager can specify that if a remote system sends a login prompt, expect should reply with a manager's login ID, but if a remote system sends an error message, the expect script should inform the user that a problem has occurred and cease interaction with the remote system. The point is:

> *In addition to interacting with a remote system, an expect script can interact with a human manager.*

13.9 Example Expect Script

A short example will clarify the concept. To simplify the example, consider a script that interacts with a remote system's CLI as follows: the script logs into a remote system, runs the command *ifconfig* to enable a network interface, and then logs out.

We assume that the CLI on the remote system is designed to interact with a human. Normally, a human initiates the login procedure by typing the *ENTER* key, and the system responds by displaying a login prompt on the console. Thus, to initiate interaction, the script sends a *newline* character (a character that corresponds to typing the *ENTER* key), and the system responds with the string:

```
Login:
```

The script sends a login ID (our example uses login ID *manager*), and the system prompts for a password:

```
Password:
```

Our example script sends the password *lightsaber*. Once the login has completed, the system sends a command prompt that consists of a greater-than character, >, and is ready to process commands.

Recall that our example script sends a command, and then terminates the session. To terminate a session, the script sends:

```
logout
```

The command the script runs, *ifconfig*, specifies that the primary network interface on the device should be enabled. The exact form of the command is:

```
ifconfig hme0 up
```

The remote system responds to the *ifconfig* command by emitting a response that specifies information about the network interface, including the IP address, address mask, and broadcast address. The output is formatted into two lines of text as the following example illustrates:

```
hme0: flags=1000843<UP,BROADCAST,RUNNING,MULTICAST,IPv4> mtu 1500 index 2
        inet 128.10.2.26 netmask ffffff00 broadcast 128.10.2.255
```

Figure 13.1 contains an expect script that performs the steps required to log in, enable an interface, and log out. In theory, the script only needs to send text to the remote system. In practice, however, the script must verify that the remote system has responded as anticipated during each step of the interaction. In addition, a script should inform the user about progress and the outcome.

The example code uses three basic instructions: *send*, *send_user*, and *expect*. The *send* instruction takes a string of characters as an argument, and transfers the string to the console on the remote system as if a human had entered the characters. The *send_user* instruction displays a string of characters as output on the manager's screen. Finally, the *expect* instruction monitors output from the remote system, and responds accordingly. The language follows the Unix convention of using a backslash to escape control characters. Thus, the two-character sequence \n at the end of a string corresponds to a *NEWLINE* character, the equivalent of pressing the *ENTER* key on the keyboard.

In the figure, each line following the keyword *expect* contains a pattern followed by an instruction. For example, the first occurrence of *expect* has two patterns, the string *Login:* and an asterisk, which matches any string. Thus, if the remote system emits *Login:*, the script responds by sending the string *manager*. If the remote system sends anything else (e.g., an error message), the script displays an error message for the manager and exits.

The expect program provides many features in addition to the few that Figure 13.1 illustrates. For example, a script can set a timer to take action in case the remote system does not respond. An expect script can also allow a manager to interact directly with a remote system. For example, a script can be created that logs into a remote system, connects the manager's keyboard and screen to the remote system, and allows the manager to enter CLI commands manually. Of course, a script can execute in a mode that handles interaction automatically, and only switch to manual entry if an unexpected situation arises. The point is:

> *Because the expect program offers many features, an expect script can provide sophisticated functionality.*

13.10 Management Scripts, Homogeneity, And Expect

Many sites use expect scripts to handle mundane management tasks. For example, an expect script named *passmass* is available that can change a user's password on multiple computers — the script takes a set of hosts as arguments, and performs the same password change on each host.

```
#
# Example expect script that logs in, turns on an interface, and logs out
#

send_user "attempting to log in\n"

send "\n"
expect {

 "Login:"    send "manager\n"

 *           {send_user "Error: did not receive login prompt\n"; exit}
}

expect {

 "Password:" send "lightsaber\n"

 *           {send_user "Error: did not receive password prompt\n"; exit}
}

expect {

 ">"         {send "ifconfig hme0 up"; send_user "performing ifconfig\n"}

 *           {send_user "Error: did not receive a command prompt\n"; exit}
}

expect  {

 ">"         send "logout\n"

 *           {send_user "Error: did not receive a command prompt\n"; exit}
}

send_user "Finished performing ifconfig on remote system\n"
```

Figure 13.1 Illustration of an expect script that interacts with a remote system. The script informs the user about each step.

Although scripts can be built to manage an arbitrary set of network elements or services, scripting is better suited to situations where the managed systems are alike or similar. For example, the password script described above assumes that the same command can be used to change the password on each system. If it were rewritten to accommodate a set of heterogeneous computers, the script would become much longer and more difficult to understand and modify. The point is:

Scripting works best when the managed systems are homogeneous. Scripts written for a heterogeneous environment tend to be longer and more difficult to create and maintain.

13.11 An Example Stand-Alone Script With Graphical Output

Although it illustrates basic concepts, the example script in Figure 13.1 focuses on command-line interaction and configuration. Scripting can also be used to devise sophisticated software systems that include graphical presentation. To explain the power of scripting, this section describes the problem of end-to-end performance monitoring, presents a script that solves the problem, and shows an example of the graphical output from the script.

How can a script help a manager monitor the overall performance of a network? One method uses a script to measure and display the round-trip delay continuously. Although it does not include all aspects of network performance, the round-trip delay across a network shows disconnections as well as congestion. In particular, a manager can use a monitoring script to measure response times from external sites. After explaining how such a script operates, we will examine sample output.

One of the chief advantages of scripting arises from the ability to combine existing tools. For example, instead of inventing a new program to assess delay, a script can use the *ping* program, which is widely available. Similarly, to plot data points in a graphical form, a script can use an existing program, such as the *gnuplot* program. As a consequence, instead of writing thousands of lines of code, a programmer can create a short script that gathers, processes, and displays information.

An example will clarify the concept and show the relative size of scripts. Our example employs two separate scripts: a monitoring script that gathers data about network performance and a plotting script that formats the results in graphical form for a human to view. We will examine the monitoring script first, and then consider the plotting script and the resulting output.

The monitoring script uses *ping* to probe a set of destinations that a manager specifies. The script takes action periodically: once every five minutes, it invokes *ping* to check each destination. For a given destination, ping sends five requests, gathers the responses, and computes the minimum, maximum, and average round-trip times. Once ping reports the results, the monitoring script extracts pertinent values and generates a single line of text that is appended to a data file for the destination. Because the data file is not meant for a human to read, each line of the file merely consists of six numbers that represent: a timestamp that gives the date and time of the probe (measured in seconds since January 1, 1970), the number of ping packets sent, the number of packets received, and the minimum, average, and maximum round-trip times measured in milliseconds. The following is an example of a line of text written by the monitoring script:

1143019606 5 5 36.007 48.816 66.116

In the example, five ping packets were sent, five were received, the minimum round-trip time was 36.007 ms, the average was 48.816 ms, and the maximum was 66.116 ms.

Figure 13.2 contains the code for the monitoring script, which uses *expect* to process the output from *ping*. Although the script contains almost 200 lines of text, the majority are comments that have been added to help readers understand the code.

```
#!/usr/bin/expect -f
#
#
# monitorscript - expect script that uses ping to monitor a set of hosts
#
#
# use:           monitorscript config_file
#
# where config_file is a text file that contains a list of hosts to
# be monitored, with one host name or IP address per line
#


#
# Check for an argument and set variable hostfile to the argument
#
if {[llength $argv] == 0} {
        puts stderr "usage: ping.ex <config file>";
        exit 1
}

set hostfile [lindex $argv 0]

#
# load_config - read the configuration file, place the contents in list
#       'hosts' and create an output file to hold ping results for each
#       host in the list.
#
```

```
proc load_config {} {
    global hosts host_out hostfile

    # declare a list named 'hosts', or empty it, if it exists

    set hosts [list]

    # open the configuration file and append each line to list hosts

    set cf [open $hostfile r]
    while {[gets $cf line] >= 0} {
        lappend hosts $line
    }

    # for each host, X, create an output file named  monitor-X.raw

    foreach i $hosts {
        set host_out($i) [open "mdir/monitor-${i}.raw" a]
        fconfigure $host_out($i) -buffering line
    }
}


#
# reload_config - close the existing output files and reload the
#        configuration (i.e., change the configuration file while
#        the script is running).
#

proc reload_config {} {
    global hosts host_out reload
    foreach host $hosts {
        close $host_out($host)
    }
    unset hosts host_out
    load_config
    set reload 0
}


#
# check_status - check the global status variables and take action
#

proc check_status {} {
```

```
        if {$::die} exit
        if {$::reload} reload
}


#
# lremove - remove the first occurance of an item from a list, and
#        return the modified list
#
proc lremove {l v} {
    set i [lsearch $l $v]
    lreplace $l $i $i
}


#
# Find a host ID in a list of IDs
#
proc host_by_id {idlist id} {
    lindex $::hosts [lsearch $idlist $id]
}


#
# Program begins here: load a set of host names from the config file
#
load_config


#
# Initialize global variables and set traps to catch interrupts
#
set die 0
set reload 0

trap {set die 1; set wakeup ""} {SIGINT SIGTERM}
trap {set reload 1} {SIGHUP}


#
# Main loop: repeatedly ping the target hosts
#
set wakeup ""
while {1} {
    check_status

    # get the current time (Unix epoch on Unix systems - seconds since
    # Jan 1, 1970)
```

```
set time [clock seconds]
after 300000 { set wakeup "" }
set host_ids [list]

# ping each host on the list five times and record the results

foreach host $hosts {
    spawn -noecho ping -n -c 5 -i 5 -W 10 $host
    lappend host_ids $spawn_id
    wait -i $spawn_id -nowait
    set results($host) [list]
}

# create a list of hosts for which ping has been executed, and
# iterate until a response has been received from each.

set valid_ids $host_ids

# continue iterating until the list is empty

while {[llength $valid_ids]} {

    # use expect to analyze the output from ping

    expect -i $valid_ids \
        eof {
        # case 1: when an end-of-file condition is encountered (i.e.,
        # all output for a given host has been processed), remove the
        # host from the list.
            set valid_ids [lremove $valid_ids $expect_out(spawn_id)]
        } \
        -indices -re {([0-9]+) packets transmitted, ([0-9]+) received} {
        # case 2: if the next item in the ping output is a line that
        # gives packets transmitted and received, append the data to
        # the record for the host.
            set host [host_by_id $host_ids $expect_out(spawn_id)]
            set results($host) [list $expect_out(1,string) \
                $expect_out(2,string)]
        } \
        -indices -re {min/avg/max/mdev = ([0-9.]+)/([0-9.]+)/([0-9.]+)} {
        # case 3: if the next item in the ping output is a line of
        # statistics that gives the minimum, average, and maximum
        # round-trip times, append the values to the record for the
        # host.
```

```
                lappend results($host) $expect_out(1,string) \
                    $expect_out(2,string) $expect_out(3,string)
         }
    }


    #
    # go through host list and write nonempty responses to output file
    #

    foreach host $hosts {
        if {[llength $results($host)] > 2} {
            puts $host_out($host) "$time $results($host)"
        }
    }

    #
    # see if user aborted or requested a reload during the cycle
    #

    check_status

    #
    # wait for next iteration to begin
    #

    vwait wakeup
}
```

Figure 13.2 An example script that uses ping to monitor a set of hosts and
collect data for display. The script uses a configuration file to
determine which remote hosts to ping.

To permit a manager to control the set of destinations that will be probed, the
script uses a separate configuration file. Each line of the configuration file contains a
domain name or an IP address; the script reads the configuration file, creates an internal
list of destinations to ping, and then begins.

Interestingly, the script allows a manager to reload the configuration file at any
time by sending a signal. That is, a manager does not need to restart the script. Instead, once a manager edits the configuration file and sends a signal, the script stops
probing the current set of hosts, rereads the configuration file, and begins probing the
new set.

The script uses the names given in the configuration file when creating the corresponding data file. For example, if the configuration file contains a line with the domain name *cnn.com*, the script places the corresponding data in a file named:

ping-cnn.com.dat

Once the monitoring script has gathered data and created a file for each destination, a manager uses a second script to convert the data into graphical form that can be displayed for a human. The plotting script reads the same configuration file as the monitoring script. Thus, if the configuration file contains *cnn.com*, the plotting script will open file *ping-cnn.com.dat* and create a plot of the data in file:

rtt-cnn.com.png

The resulting plot is created in a form that can be displayed by a standard web browser.

Figure 13.3 contains the code for the plotting script.

```
#!/bin/sh
#
# Invoke the Gnu plot program to display output from monitorscript
#
# use:   plotscript configfile [directoryname]
#
# where the argument configfile is a monitorscript configuration file,
# and the argument dirname is the name of a directory in which
# monitorscript has stored output files.
#
DIR=monitordir
case $# in

    1|2) if test "$#" = "2"; then
                DIR="$2"
         fi
         CONFIG="$1"
         ;;

    *)    echo 'use is: plotscript hostname [directoryname]' >&2
          exit 1
          ;;

esac
#
# Run gnuplot to place a plot of the data for each host in the
# monitor directory
```

```
#
for HOST in `cat $CONFIG`; do
    gnuplot > /dev/null 2>&1 <<EOF
        set timefmt "%s"
        set xdata time
        set format x "%m/%d %H:%M"
        set xtics rotate
        set title "RTT data for $HOST"
        set xlabel "Time and Date (EST)"
        set yrange [0:1000]
        set ylabel "RTT (ms)"
        set y2range [0:100]
        set y2label  Loss (%)"
        set terminal png size 800,600
        set output "$DIR/rtt-$HOST.png"
        set key   topleft
        set key box

        plot "$input" using (\$1 - 18000):4 title "Min. RTT" with lines, \
             "$input" using (\$1 - 18000):5 title "Avg. RTT" with lines, \
             "$input" using (\$1 - 18000):6 title "Max RTT" with lines, \
             "$input" using (\$1 - 18000):(\$3/\$2) title "Loss to $HOST" \
                 axes x1y2 with lines
EOF
    graphfiles="$graphfiles \"$IN\" \
using (\$1 - 18000):5 title 0g RTT to $HOST\" with lines,"
done

graphfiles=`echo $graphfiles | sed -e 's/,$//'`

#
# Run gnuplot again to produce a summary graph for all hosts
#
gnuplot > /dev/null 2>&1 <<EOF
    set timefmt "%s"
    set xdata time
    set format x "%m/%d %H:%M"
    set xtics rotate
    set title "Aggregate RTT data"
    set xlabel "Time and Date (EST)"
    set ylabel "RTT (ms)"
    set terminal png size 800,600
    set output "$DIR/rtt-all.png"
    set key top left
    set key box
```

```
        plot $graphfiles
EOF
```

Figure 13.3 An example script that plots data collected by the monitoring
script. The script uses the same configuration file as the monitoring script.

Output from the script consists of a graph that can be viewed on a user's screen.
Figure 13.4 illustrates how the output might appear†.

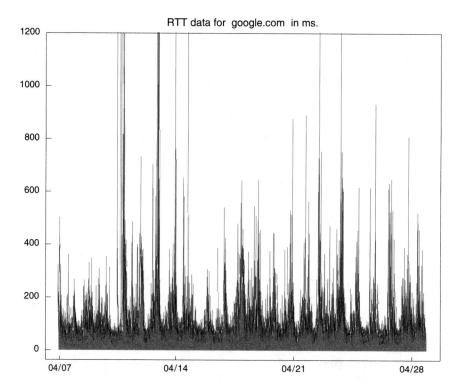

Figure 13.4 Illustration of a plot produced by the script in Figure 13.3. Gray
is used to indicate average round-trip times, and blue is used to
indicate maximum round-trip times.

In the figure, output extends over multiple days, with each week indicated along
the x-axis. The y-axis indicates the round-trip times, with average values plotted in
gray and maximum values plotted in blue. On a manager's display, multiple colors are
used to indicate minimum, average, and maximum delays.

---

†The plot in the figure is from actual data obtained by using the monitoring script to measure RTT
between a computer in West Lafayette, Indiana and Google.

In addition to creating one plot for each destination, the script in Figure 13.3 creates a summary plot that contains data for all destinations in the configuration file. A separate color is used for each destination. The point is:

> *Scripts that use existing programs to gather and display management information can be much smaller and easier for a programmer to create than conventional software.*

13.12 Using Scripts As An Extension Mechanism

Although stand-alone scripts are useful and lower software production costs, the most intriguing aspect of scripting arises from the use of scripts as an extension mechanism for network products. In essence, a vendor creates a product that contains a set of predefined *extension points*, which are known informally as *hooks*. When configuring the product, a network manager can specify a script to be invoked for each extension point. Once configuration is complete, the product runs the scripts automatically — whenever it reaches an extension point during processing, the product invokes the corresponding script.

Earlier in the chapter, we said that script invocation works best for products that operate at low speed or handle few packets per second. We now see why: because they are usually written in an interpretive language, scripts execute slowly. In particular, scripting works well as a server extension because requests tend to be small (i.e., a few packets) and a server tends to perform significant computation before returning a response. Thus, the added overhead of scripting is not significant. It is also easy to understand why scripting extensions are well-suited to most servers: a server runs as an application, which means that the interface to a script is trivial compared to the interface between a hardware mechanism and a script. To summarize:

> *A network product that allows scripting extensions includes a set of extension points at which the product can invoke a script. Scripting extensions are especially appropriate for a server that is implemented as an application.*

13.13 Example Server With Scripting Extensions

To understand scripting extensions, consider an example. Suppose a vendor decides to create an extensible DHCP server†. The primary purpose of such a server consists of supplying an IP address to a computer when the computer boots. Although a DHCP server also handles renewal requests, it will be sufficient only to consider new

---

†Our example is loosely based on Cisco's CNS Network Registrar (CNR) product, but the description has been simplified.

requests. Thus, from a server's point of view, an incoming packet contains a request for an address, and an outgoing packet carries a response to the client.

Despite its seeming simplicity, a DHCP server performs several processing steps when a packet arrives. Figure 13.5 lists the sequence of steps that a server takes to process a new DHCP request.

1. Receive the next incoming packet and verify that the packet contains a valid DHCP request.

2. Decode the packet by extracting information and placing the values in an internal data structure.

3. Identify a class for the client (i.e., associate the client with a particular set of address leases).

4. Look up an address for the client, calculate a lease, and begin to gather information for a response.

5. Add additional information (e.g., boot file name) to the set of items needed for a response.

6. Form a reply packet by encoding the response information into a valid DHCP message.

7. Update information about the lease in a nonvolatile data store (i.e., information on disk), and send the response.

8. Perform dynamic DNS update to create a DNS entry for the assigned address.

Figure 13.5 A list of the processing steps a DHCP server takes when a packet arrives with a request for a new address. The figure omits many details that are required in a production server.

Most steps in the figure are self-explanatory. When a packet arrives, the server checks validity. If the request is valid, the server optimizes processing by extracting fields from the packet and placing the items in an internal data structure. Successive processing steps refer to items in the data structure without manipulating fields in the original packet.

Step 3 is perhaps the most confusing. To understand why the step is needed, observe that a single DHCP server can manage multiple sets of IP addresses. In the simplest case, each set of addresses corresponds to an IP subnet, and a server uses the subnet to which a client is attached when choosing an address. In a more complex situation, an ISP might choose to assign each customer to a set of addresses, and then use the assigned addresses to control routing or priority. In any case, when a request arrives from a client, a DHCP server uses information in the packet to associate the client with a particular set of addresses. Following commercial nomenclature, we use the term *class* to refer to a set of addresses, and say that the server associates the client with a specific class.

Once a class has been identified for the client, the server can look up an address and calculate the lease time for the address. The server creates an internal data structure to hold the items for a response, and fills in the information. Once all items have been gathered and verified, the server forms a reply message by encoding each item according to the DHCP protocol standard. Immediately before sending the response packet, the server stores the lease information on disk. Thus, if it crashes and reboots, the server has a record of the address lease.

The final step in Figure 13.5 specifies that the server should perform a DNS update. Typically, a DHCP server installs both a forward and reverse mapping in a DNS server. Updating DNS is important in case the client computer contacts a server that uses DNS to authenticate communication (e.g., some email servers use reverse DNS to authenticate a client).

13.14 Example Of Server Extension Points

Now that the main processing steps a DHCP server takes have been identified, it is easy to understanding how extension points can be added to a server. Figure 13.6 illustrates seven extension points.

The first extension point, *post-packet-decode*, occurs after a request has been received, but before address lookup occurs. The main purpose of such an extension arises from the need for a filtering policy: a script can examine an incoming request and decide whether to accept or reject it (i.e., decide whether to allow processing to continue or declare the request invalid). Because an external script handles the extension, a manager can create a script that implements an arbitrary policy. For example, to prevent an unauthorized computer from obtaining an address, a manager might choose to block certain computers that are known to pose a security risk or might require each user to register their computer before honoring DHCP requests.

Other extension points allow a manager to control the server at each processing step. For example, *pre-client-lookup* allows an external script to choose an address class for a packet, which gives a manager the ability to make exceptions from a general policy. *Pre-packet-encode* gives a manager the ability to override choices the server has made before a response is sent (e.g., override the default router field). Figure 13.6 illustrates the overall processing, and indicates when each extension can be invoked.

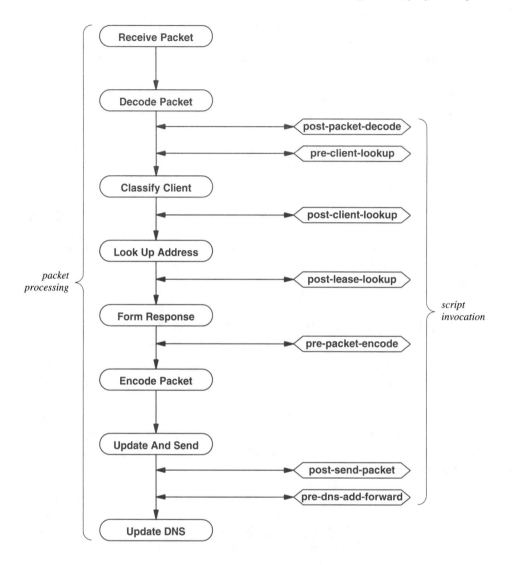

Figure 13.6 Illustrations of extension points in a DHCP server at which a
script can be invoked. A script can modify values and control
processing.

13.15 Script Interface Functionality

Figure 13.6 gives a generic overview of extension processing; an actual server contains many details not shown. For example, in addition to allowing a script to examine
and alter items associated with a request, the interface between a server and a script can

provide a mechanism that allows a script to reject a request. That is, when it returns, the script can pass back a code that instructs the server to stop processing the request and discard the packet. Alternatively, an interface can allow a script to request that the server stop processing the request and send an error message back to the client.

Although a script can examine and alter arbitrary values associated with a request, the interface between a server and a script should protect the server from scripts that misbehave. One protection technique uses isolation: the server limits the values that a script can change. For example, before invoking a script, a server can create a new namespace (e.g., a new *dictionary* of variables), copy the data associated with the current request into the dictionary, and run the script in an environment that only has access to the new namespace. Because it only has access to the copy, the script cannot change the original data in the server. When the script finishes, the server can examine values in the copy and decide whether they are valid before making the same change in the original data.

We can summarize:

> *Although the interface between a server and a script can allow a script to reject requests and otherwise control processing, the interface should also protect the server from scripts that misbehave.*

13.16 Example Server Extension Script

To clarify the concepts, consider the script in Figure 13.7 that enhances the safety and security of a DHCP server by discarding all *DHCPDECLINE* messages. Although the protocol uses such messages to permit a client to terminate use of an address, a malicious host can send a series of decline messages to mark addresses as unavailable. To prevent such an attack, a site can use the script as a server extension, causing the server to ignore each decline message.

```
#
#       Example discard script for Cisco's DHCP server (CNR product)
#
#
# Purpose:
#           Security/safety enhancement that prevents a malicious client
#           from declaring all leases in a scope unavailable.
#
# Operation:
#           Causes server to ignore all DHCPDECLINE messages.
#
# Use:
#           Attached to the server's post-packet-decode extension point.
```

```
#           Refer to the vendor's documentation for notes on how to
#           configure and enable the extension.
#
# Arguments:
#           Dictionaries for the request, the response, and the server
#           environment.  Refer to the vendor's documentation for the
#           set of items in each dictionary.
#
# Note:
#           To enable logging, change global variable LogDeclineDrops to "1"

set LogDeclineDrops "0"

proc DropDecline { request response environ } {
global LogDeclineDrops

    # Set variable msgtype to the message type from the incoming packet

    set msgtype [ $request get dhcp-message-type ]

    # if the message type is DHCPDECLINE (value 4), drop the packet
    # and send a log message (provided logging is enabled)

    if { $msgtype == 4 } {

        $environ put drop true

        # if logging enabled, generate a log message.

        if { $LogDeclineDrops } {

            $environ log LOG_INFO "DropDecline: dropping a DHCPDECLINE \\
            message from host with address'<[ $request get chaddr ]>'"
        }
    }
}
```

Figure 13.7 An example extension script for Cisco's DHCP server written in
Tcl. The script causes the server to discard all DHCPDECLINE
messages (i.e., messages with a type field of 4).

The exact details of the programming language that can be used for an extension
and the interface between the server and a script are defined when a server is created.

For example, although code in the figure is written in the *Tool Command Language* (*Tcl*), Cisco's server also permits extensions to be coded in C or C++.

In the figure, a hash mark, #, defines the beginning of a comment; text following a hash mark can be removed without changing the behavior of the script. In addition, blank lines have been inserted and the code has been indented to make it readable. As the figure shows, a script does not need to be long — even with each closing brace placed on a separate line to improve readability, the executable code occupies only twelve lines.

The extension script, named *DropDecline*, is called after the server has received a packet and decoded the DHCP message. In the vendor's terminology, a manager must configure the server to attach the script to the *post-packet-decode* extension point. To make the correspondence obvious to a manager, a file name can be chosen for the script that reflects the extension point. For example, the script in the figure might be placed in file *post-packet-decode-drop-decline.tcl*.

The example code is constructed for a server that passes three arguments to the script. Each argument is a *dictionary*. That is, each argument defines a namespace that contains pairs of:

$$(\,name,\ value\,)$$

A dictionary contains additional information for each item to specify whether the script can read the item, change the item, or both.

The first dictionary, named *request*, contains items in the DHCP request, and the second, named *response*, contains items being gathered for a reply. After a packet arrives, the server decodes the packet by creating items in the request dictionary for each field in the packet. For example, the request dictionary contains an item for the client's MAC address, each field in the DHCP message header, and so on.

The response dictionary also contains variables that correspond to fields in a DHCP packet. However, items in the response are not obtained from a packet that has arrived. Instead, the items correspond to values that will be placed in the reply packet (i.e., the server uses the response dictionary to gather information for a reply).

The third argument, named *environ*, is analogous to the *environment* found on a Unix or Windows system — the argument contains a set of named items that characterize the run-time environment of the server and control server processing. For example, the environ dictionary contains a Boolean variable named *drop*. To specify that the server should discard the request, a script must set variable *drop* to *true* before returning control to the server. In Figure 13.7, a single line of code makes an assignment to the *drop* variable to discard a message:

`$environ put drop true`

The operation of the example script is trivial. The script begins by extracting the message type from the request dictionary. That is, the script looks up the DHCP message type field in the request dictionary, and copies the value into local variable *msgtype*. Provided the message type is 4, the script sets the *drop* variable to *true*.

Note that from a script's point of view, the code that discards a packet is trivial. In fact, the script merely assigns a value to a variable. The server handles all internal details of cleaning up the state (e.g., erasing the message and recovering the buffer). The point is:

> *In many cases, a script merely decides what should be done, and the server performs the necessary action. For example, to discard a packet, a script sets a variable and the server handles details such as buffer deallocation.*

13.17 Example Script That Manipulates A Reply

The example script in Figure 13.7 focuses on an incoming packet (i.e., a request). To understand why a manager might need to alter an outgoing packet (i.e., a response), consider a network where clients run the Unix operating system. When a DHCP server allocates an IP address, Unix expects the message to contain a valid *host name* field. Thus, on a network with Unix clients, a manager must arrange for the DHCP server to include a host name.

How can a script add a host name to a packet? It might seem that a server would create a packet and then allow a script to make changes. However, the DHCP server described above does not allow a script to modify an outgoing packet directly. Instead, a script can only access the information that the server is gathering for a reply. The script can read or change values before a packet is created. Once the extension script finishes making changes, the server uses the modified information to construct the final packet. Thus, to control an outgoing packet, a script only needs to change values in the *response* dictionary. For example, to force the server to include a host name in an outgoing packet, a script only needs to assign the name to a variable in the *response* dictionary. The example script in Figure 13.8 contains code that will ensure a host name appears in each DHCP reply that carries an IP address to the client.

```
#
#             Example script to insert a host name in a DHCP reply
#
#
# Purpose:
#             Accommodate clients such as Unix computers that expect a
#             DHCP reply message to contain a valid host name.
#
# Operation:
#             Force server to include the host name in outgoing reply
#             messages.
#
# Use:
#             Attached to the server's pre-packet-encode extension point.
#             Refer to the vendor's documentation for notes on how to
#             configure and enable the extension.
#
# Arguments:
#             Dictionaries for the request, the response, and the server
#             environment.  Refer to the vendor's documentation for the
#             set of items in each dictionary.
#

proc AddHostName { request response environ } {

    # Set variable msgtype to the message type in the outgoing packet

    set msgtype [ $response get dhcp-message-type ]

    # if the reply message type is not DHCPDECLINE (value 4) or
    # DHCPNACK (value 6), copy the client host name value from the request
    # dictionary into the host name field in the response.

    if { $msgtype != 4 &&  $msgtype != 6 } {

        $response put host-name [ $request get client-host-name ]
    }
}
```

Figure 13.8 An example extension script for Cisco System's DHCP server
that causes the server to include a host name in each reply that
carries a lease. The script is written in Tcl.

Observe that the code in the figure does not blindly set the host name option in every outgoing message. Instead, the script only sets the host name in messages that carry an IP address to the client. For example, if the server denies a request, a message that carries the denial should not have the host name option.

To enforce the restriction, the script examines the message type and only sets the host name if the message type is other than *DHCPDECLINE* or *DHCPNACK*. Because it is focused on handling output packets, the script does not examine the message type in the arriving packet. Instead, the script uses the *response* dictionary when extracting the message type. That is, the script checks the message type that will appear in the outgoing message rather than the message type that appeared in the incoming message.

Once it has determined that the outgoing message should indeed carry a host name, the script executes the following line of code:

$response put host-name [$request get client-host-name]

In essence, the code specifies that the value of variable *client-host-name* in the request dictionary should be copied into variable *host-name* in the response dictionary.

The code cannot be understood until we know more about the meaning of variables. How did the programmer know that the message type for the outgoing packet had been stored in the response dictionary? How did the programmer know to copy the client host name from the request dictionary to variable *host-name* in the response dictionary? How did the programmer know that the client name variable in the request dictionary was valid?

The answer to all three questions is that the server vendor specifies the exact semantics of each item in a dictionary, including the meaning of the item, the possible values that can be assigned, and the times at which the item is valid. Thus, to write correct and meaningful code, a programmer must understand the assumptions and guarantees that the server interface defines for each variable. We can summarize:

> *Details of dictionary variables and their semantics are dictated by the vendor; before they can create correct extension scripts, programmers must become familiar with the names and exact meaning of the variables in each dictionary.*

13.18 Handling Multiple Tasks With A Single Script

Production scripts are usually much more complex than our examples. The primary reason is that a server restricts each extension point to a single script. Thus, a production script typically contains a set of tasks.

A production version of the example script in Figure 13.8 might contain additional code to check for other unwanted arrivals. An expanded script might also drop packets from a specific client or packets for Microsoft's RAS service. An expanded script might also check the client ID, and use the ID to associate the packet with a specific address class. Thus, an expanded script might have an overall structure of conditional tests, similar to the following:

```
if ( message is DHCPDECLINE)
    drop the packet and send a log message
if ( message is an RAS message)
    drop the packet and send a log message
if ( client ID is for a Cable customer )
    set the address class to cable_subscriber
```

The point is:

Restricting scripts to one per extension point results in each script handling multiple, possibly unrelated, tasks. A typical extension script is structured as a series of conditional tests and actions.

13.19 Script Timing, External Access, And Overhead

Because they are trivial, the example scripts presented in the chapter require little execution time. Even with the overhead of invocation and interpretive execution, the example scripts do not significantly increase the time a server needs to process a request and send a reply. However, overhead can be important if a script performs complex computation. Thus, before configuring extensions, a manager must be aware of the potential overhead and decide whether extra delay is justified.

The added delay is especially important in the case of an extension that accesses external resources. For example, an extension script can be constructed that maintains permanent state on a nonvolatile device such as an external disk. Doing so can increase the cost of access by several orders of magnitude. As an alternative, a script can use the network to access another service. For example, to make a decision about a request, an extension script might access a remote database that stores information about clients along with a record of how to respond to each. As with external storage, accessing remote services can increase processing time by several orders of magnitude.

We can summarize:

A script that accesses data on secondary storage or uses a network to access a remote database or other remote services can substantially increase the time required to process a request.

13.20 Summary

Because a designer chooses configuration parameters when a product is built, the scope and generality of a product is limited by the designer's ability to anticipate future needs and uses. Consequently, configurable products follow an iterative upgrade cycle in which the range of possible uses only changes in successive versions of the product as configuration parameters are altered or added.

Scripting technologies provide an alternative to strict configuration. Scripting lowers the cost of creating and modifying software, but also results in lower run-time performance. There are two broad categories of scripting used in network management: stand-alone scripts and extensions. A stand-alone script, which operates like an application program, is especially helpful for automating repetitive management tasks.

The expect program is a popular scripting technology used with command-line interfaces. Expect can interact with one or more remote network elements as well as with a manager. Instructions to expect are kept in a command file that is known as an expect script. An expect script does not blindly send keystrokes to a remote system. Instead a script can use the response(s) from a remote system as conditions that determine how the script operates. Expect scripts work best in a homogeneous environment where all network elements offer the same CLI.

One of the most interesting uses of scripting involves an extension mechanism for network products. To use scripting, a product must define extension points, each of which allows a script to be attached. Because scripts operate slowly and interfacing a script with an application program is easier than interfacing with a hardware system, extension works best with lower-speed products such as servers that are implemented as application programs.

We examined simple extension scripts designed to work with the DHCP server that is part of Cisco' CNR product. The interface to a script does not permit the script to access the server's internal data structures. Instead, the interface consists of three dictionaries that store pairs of name and value. One dictionary contains items from a request packet that has arrived; one contains items being gathered for a reply packet; and the third contains items from the server's run-time environment. To examine an incoming message, a script consults items in the request dictionary; to add or change fields of the reply message, a script modifies items in the response dictionary. Finally, to control processing, a script changes items in the environment dictionary; the server uses values in the dictionary when deciding how to proceed. Although scripting provides a convenient mechanism to extend products, allowing a script to reference external storage or remote services can increase processing delay significantly.

FOR FURTHER STUDY

Information about the *expect* program can be found at the expect home page:

$$http://expect.nist.gov/$$

Examples of network management tools that are built using expect scripts can be found at:

$$http://www.tcl.tk/customers/success/netmanage.html/$$

Cisco's CNR product, which offers extensions, provides IP address management, including DHCP and DNS servers. A description can be found at:

$$http://www.cisco.com/en/US/products/sw/netmgtsw/ps1982/index.html/$$

In addition to scripting mechanisms offered by commercial vendors, the open-source community has produced scripting facilities. For example, the Scotty system that uses scripting for network management was developed at the Technical University of Braunschweig in Germany and the University of Twente in the Netherlands.

Part III

An Examination Of
Future Possibilities
For Automated
Network Management Systems

Chapter Contents

14.1   Introduction, 239

14.2   Network Automation, 240

14.3   Dividing The Problem By Network Type, 241

14.4   Shortcomings Of Existing Automation Tools, 242

14.5   Incremental Automation Vs. A Blank Slate, 243

14.6   Interface Paradigm And Efficiency, 244

14.7   The Goal Of An Automated Management System, 246

14.8   Desiderata For An Automated Management System, 248

14.9   Multiple Sites And Managers, 250

14.10   Authority Domains And Role-Based Access Control, 250

14.11   Focus On Services, 251

14.12   Policies, Constraints, And Business Rules, 251

14.13   Correlation Of Multiple Events, 253

14.14   Mapping From Logical To Physical Locations, 253

14.15   Autonomy, Manual Override, And Policy Changes, 254

14.16   Summary, 255

14

Network Automation: Questions And Goals

14.1 Introduction

The first part of the text characterizes network management by defining the problem and providing general background. Chapters review the FCAPS model, and consider each aspect. The second part of the text examines extant tools and technologies, including scripting technologies that managers can use to devise stand-alone management systems or to extend existing products.

The third part of the text focuses on the future of network management. Instead of presenting solutions, chapters consider the broad challenge of automating network management. This chapter begins the discussion by considering the question of whether network management can be automated and the conditions under which automation might be possible. The chapter also reviews desirable characteristics of an automated network management system.

Successive chapters examine possible software architectures that can be used for network management and the representation of network state. The chapters discuss the translation between the internal representation of a network that is kept by the network management system and the underlying network elements. In addition, a chapter discusses engineering tradeoffs that must be made when designing a practical system.

The final chapter of the text summarizes the discussion of automation by presenting a set of open problems. As we will see, many basic questions remain unanswered, and much research is still needed.

14.2 Network Automation

Many questions surround the issue of *network automation*. Can networking be completely automated? That is, can software or hardware systems be devised that replace the human intelligence currently required to create and operate a network? If not, is the problem so inherently complex that automated solutions will never exist, or are we merely unable to create an automated solution at present? The questions have been debated since the inception of data networking.

As we have seen, tools have been created that automate repetitive, low-level tasks. Thus, it is more accurate to ask which networking functions can be automated and which cannot. One way to tackle questions about automation is to divide the problem into subproblems. For example, it might be easier to consider two major aspects of network management separately:

- Initial planning and deployment
- Day-to-day operation and maintenance

Initial Planning And Deployment. Planning a network includes assessing probable uses, estimating traffic, designing a topology, and choosing technologies. Often, input to the planning process is derived from guesswork, and the initial design choices are made without detailed knowledge. Thus, some engineers think that initial planning will be difficult to automate.

Other engineers take the opposite view. They point out that in many cases, initial network designs are often copied from existing networks — a designer, who is familiar with the networks at several organizations, chooses one of the existing networks as the basis for a new network. An automated design system might follow the same approach by starting with a small set of generic network plans and selecting the plan most appropriate for a given situation.

Day-To-Day Operation And Maintenance. Even if initial planning is automated, the complex problem of managing an operational network remains. Interestingly, some of the complexity in day-to-day management arises from an opposite situation than complexity in planning: instead of having too little data, day-to-day management is plagued by too much. It is possible to obtain detailed statistics such as a count of packets that travel across each link or information about individual flows that traverse each switch. When trying to understand a network, large volumes of detailed data can be overwhelming, making it difficult to observe important events and trends.

Proponents of network automation assert that computer software is ideally suited for sifting through massive amounts of data. A program can extract key items and monitor trends better than humans. Detractors argue that automated software cannot be created to handle day-to-day operations until the basic problem is better understood — no one has discovered algorithms or methods that can sift through management data and extract significant items from the plethora of detail.

We can summarize:

> *Although automation is a laudable goal, a question arises about how much of network management can be automated. One approach divides the problem into planning/deployment and day-to-day operations/maintenance.*

14.3 Dividing The Problem By Network Type

Another approach to the question of network automation uses broad classes of networks to divide the problem into subproblems. For example, the question of automation might become tractable if the scope were limited to a class such as:

- Edge network
- Core network
- Enterprise network
- Provider network

Edge Vs. Core. As we have seen, a core network and an edge network differ dramatically. A core network is focused on high-speed packet forwarding and inter-domain issues. Core networks are likely to use a traffic engineering approach and to base accounting on aggregate traffic measurements. Edge networks are likely to use conventional routing and to base accounting on individual flows rather than aggregates. Furthermore, the edge of a network is likely to filter traffic and handle tasks such as address assignment. Thus, partitioning networks into edge and core classes might reduce the complexity of automation by separating management tasks.

Enterprise Vs. Provider. Another possible approach to reducing complexity separates management tasks into those needed by an enterprise and those needed by a service provider. An enterprise must handle traffic destined to the Internet from the local site and traffic destined to the local site from the Internet. A provider handles traffic among customers and peers. Thus, limiting the scope to a particular type of network may reduce the complexity, and make automation feasible.

We can summarize:

> *Another approach to automation focuses on using the type of network to divide the problem into subproblems. Potential types include edge, core, enterprise, and provider networks.*

14.4 Shortcomings Of Existing Automation Tools

Although some automation exists, current tools and technologies have severe shortcomings. In general, extant network automation can be characterized as:

- Piecemeal solutions
- Focused on individual network elements
- Automating over a manual interface

Piecemeal Solutions. Existing automation tools tend to solve one small part of the network management problem without regard to other problems. As a result, automation is a patchwork. In some cases, tools overlap, with two or more tools interfering as they attempt to handle related problems or control a given element. In other cases, problems remain unsolved, and aspects of network management rely on manual intervention because a set of tools fails to handle all details or all elements.

Focused On Individual Network Elements. Instead of treating a network as a uniform fabric, current automation tools tend to interact with one network element at a time. Propagating a change through the entire network requires the management system to reconfigure one element and then another. During reconfiguration, the network remains in an inconsistent state, with only some elements modified. More important, because managers are required to specify the set of elements that a given tool should handle, manual configuration is needed whenever new elements are added to the network or old elements are removed — for each automation tool, a manager must update the set of elements that the tool handles.

Automating Over A Manual Interface. The management interface in many network elements is designed for human interaction. Thus, current automation systems are an afterthought — an automation tool is retrofitted to use an existing interface (e.g., an expect script parses messages intended for humans). As a result, tools are often clumsy. Furthermore, because tools process text syntactically without understanding the content or meaning, each tool must be changed when a vendor introduces new messages or modifies the wording or format.

The point is:

Current network automation technologies focus on individual network elements and provide automation over existing interfaces. Existing tools provide a patchwork of solutions in which some tools overlap and problems remain unsolved.

14.5 Incremental Automation Vs. A Blank Slate

One of the primary questions surrounding automation involves the overall approach: is it possible to automate management of existing networks or is a complete redesign of networks needed? Proponents for managing existing networks argue that the Internet is already so entrenched that a redesign is hopeless. They note that for ten years, vendors have tried and failed to convince customers to adopt IPv6. To avoid a similar embarrassment, they argue that new management technologies must face the reality of an existing network and make incremental improvements.

Proponents of starting with a blank slate argue that an incremental approach is fundamentally flawed — starting with current networking technologies limits the scope and functionality of a management system. They point out that many of the assumptions and principles that underlie the original Internet were derived over twenty-five years ago, well before packet networks were common and large. They assert that to accommodate dramatic growth during the intervening years, the original technologies have been patched and extended until the resulting systems are inherently complex. Thus, management cannot be automated easily. For example, they point to a situation where firewall rules must be managed in a network that allows outside connections to enter via a VPN and then sends incoming traffic across an MPLS tunnel through a NAT box that separates the edge of the network from the core; the example contains such a hodge podge of technologies that no management system can hope to provide sensible controls.

Even if it is not practical to redesign all network technologies and protocols, fundamental questions remain that underlie all discussions of network management:

- How do existing network protocols and architectures limit our ability to build automated systems?

- How much increased management functionality can be achieved in a new, redesigned Internet?

Another way to look at the issue focuses on individual aspects of the existing networking infrastructure. Perhaps the source of management complexity can be identified. Thus, it might be worthwhile to analyze the management consequences of individual choices. That is, instead of redesigning existing networks, consider whether manageability can be improved by eliminating, modifying, or replacing a given technology, protocol, or architectural component.

The point is:

A fundamental question focuses on the limitations that extant technologies impose: would substantially more automation be possible if some or all networking technologies were redesigned?

Of course, it may turn out that management complexity arises from combinations of technologies rather than from an individual technology. In the example cited above, for instance, complexity arises from a combination of firewall, VPN, MPLS, and NAT technologies. Thus, it may be important to consider the management limitations imposed by combinations of technologies.

Interestingly, although combinations of technologies present the potential for complexity, actual complexity arises from interaction. For example, consider the interaction between a firewall and a VPN. Suppose a site segregates its network into *internal* and *external* areas, with a firewall between the two. Furthermore, suppose the site uses VPN technology to provide employees with access to the internal area from home. Interactions between the firewall and VPN technologies only occur if packets carrying data to the VPN cross the firewall.

All technologies affected by an interaction must work together or a problem results. Management is especially difficult because a change in any technology can affect the interaction. For example, the author experienced a situation in which a change in a firewall policy caused a VPN to exhibit odd behavior: although it was still possible to establish a VPN connection, the firewall blocked all successive packets. To a user, the behavior appeared bizarre — the VPN software assured the user that a connection was in place, but no application worked.

One approach to increasing manageability reduces or eliminates interaction. Thus, if a site needs to use both VPN software and a firewall, the site can increase manageability by ensuring that the two do not interact. For example, to eliminate direct interaction, an incoming VPN connection can terminate outside the firewall and traffic can then be routed around the firewall to the internal area. Alternatively, incoming traffic can be divided so that VPN traffic travels through a special firewall and other traffic travels through a firewall that enforces the site's general policies.

The point is:

> *Because interactions among technologies contribute to the complexity of managing existing networks, restricting or eliminating interactions can increase the ability to automate management tasks.*

14.6 Interface Paradigm And Efficiency

A key part of the question about automation of existing networks centers on the interface that network elements provide to a manager. The management interface plays an especially important role in determining the overall functionality that can be included in an automated management system. Consequently, the question of an interface forms a fundamental focus in the discussion of network automation.

To understand the issue, consider an extreme: a network *appliance* that is intended for use by a consumer rather than a network manager†. Often, the management interface on an appliance is limited to a few configuration parameters, and does not permit a user to inspect or override values such as routing table entries.

As the example illustrates, the interface on a network element can severely restrict the set of tasks for which automation is feasible. More important, we will see that the interface can have a significant impact on the efficiency of an automation system. Thus, even if automation is possible, the management interface can make the resulting automation system impractical.

We can summarize:

> *When considering the automation of existing networking technologies, the interface a network element exports is crucial because the interface determines the set of management tasks that can be automated and the practicality of doing so.*

The importance of a management interface to the question of automation means that it is helpful to understand the precise relationship between interface capabilities and the functionality of a management system. The issue has both theoretical and practical aspects. For example, a theorist might be able to establish a mathematical relationship between a set of functions that an interface provides and the class of management tasks that can be carried out. A systems designer might be able to analyze the computational overhead that various interfaces induce on a given management task. Pertinent questions include:

- Is it possible to characterize the set of management tasks that a given interface can support?

- Is it possible to state the computational cost of performing management operations with a given interface?

The question about the impact of a network element interface on management functionality can be inverted. Instead of considering the consequences of an existing design, we can consider the benefits of modifying an interface:

- Can the management interface on a network element be redesigned to improve efficiency?

- If an element's interface can be redesigned, what capabilities should be included to guarantee that automated software can perform arbitrary management operations?

---

†A network appliance is sometimes called a *dumb device*.

14.7 The Goal Of An Automated Management System

Before answering the questions of whether automation is possible with existing networks or whether redesigning element interfaces can increase the functionality or efficiency of a management system, it is necessary to understand the problem to be solved. This section discusses the goals of network automation, and later sections provide an example list of desirable characteristics.

The search for an automated system begins with two broad questions, one that focuses on the scope of a management system and one that focuses on the human interface:

- In an ideal world, what functionality should an automated network management system provide?

- How should such a system interact with managers?

The question of functionality may seem trivial. When asked to imagine an ideal automation system, many managers envision a mechanism that handles all aspects of FCAPS. They dream of a system that automatically configures network elements and services, detects and corrects faults, provides the form of accounting a manager chooses, automatically optimizes performance, and guarantees that the entire network and all services are secure.

The second question ties an ideal system to reality. Although managers desire a system that handles all problems automatically, the system cannot act without input; many management choices are made to accommodate the needs of an organization and business goals rather than to accommodate the underlying technology. In addition, physical and financial limitations can exist that constrain the possible choices. Thus, even if a system can be designed to handle management automatically, a manager must be able to specify nontechnical limitations. To summarize:

Although it is possible to imagine an automated system that handles all aspects of FCAPS without intervention, a realistic system must allow a manager to specify goals and constraints.

A second aspect of the interaction between a manager and an automated network system concerns how a manager handles situations in which the automated system is either unable to cope with conditions or makes choices that are unsatisfactory. The underlying concept is *manual override*, and several questions arise:

- To what extent should an automated system allow a manager to override decisions or choices?

- What interface should an automated system provide to permit a manager to override decisions manually?

- If a manager manually overrides choices that have been made, how does the automated system assess and accommodate the changes?

The second question focuses on the issue of how a manager specifies a manual override. Two broad approaches exist. In an *integrated approach*, a manager interacts with the automated system by specifying changes that are desired and the system makes the changes on the manager's behalf. In a *tiered approach*, a manager interacts with the underlying network elements or services to make changes directly.

Integrated Approach. An integrated approach requires that manual override be included as part of the functionality of an automated system. Combining override functionality into an automated system has the advantage of allowing the system to check the input and issue warnings if a manager enters incorrect values. However, the integrated approach has two drawbacks. First, if the system designers do not provide a way to override a particular value, a manager has no recourse. Second, if manual override is needed because part of the automated system has failed, the failure may prevent manual override from working correctly.

Tiered Approach. A tiered approach gives a manager direct control in situations where manual intervention is required, without relying on the automated system to act as an intermediary. However, a tiered approach has two drawbacks. First, allowing a manager to enter arbitrary values means that a manager can inadvertently specify values that conflict with other choices of the automated system. Second, additional mechanisms are needed to prevent the management system from reverting back to original values automatically (e.g., parameters that a manager changes can be protected so that no further updates are permitted until a manager approves).

We can summarize the question regarding an interface that allows a manager to exert manual control:

> *Should an automated management system include facilities for manual override, or should the interface between the automated system and network elements be designed to allow a manager to examine and modify the configuration directly?*

The third question, which centers on how an automated system copes with manual override, is interesting because it raises several possibilities. If the automated system is tightly integrated with the underlying facilities, it is possible to analyze each override request that a manager issues. The system can check the validity, compute the potential impact, and inform the manager about the consequences that the change will incur. The system can issue a report to the manager before a change is instantiated (to allow a manager an opportunity to review the change) or after a change is instantiated (to alert a manager about potential repercussions and situations that should be monitored).

Some engineers argue that because a tiered architecture provides a back door through which a manager can control individual elements, management cannot be completely automated. They assert that automation implies a tight coupling to underlying network elements. Others argue that even if management is automated, the ability to make changes directly is needed to accommodate situations in which automation fails. In any case, if a tiered architecture is used, the automated management system must be able to learn about manual changes. Either, a network element propagates change information to the system or the system detects changes (e.g., interrogates underlying elements repeatedly to determine which parameters have been modified).

Once it detects a change, the management system must attach meaning to new values. In essence, a loosely-coupled architecture forces the management system to induce meaning from details: instead of starting with a manager's request and computing a set of changes that must be applied to elements, the system starts with a set of changes and attempts to derive a reason the modification was made. If the interface to a network element is not chosen well, the inverse computation can be difficult or impossible. We can summarize:

> *An automated system can react to manual overrides by informing a manager about potential consequences. A loosely-coupled tiered architecture can make reaction difficult because a management system must calculate meaning from the new values.*

14.8 Desiderata For An Automated Management System

Suppose we ignore the question of whether an automated network management system is feasible, and imagine the functionality that is desirable. What properties should an automated management system possess? An ideal system can be characterized as:

- Comprehensive
- Universal
- Scalable
- Versatile
- Adaptable
- Intelligent
- Standardized

Comprehensive. Unlike current tools and technologies, an ideal management system will handle all aspects of FCAPS. More important, the system will not appear to be a collection of multiple, independent subsystems. Instead, the system will be capable of configuring a network, detecting faults, and monitoring performance in a consistent, seamless manner.

Universal. An ideal automated management system will be capable of managing all types of networks. Thus, in addition to managing an enterprise network, a service provider network, a network at the core of the Internet, or a network at the edge, an ideal system will permit arbitrary network topologies.

Scalable. An ideal system will accommodate all sizes of networks, ranging from the smallest network to the largest. In particular, scalability means that an automated system must accommodate a network that spans multiple sites.

Versatile. An ideal system will not be restricted to managing a subset of network resources. Instead, an ideal system will handle arbitrary network technologies and arbitrary network elements, including high-level services as well as low-level devices in a uniform manner, without exposing boundaries.

Adaptable. Because networking continues to change, an ideal system will be designed to adapt to changing infrastructure and specifications. The system will be extensible to accommodate new hardware and software technologies as they appear. In addition, an ideal system will accommodate changes in business goals and financial constraints.

Intelligent. Although routing has been automated, technologies that handle other aspects of management usually are designed to help managers make decisions; they rely heavily on human intelligence. An ideal management system will automate decision making, and minimize the need for human intervention.

Standardized. Most networks contain a collection of hardware and software products developed by multiple vendors. To accommodate heterogeneity, an ideal management system will provide a vendor-independent standard that spans all vendors and allows their products to be integrated smoothly.

To summarize:

> *If we ignore the question of feasibility and imagine an ideal network management system, we envision a system that will be comprehensive, universal, scalable, versatile, adaptable, intelligent, and standardized across all vendors.*

The next sections expand our understanding of an ideal network management system by examining specific, desirable features.

14.9 Multiple Sites And Managers

One of the most challenging aspects of network management arises from large networks that span multiple sites. For example, consider the internal network of a multinational corporation that has campuses on three continents. Such a configuration poses several difficulties for network management. First, although each site has a manager whose primary duty corresponds to the local site, all managers must coordinate. Second, if sites span multiple time zones, working hours at one site may not correspond to working hours at another, making it difficult to reach a human if a problem occurs. Third, because communication among sites often uses the Internet, latency can be high.

An ideal management system will handle the problem of multiple sites in a uniform manner. More important, an ideal system will understand site boundaries and the interconnection mechanism. Thus, if the global Internet is the interconnection mechanism and each site has an address prefix assigned by a local ISP, the automated system will correctly identify sites of the organization's network and will use the appropriate mechanism (e.g., a VPN tunnel between each pair of sites) to transfer traffic.

The point is:

> *An ideal management system will handle multiple sites in a uniform, coordinated manner, will understand site boundaries, and will automatically provide an appropriate transfer mechanism among sites, such as an encrypted tunnel.*

14.10 Authority Domains And Role-Based Access Control

As the previous section states, each site of a network can have one or more managers. Each manager is assigned a *domain of authority* that specifies the functions the manager can perform. For example, the domain of authority for a given manager can specify whether the manager's authority is limited to a single site or extends across multiple sites in the organization. As an alternative, a domain of authority can specify the type of equipment rather than physical locations (e.g., DSL modems at any site in the organization).

In addition to specifying the subset of equipment over which a manager has control, a domain of authority specifies the set of functions that a manager can perform. For example, in a large network, management responsibility might be divided into management of routing, management of security, and management of faults, with one manager assigned to each.

To control a manager's authority, an ideal management system will adopt an approach that uses *Role-Based Access Control* (*RBAC*). In addition to making the assignment of authority straightforward and unambiguous, an ideal system will include facilities that allow a manager to pass privileges to another manager temporarily.

The point is:

> *An ideal RBAC environment will offer a high-level interface that is easy to understand and permits roles and privileges to be defined without specifying low-level details.*

14.11 Focus On Services

Perhaps the most significant features of an ideal network management system arise from the focus on services rather than hardware. That is, instead of providing an interface that requires a manager to configure individual network elements, an ideal system will allow a manager to specify the ultimate goal and will automatically configure network elements to achieve the goal.

To achieve a high-level interface, an ideal management system will focus on network-wide services rather than protocols and network elements. For example, an ideal system will allow a manager to request that an IP voice service be deployed across the network without requiring the manager to identify individual elements that are used to provide the service. Similarly, an ideal system will automatically handle all details needed for the service such as reserving bandwidth on individual links and configuring the gateways.

We can summarize:

> *The interface between a manager and an ideal management system will allow a manager to request that high-level services be deployed across an entire network; the management system will handle the necessary details.*

14.12 Policies, Constraints, And Business Rules

How can a management system decide whether to honor a request for a new network-wide service? What happens if the deployment of a new service conflicts with existing services (e.g., insufficient resources exist to accommodate a new service and existing services)? The answer lies in the use of policies: before a management system can deploy services, a manager must define policies and store them in a form that the management system can access. Figure 14.1 illustrates the conceptual organization of a network management system that uses a policy subsystem.

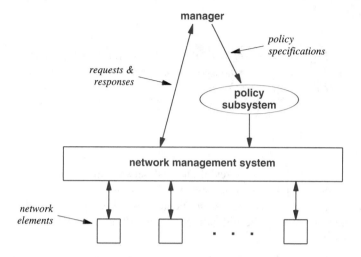

Figure 14.1 Illustration of the interactions between a manager, a policy sub-system, and an underlying management system.

An ideal policy subsystem will offer managers the opportunity to state local as well as global policies; the management system will use both to guide decisions. A global policy applies across an entire network, and a local policy applies to a subset of the network. For example, a manager might choose to establish a local policy for an entire site. Alternatively, a manager might choose to use local policies for each group of links within a site.

To allow an automated management system to check deployments against policies, the policies must be expressed in a language that is precise and unambiguous. A precise specification of policies has an interesting advantage: the policies can be analyzed and a manager informed about policy conflicts. In particular, before attempting to deploy services, the policy subsystem can analyze the set of policy statements and report internal inconsistencies to a manager.

An ideal policy subsystem will be *dynamic* in the sense that the system will allow a manager to change a policy at any time. Of course, each policy change must be validated to ensure that the change does not conflict with other policies. Furthermore, each change must be validated against the existing network deployment to ensure that the network adheres to the new policies.

The phrase *policy-constrained management* is used to characterize a scheme in which a management system validates each request from a manager against a set of policies before honoring the request. The result of policy-constrained management is a guarantee that the network adheres to the policies. To summarize:

An ideal management system will include a dynamic policy subsystem that allows a manager to specify or change policies; to guarantee that the network operates according to policy, the system will use the policies to validate subsequent requests and decisions.

A policy subsystem forms an explicit link between business practices and a network within the business. We use the term *business rules* to denote the formal statement of business practices, goals, and constraints; we say that a policy subsystem encodes business rules as they apply to a network. When creating policies for a network, a manager translates business rules into precise statements. In an ideal system, the policy language will make the translation of business rules to networking policies straightforward. To summarize:

The chief purpose of an ideal policy subsystem will be to ensure that a network adheres to the business rules of the organization that owns and operates the network.

14.13 Correlation Of Multiple Events

An ideal network management system will be capable of observing a network, interpreting the observations, and generating reports that are easy for a manager to understand. Intelligent interpretation of events involves correlating events across an entire network. For example, consider a series of events that arrive from client software indicating that a server does not respond. If similar events arrive from multiple host computers, the server is either down or unreachable. An intelligent system will determine the exact cause of the problem by correlating incoming events with reports of reachability and element status.

The point is:

When interpreting event data, an ideal management system will correlate events across a network to arrive at an intelligent interpretation.

14.14 Mapping From Logical To Physical Locations

The interface on an ideal management system will present information in a form that is easy for a human to understand. One particular aspect of interaction is important: the ability to relate logical items to physical locations. For example, if a hardware device fails, an ideal management system will be able to specify the exact physical location of the device, including details such as the building, room, and rack in which the device is located.

Relating each logical entity to a physical location requires a network management system to understand the physical inventory and physical relationships. For example, a management system must understand that the hardware interfaces on a switch are physical entities accessible to a network manager. Similarly, a management system must know that a switch is located in a rack, and a rack is located in a room. An ideal management system will understand both logical and physical *inventory*, and will allow a manager to determine the physical location of a device, provided one exists.

The point is:

> *An ideal management system will understand physical relationships, and will help a manager by relating each logical entity to a physical location.*

14.15 Autonomy, Manual Override, And Policy Changes

How should an ideal network management system deal with manual override? An ideal system will automatically handle problems and optimize performance according to the policies a manager establishes. If a situation arises that cannot be handled within the policy constraints, an ideal system will permit a manager to change the policies. In particular, an ideal system will inform a manager that the solution lies outside current policies, and will allow the manager to override the policies.

As an example, consider route configuration during an emergency, such as a natural disaster that causes massive power outages. Under normal conditions, a particular link may be reserved for traffic from a specified set of sources (e.g., from one customer). In an emergency situation, however, it may be important to route arbitrary traffic across the link. Rather than allow a manager to override routes explicitly, an ideal system will propose a solution and will allow a manager to decide whether to override existing policy temporarily.

Keeping the management system involved in temporary changes has two benefits: accountability and consistency. Accountability is achieved because a manager making a temporary policy change can be authenticated, and the change can be recorded. Thus, it is possible to determine who authorized each change. Consistency is achieved because the management system retains control of individual network elements. Thus, the system will protect the network by coordinating changes to ensure that the global state is consistent and correct. We can summarize:

> *Instead of allowing a manager to make manual changes in individual network elements, an ideal management system will inform a manager about options that violate policy and will permit the manager to change policy permanently or override policy temporarily.*

14.16 Summary

Many questions arise regarding network automation. If network management cannot be completely automated, how should the problem be decomposed into simpler subproblems? Possible approaches include separation into deployment and operation or division by network type. Current management tools provide piecemeal solutions that focus on individual elements rather than high-level services. Can diverse tools be integrated into a single management system? Is it possible to automate current networks, or is a redesign needed? Does the current management interface that network elements provide impose limits on management automation?

Two broad questions arise when considering an automated management system: what functionality should the system provide, and how should such a system interface with a manager? An integrated design provides a single, high-level interface for managers; a tiered design also provides a manager with low-level access that allows the manager to configure individual elements.

If we envision an ideal network management system, the system can be characterized as comprehensive, universal, scalable, versatile, adaptable, intelligent, and standardized across multiple vendors. Such a system will handle all aspects of network management and all possible devices across all types and sizes of networks. In particular, an ideal system will be able to span multiple sites and will provide role-based access control to allow multiple managers to coordinate effectively without interference. Such a system will correlate multiple events, and will be able to report the physical location of equipment. It will focus on network-wide services rather than individual elements, and will use a policy subsystem to provide policy-constrained management. Finally, an ideal system will operate autonomously: instead of allowing a manager to override network element configurations manually, the system will inform a manager about items that violate policy, and allow a manager to change or override the current policy.

Chapter Contents

15.1   Introduction, 257
15.2   Paradigms For Management System Design, 258
15.3   Characteristics Of A Top-Down Approach, 258
15.4   Characteristics Of A Bottom-Up Approach, 259
15.5   Selecting Any Or All In A Bottom-Up Design, 260
15.6   Weaknesses of The Two Design Paradigms, 260
15.7   A Hybrid Design Methodology, 261
15.8   The Critical Need For Fundamental Abstractions, 262
15.9   An Analogy To Operating Systems, 263
15.10 Separation Of Management From Elements, 264
15.11 Mapping From Abstractions To Network Elements, 264
15.12 Northbound And Southbound Interfaces, 265
15.13 A Set Of Architectural Approaches, 266
15.14 Useful Implementation Techniques, 273
15.15 Late Binding Of A Programmatic Interface, 275
15.16 Validation Of External Expectations, 276
15.17 An Architecture Of Orthogonal Tools, 278
15.18 Summary, 279

15

Architectures For Network Management Software

15.1 Introduction

Chapters in this part of the text consider the future of network management, with emphasis on systems that will handle management tasks autonomously, minimizing the need for human intervention. The previous chapter begins the discussion by posing fundamental questions about whether automation is feasible and whether the problem must be divided into smaller subproblems; it characterizes an ideal management system, and reviews features such a system will possess.

This chapter continues the discussion of future systems by considering possible approaches, architectures, and techniques that can be used. The chapter examines the bottom-up and top-down design paradigms, and explains the advantages of each. It discusses the structure of a management software system, considers ways a system can be structured, and examines techniques that can be used to build and optimize an automated management system.

Later chapters expand the discussion by focusing on systems in which data definitions fill a central role. The chapters discuss the internal representation of a network, the semantics attached to an internal definition, and design tradeoffs. The text concludes with a discussion of open problems.

15.2 Paradigms For Management System Design

The creation of a new management system can proceed in one of two basic ways:

- Top-down
- Bottom-up

The Top-Down Paradigm. A design is classified as *top-down* if a designer starts with a list of fundamental requirements, devises abstractions that are sufficient to solve the problem, and then creates a management system that implements the abstractions. A top-down design does not need to be comprehensive — the general problem can be partitioned into subproblems, and the paradigm can be applied to one subproblem at a time. Because it starts with a blank slate, a top-down approach tends to be favored by designers who have a more theoretical background.

The Bottom-Up Paradigm. A design is classified as *bottom-up* if a designer starts with network elements, interfaces, and technologies, and creates new management facilities to configure, monitor, and control existing systems. Bottom-up design is not limited to hardware devices — a designer can include high-level services and other software mechanisms in the set of facilities to be managed. Like a top-down design, a bottom-up design can focus on some aspects of network management, while omitting others (e.g., include only configuration and fault management). Because it starts with existing systems, the bottom-up paradigm tends to be favored by designers who have an engineering background.

To summarize:

> *The design of a new management system can proceed* bottom-up *by starting with functionality in existing systems, or* top-down *by starting with fundamental requirements and creating new abstractions.*

15.3 Characteristics Of A Top-Down Approach

A top-down paradigm has the following characteristics:

- Begins with a set of basic requirements
- Accommodates arbitrary management functionality
- Transcends limitations of existing systems
- Extends the scope of management with new abstractions
- Recommends new functionality needed in element interfaces

In the simplest case, a top-down design merely documents and names functions that are needed for management tasks. For example, suppose the operational requirements state that it should be possible to monitor the performance of each link in a network. A designer can create a set of abstract link monitoring functions and describe the output from each function, without specifying how the functions collect or generate the required output. Similarly, if the requirements specify that managers must be able to control elements, a designer can specify an abstract set of control functions and configurable parameters, without giving details of their implementation and without attempting to relate the abstraction to parameters in existing network systems.

The chief advantage of the top-down paradigm lies in its freedom: a designer can imagine a fresh, new management scheme that is unfettered by current reality. A designer can envision new management facilities and services, even if they are not supported by current network elements. Once a set of abstractions has been derived and refined, a designer can proceed to look for efficient ways to map the abstractions onto hardware and software.

15.4 Characteristics Of A Bottom-Up Approach

A bottom-up paradigm, which follows a conventional engineering approach, has the following characteristics:

- Generalizes from existing systems
- Retains existing elements and services
- Accommodates heterogeneity and multiple vendors
- Exploits current management interfaces
- Permits incremental extension of functionality

In the simplest case, a bottom-up design merely accommodates minor differences among manufacturers or models of equipment. For example, consider firewall systems designed by two separate vendors. Each system has an interface that allows a manager to specify firewall rules. Even if the two system have approximately the same basic capabilities, the interfaces on the two systems may differ dramatically. A bottom-up design examines the two interfaces, and devises a new system that incorporates features from both.

In more complex cases, a bottom-up approach can be used to derive a generalization that handles more than the specific instances at hand. For example, suppose a designer observes that existing systems include a parameter, P, and that five possible values can be assigned to P. To generalize the parameter, the designer can increase the set of values, either by giving additional values and meanings explicitly or by stating that up to sixteen values can be assigned, but only giving meanings for the first five.

15.5 Selecting Any Or All In A Bottom-Up Design

One of the primary choices that must be made in a bottom-up design concerns the functionality to be extracted from existing systems. The two choices can be characterized as including functionality found in *any* of the underlying systems or including functionality common to *all* of the underlying systems. That is, a designer can form a set of management capabilities by extracting a union or an intersection of functions offered by existing systems.

Neither approach solves all problems. On one hand, choosing to include functions from any of the underlying systems appears to make the resulting management system more powerful. However, it means that the management system can contain functions that cannot be applied to all systems. On the other hand, including only the functions that are common across all underlying systems restricts the management system to the lowest common denominator. However, it means that a function in the management system can be applied to an arbitrary underlying system.

To summarize:

> *When using a bottom-up paradigm, a designer can choose to include management for the functionality found in each of the underlying systems or can restrict management to the functionality that is common to all existing systems.*

15.6 Weaknesses of The Two Design Paradigms

Each design paradigm has weaknesses. Critics point out that a bottom-up design tends to be *incremental* without adding significant value beyond the existing management interfaces. That is, because the bottom-up approach leaves network elements and services unchanged, the resulting management system tends to become a thin veneer that provides a user interface without introducing new functionality. More important, vendors tend to choose interfaces that customers find familiar. Thus, once an interface becomes widely accepted, other vendors will follow the same pattern, even if a better interface exists. Consequently, critics point out that:

> *Instead of creating new approaches, a bottom-up paradigm tends to reinforce market popularity.*

The top-down paradigm also has weaknesses. Critics point out that a top-down approach tends toward the *theoretical* and *impractical*. That is, because top-down designs are derived from users' desires rather than from existing systems, new functionalities can be created at an arbitrarily high level of abstraction, without regard to the overhead that will be required to implement them. For example, it is possible to envision a management system in which the system has instant access to data from all elements in a network. In practice, however, gathering such data can be impractical, if the network has insufficient bandwidth, or impossible, if latency between sites is sufficiently high. The point is:

> *Because the top-down paradigm is not constrained by the reality of existing systems or interfaces, abstractions generated in a top-down manner can be impractical and the resulting implementation can be inefficient.*

15.7 A Hybrid Design Methodology

How can a designer overcome the weaknesses of the top-down and bottom-up paradigms, while capitalizing on their strengths? The solution lies in a hybrid paradigm: when designing a management system, strive to create new abstractions that satisfy the high-level requirements, but keep the design anchored in reality. That is, use the question of practicality as the litmus test for new abstractions.

To begin, survey the management mechanisms and interfaces that existing systems provide. In addition, consider practical constraints imposed by large networks that span multiple sites. Finally, gather a list of needs and desires from practitioners. Once the information is in hand, follow a top-down paradigm to propose new, high-level mechanisms that solve various aspects of the problem. Instead of merely imagining possible mechanisms, however, follow a bottom-up paradigm to map each mechanism onto real networks. Consider the overhead and the efficiency that will result when the proposed mechanisms are implemented. Iterate through the process: use the analysis of efficiency to refine the proposed mechanisms or create alternatives that are more efficient; discard a proposed abstraction unless an efficient implementation can be found.

Of course, the hybrid approach outlined does not guarantee a solution. In fact, a paradox can arise. On one hand, if all proposed mechanisms are inefficient, a designer is left with a set of useless abstractions that must be discarded. On the other hand, if all proposed mechanisms can be implemented directly and efficiently on existing network elements, the mechanisms are incremental and insignificant because the proposed design does not differ dramatically from existing systems. Thus, a designer faces a difficult task of proposing mechanisms that simultaneously embody new ideas and allow a practical implementation on real networks. We can summarize:

> *Although it helps keep new proposals tied to reality, a hybrid approach can degenerate to undesirable extremes of useless abstraction or insignificant improvement. To avoid extremes, a designer must seek new abstractions that have practical implementations.*

15.8 The Critical Need For Fundamental Abstractions

Interestingly, the most significant problem facing network management is a lack of fundamental abstractions on which to base software systems. Although it conceptualizes network management, the FCAPS model describes and characterizes the problem space without providing abstractions that help a designer create management software. Unfortunately, no other model has been created to fill the role. Without a set of abstractions, a designer has no conceptual basis for creating management software. More important, until fundamental aspects of a system can be defined, we have no common vocabulary for comparing systems or discussing similarities and differences. Consequently, each system must be viewed as a set of features and capabilities. The point is:

The most critical problem facing network management is a lack of fundamental abstractions on which management software can be based; the absence of abstractions makes it impossible to understand conceptual differences and similarities among management systems.

Perhaps the problem of network management is so complex and unconstrained that no set of suitable abstractions exists. Perhaps abstractions could be devised, but research has been so focused on the bottom-up paradigm that researchers have not concentrated on defining abstractions. Whatever the cause, few proposals have been generated, and no consensus has arisen.

What is needed? To aid in the design and implementation of management systems, a set of abstractions should possess the following attributes:

- Limited
- Orthogonal
- Sufficient
- Intuitive
- Practical

Limited. To be useful in building a system, a set of abstractions should be small (e.g., four or five) primary abstractions. If the set is too large, the level of abstraction is not sufficiently high, and the set corresponds to a compendium of choices. That is, instead of fundamental abstractions that provide the basis for building new systems, a large set tends to arise from a bottom-up effort that catalogs existing functionality.

Orthogonal. Abstractions in the set should be independent, and abstractions should not overlap or interfere with one another. That is, each abstraction should form the basis for one aspect of the system, and no management activity should be covered by two or more abstractions.

Sufficient. The set of abstractions should be sufficient to cover all aspects of network management, and should form a sensible basis for management software. In particular, an ideal set of abstractions should be able to handle all aspects of FCAPS.

Intuitive. Abstractions are aids that help humans (designers who create management systems and managers who use such systems). Consequently, each abstraction should make an aspect of the problem or solution easier to understand — instead of forcing a person to contend with awkward or unfamiliar concepts, an abstraction should appeal to a human's intuition.

Practical. Although abstractions that simplify complexity can help us understand problems or solutions, the fundamental abstractions being discussed are intended for designers: the point is to envision abstractions that help designers create automated management systems. Consequently, abstractions must be practical in the sense that it is possible to devise an efficient implementation of the abstraction. There are several aspects of implementation, including the computation and storage required as well as the impact on a network (e.g., the traffic generated or the latency needed).

To summarize:

> *A set of abstractions should be limited, orthogonal, sufficient, intuitive, and practical.*

15.9 An Analogy To Operating Systems

An analogy will clarify the importance of fundamental abstractions. When computing was in its infancy, approaches were not standardized — each vendor designed a processor and I/O devices anew. Once hardware had been devised, control software was created to help programmers use the hardware. Usually, control software incorporated low-level functions that exactly matched features of the underlying hardware. For example, on a computer that included a secondary storage device such as a disk, control software might include commands to start or stop the disk, move the arm, and transfer data.

In the 1960s, control software matured. Gradually, vendors started to include higher-level abstractions and more sophisticated functionality. Eventually, researchers (especially researchers working on Project MAC) identified powerful abstractions such as *process*, *address space*, *user account/login*, *file*, and *device-independent I/O*. Because they capture the fundamental aspects of operating systems, the abstractions provide a cornerstone of modern operating system design. An OS designer begins by creating a precise definition for each abstraction, and then chooses ways to bind them together (e.g., to associate an address space with a process).

The abstractions that have been created for operating systems illustrate what is needed for network management. A limited set of operating system abstractions have emerged that are orthogonal, sufficient for a wide range of systems, intuitive for both users and designers, and practical in the sense that efficient implementations are possible.

> *A set of abstractions is needed for building network management that are as powerful and fundamental as the abstractions used to build operating systems.*

15.10 Separation Of Management From Elements

One of the key questions surrounding the creation of a network management system concerns the overall structure: does the management system exist outside network elements, or is the management system integrated into the elements? In theory, the distinction is unimportant — instead of assuming an independent distributed system to handle management, one can imagine that each element contains an additional management processor and that the management processors on network elements communicate with one another. Thus, a management system that can be implemented by an independent, distributed system can be integrated with network elements.

In practice, however, the distinction between an independent and integrated management system is important for two reasons. First, a separate system provides the opportunity to build and deploy a management system without replacing all network elements. Second, if network elements are separate from the management system, it is easier to monitor and control the interaction between the two. The point is that although they may be irrelevant to theoretical work, early deployment and ease of monitoring are key ingredients in a practical research effort.

The presentation of architectures in this chapter and discussions in later chapters adopt the practical approach. That is, the discussion tacitly assumes that a management system is separate from the network elements being managed. To summarize:

> *Throughout the remainder of this chapter and the text, a management system is assumed to be implemented separate from the underlying network elements. In theory, such a distinction is unnecessary, but in practice the separation eases development and deployment.*

15.11 Mapping From Abstractions To Network Elements

Thinking of a management system as separate from the underlying elements helps clarify the purpose and scope of fundamental abstractions. In essence, the abstractions are intended only for the management system. Thus, a management system can be constructed that examines and manipulates an abstract version of the network without being limited by the details of underlying network elements. In particular, the separation allows a designer to devise management software that ignores device dependencies and uses a high-level representation of the network that matches the abstractions.

If a separate management system operates on a high-level, abstract representation of the network, how does the management system control underlying network elements? The answer lies in an interface inserted between each network element and the management system. Each *element interface*, translates between operations and data representations used by the underlying network element and the high-level representation that the management system uses. Typically the translation is performed by software. Figure 15.1 illustrates the concept.

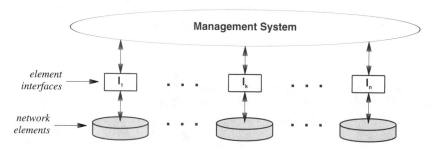

Figure 15.1 Illustration of the conceptual organization of a management system that is separate from the set of managed elements. An element interface translates between the abstract representation used by the management system and the representation used by a network element.

In addition to allowing a designer to create a new management system without changing network elements, separating the management system from network elements provides a way to accommodate heterogeneity. Elements can differ because a separate interface is associated with each element. Thus, device dependent details can be relegated to individual network elements without affecting the management system.

Note that the conceptual separation of a management system and underlying elements is independent of the paradigm used to design the management system (i.e., it does not matter whether a bottom-up or top-down paradigm is followed). In either case, an element interface isolates the management system from vendor and device details.

15.12 Northbound And Southbound Interfaces

Conceptually, an element interface is divided into two parts that are known as the *northbound* and *southbound* interfaces. The names refer to the direction that information travels: the southbound direction refers to information traveling from the management system to a network element, and the northbound direction refers to information traveling from a network element to the management system.

In general, we think of the southbound path as carrying commands, configuration information, and requests. Thus, a management system might use the southbound direction to reboot a network element, change the IP address of an interface, or request status information. Typically, the southbound path carries small amounts of information at a time.

We think of the northbound path as carrying responses to requests, status information and event data that has been generated asynchronously. For example, in addition to responses for explicit requests from the management system, a northbound path might be used to carry the equivalent of SNMP traps or NetFlow data. Thus, unlike a southbound path, the northbound path can carry high volumes of data in a continuous stream.

We can summarize:

> *The interface between a management system and network elements consists of two conceptual pieces: a southbound path carries information from the management system to the underlying element, and a northbound path carries information from the network element to the management system.*

15.13 A Set Of Architectural Approaches

How can software for a comprehensive network management system be structured? Several possibilities exist, including:

- Monolithic
- Extensible framework
- Software backplane
- Tiered hierarchy
- Database-centric

15.13.1 Monolithic Architecture

A monolithic architecture is the most straightforward — a single, large software system is constructed to control and monitor a set of network elements. The management system gathers information about the state of the network by making requests to network elements throughout the network. The system uses the information to choose actions. Once an action has been selected, the management system communicates with individual network elements to implement the action. Figure 15.2 illustrates the overall architecture.

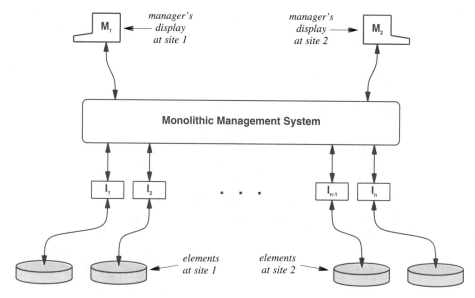

Figure 15.2 Illustration of a monolithic architecture. A single, large system interacts with managers and element interfaces.

A monolithic architecture has advantages and disadvantages. The chief advantages arise from centralization of the decision process. Data from the underlying network elements and management requests flow through a single, unified system, which means that the system can coordinate decisions and ensure consistency. In particular, because decisions arise from a single system, a monolithic architecture avoids a situation in which two or more components of a system reach conflicting decisions because the information available to each differs (e.g., components at various sites make decisions independently). More important, a monolithic system can easily coordinate among multiple managers to ensure that managers do not issue contradictory policies or commands.

Ironically, the centralization inherent in a monolithic architecture leads to its chief disadvantages: lack of resilence and flexibility. Because it has a single point of failure, a monolithic system is less resilient. In addition, a monolithic architecture is susceptible to link failures. In particular, the monolithic approach cannot easily handle a situation in which a network spans multiple sites and each site needs autonomy to continue operation even if inter-site communication fails. Finally, because all processing and human interface facilities are built-in, a monolithic system cannot be extended or changed easily.

15.13.2 Extensible Framework

An architecture known as an *extensible framework* enhances a monolithic approach by allowing a manager to customize the system. In particular, a framework includes *hooks* that allow a manager to replace modules such as a user interface or another functional unit. Figure 15.3 illustrates the architecture.

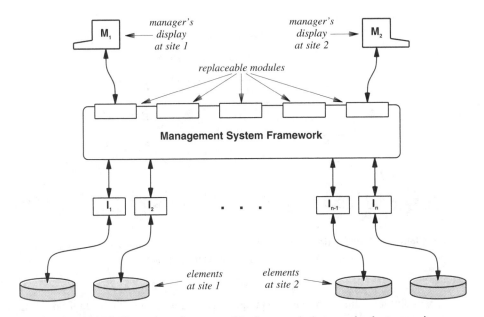

Figure 15.3 Illustration of an extensible framework that uses hooks to permit extensions. To customize the system, a manager replaces one or more of the modules.

As the figure indicates, much of the basic system can remain fixed. Thus, a manager gains the benefit of being able to customize the system, without risking a complete replacement.

15.13.3 Software Backplane

One of the more interesting architectural approaches that can be used to create a network management system is known as a *software backplane*. In essence, a management system that follows the backplane approach provides a communication mechanism analogous to the backplane in a hardware device. That is, the backplane provides communication without specific management functionality; a set of application modules that provide management functions connect to the backplane and use it for inter-module communication.

In fact, two types of modules connect to the backplane in a network management system: management applications and element interfaces. Management applications contain the logic needed to control the system, and element interfaces provide communication with network elements. An element interface can connect to a single element or, in the case of elements that do not require significant amounts of data, an interface can control a set of elements. Each element interface exports an API across the software backplane that allows management applications to send requests and receive replies. In addition, an interface can be configured to export a continuous stream of data.

Figure 15.4 illustrates the backplane architecture.

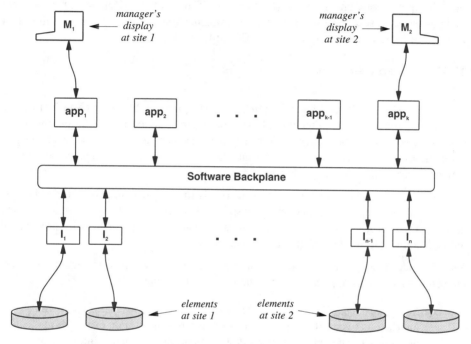

Figure 15.4 Illustration of a software backplane that provides communication among management applications and element interfaces. Conceptually, a backplane spans multiple sites.

A software backplane has two interesting features. First, although the figure shows a single entity, a backplane can span multiple network sites. That is, the backplane can be implemented as a distributed communication system with one or more nodes at each site. Second, although an application program provides the connection between a manager's workstation and the underlying systems, an application does not need to interact with a manager — applications can operate autonomously, obtaining and processing information without human interaction.

The central characteristic that distinguishes a backplane architecture from a mono-lithic system is the location of decision making. Instead of integrating all management decisions into a single system, a backplane architecture uses a set of applications that work together. The backplane only provides facilities that allow applications to com-municate with network elements and coordinate with other applications. In an extreme case, all management functionality is placed in the applications, and the backplane does not contain any management software.

The chief advantage of a software backplane architecture lies in the ease of exten-sibility. A backplane that uses late-binding allows a manager to add new applications and new element interfaces at any time. Thus, the architecture can accommodate exten-sions in applications and in network elements. The chief disadvantage of a software backplane arises from the use of a single communication paradigm — a paradigm that works well for transactions may not be efficient for bulk transfers.

15.13.4 Tiered Hierarchy

A *tiered hierarchy* architecture refines the backplane architecture described above. Recall that a backplane architecture allows a designer to divide functionality among ap-plications, some of which interact with a human manager and some of which operate autonomously. A tiered architecture formalizes distinctions among management appli-cations by organizing them into levels of a hierarchy.

In a tiered architecture, each tier corresponds to a logical function within the sys-tem. To implement the architecture, a designer chooses a set of logical functions and arranges them in a hierarchy. Applications are divided among the tiers by associating an application with the logical function it performs.

To understand a tiered approach, consider Figure 15.5 which illustrates a tiered ar-chitecture that divides applications into three basic functional types:

> *User Interface.* The interface tier contains applications that handle the interface between the system and a human manager. For example, ap-plications in the interface tier allow a manager to make requests, and format data for graphical presentation.

> *Aggregation.* The aggregation tier contains applications that gather, analyze, and correlate data from multiple devices. Typical applications found in the aggregation tier filter and select items of interest, and sum-marize the results. For example, an application might accept NetFlow data, select specific flows, and analyze the selected items.

> *Access.* The access tier contains applications that interact with underly-ing network elements to control the element or gather information. For example, an application in the access tier might configure network ele-ments to report events, and then arrange to forward the events to an ap-plication in the aggregation tier.

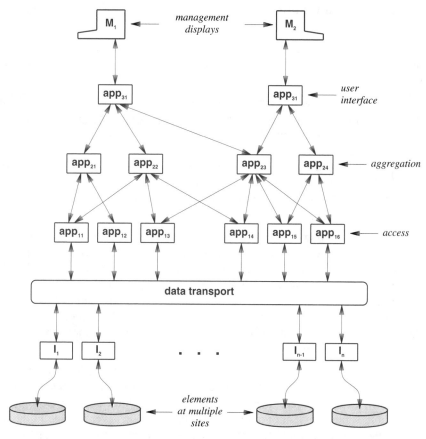

Figure 15.5 Illustration of a tiered hierarchy architecture with applications divided into three tiers. Each tier of the hierarchy corresponds to a logical function within the system.

The chief advantage of a tiered hierarchy arises because the architecture allows a design that eliminates duplication — a single point in the hierarchy can aggregate or summarize raw data and make the summary available for many uses. The chief disadvantage lies in the introduction of extra levels for all management applications: although aggregation of raw data can be helpful for performance analysis, an aggregation layer merely imposes overhead for straightforward transactions.

15.13.5 Database-Centric

A *database-centric* architecture is perhaps the most interesting and novel. It formalizes the concept of an internal network representation, focuses on uniformity of the data, and uses conventional database technology to store the information.

To understand how a database can be used for management, recall the paradigm that SNMP follows. Instead of providing a large set of management commands, SNMP defines a Management Information Base (MIB) that contains a set of abstract variables, and phrases all operations in terms of *GET* and *SET* requests on MIB variables. A database-centric architecture extends the concept of using MIB variables by allowing a designer to create abstract variables for each item in a network, including variables that correspond to hardware items, configuration parameters, protocols, high-level services, and network measurements.

Instead of adopting SNMP's approach of defining agents that run in each network element, a database-centric design arranges to store abstract variables in a general-purpose distributed database system. That is, a database schema is created with fields that correspond to the abstract variables. From an application's point of view, using a database is similar to using SNMP. When a management application needs information about the network, the application performs a *fetch* from the appropriate record in the database. Similarly, when it needs to make a change, a management application issues a *store* to the appropriate database record.

Having a database of values manipulated by management applications is insufficient unless values in the database are tied to network elements. Thus, the database is extended by adding element interfaces. As in other architectures, an element interface handles both southbound and northbound directions. Whenever a value in the database changes, the southbound interface propagates the change to an underlying network element; whenever an element detects a change in the network, the northbound interface stores the new value in the appropriate record in the database. Figure 15.6 illustrates the architecture†.

A database-centric architecture has two principal advantages and a disadvantage. First, because it relies on standardized technology (i.e., a relational database system) to solve the problem of long-term persistence for management data, the architecture avoids reinventing a persistent storage system. Second, because distributed database systems have been honed to handle synchronization and concurrency, a database-centric architecture effectively solves the problem of creating a distributed management system that spans multiple sites. The chief disadvantage of a database-centric architecture lies in the extra overhead introduced for items that do not need persistent storage (e.g., straightforward transactions).

The next chapters expand the discussion of a database-centric architecture by considering the questions of how information about a network is loaded into a database initially and how semantic constraints can be associated with data items.

---

†Although the figure shows all applications at the same level, a tiered hierarchy of applications can be used with a database-centric architecture.

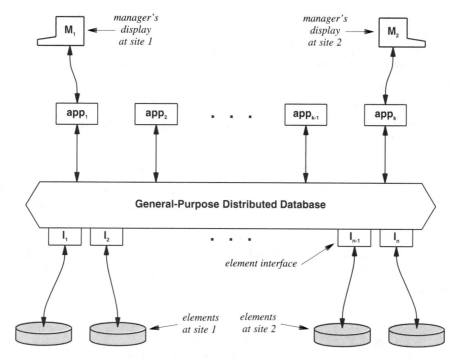

Figure 15.6 Illustration of a database-centric architecture. Element interfaces are coupled directly to the database to ensure that values in the database remain synchronized with the underlying network.

15.14 Useful Implementation Techniques

The architectural descriptions above focus on the overall structure of an automated management system without giving details. Several techniques can be used to enhance a system architecture and optimize performance or flexibility. For example, useful techniques include:

- Automatic replication
- Data caching
- Code migration

Automatic Replication. One question that arises when considering a software architecture concerns the amount of replication that should be used. For example, Chapter 11 discusses the use of remote flow collectors that aggregate flow data before forwarding statistics to a central management system. The fundamental questions in such instances focus on how many aggregation points to use and where to place them.

Automatic replication avoids the need to choose aggregation points a priori. In essence, automatic replication begins with a fixed set of aggregation points, possibly none, and monitors traffic. If the amount of management traffic exceeds a predefined level, the system increases the number of remote aggregation points automatically†. Thus, the replication structure grows as needed.

Data Caching. The general idea of data caching is straightforward: whenever data is transferred to a remote location, the remote location keeps a copy of the data and successive requests are handled from the copy. Of course, a cached copy cannot be used if the data has become *stale* (i.e., invalid), so a caching scheme must include a mechanism that allows the system to determine when cached data is valid.

Caching is particularly important for a multi-site network where a management system permits a manager to examine management data repeatedly. For example, consider a flow analysis application that allows a manager to reanalyze flow data after changing the aggregation criteria. If the analysis and display functions occur at one site and some of the flow data is collected from other sites, caching can improve performance significantly. Caching offers a similar improvement for other forms of management information that does not change often, including meta-information such as policy data, access lists, directories, and accounting information.

Code Migration. Although an architecture does not specify details such as the type of hardware systems on which management software runs, our discussion of architectures implies a traditional model of computation: a fixed set of computers are dedicated to running a management system, and each computer is preassigned a set of management tasks. Thus, the discussion assumes that a manager will be able to compute the resources needed to run the management software and the software can be statically assigned to each of the computers. Although automatic replication reduces the need to know the exact hardware resources required to run management software, replication does not add flexibility to the overall design.

To understand how an architecture can be created that has significantly more flexibility, consider a system that binds management software to hardware dynamically. That is, assume code is interpreted, making it possible to run the code on an arbitrary management processor. Rather than structure the management system to optimize data transfer, a management system can be built that migrates code to the point at which processing is needed. To use the flow analysis example again, consider the tasks of selecting and summarizing the flow data. Instead of sending all the data to a central point where the analysis is performed, a system can be constructed that transfers an analysis program to remote locations. When run, the program processes and summarizes the data, and only transfers the summary back to the central site for display.

The chief advantage of code migration arises in a system that dynamically assigns tasks to management hardware. For example, if the rate of management events increases at one site, copies of an event analysis program can be propagated at the site. Similarly, if the rate of a given management activity decreases, the system can choose to consolidate copies of code that handle the activity.

---

†If available hardware cannot support additional aggregation points, the management system can recommend adding more hardware.

The point is:

> *Techniques are available that can increase the flexibility and efficiency of a management system. Examples include automatic replication, data caching, and code migration.*

15.15 Late Binding Of A Programmatic Interface

Applications play a key role in all the architectures presented in the chapter. In fact, the key difference between current management systems and automated systems arises from the shift in focus away from humans — managers only specify policy; the software system implements the policy. Thus, because applications form the heart of an automated system, the interface that a system provides to applications is important.

Engineers use the term *programmatic interface* to describe the interface that an application program uses to access a management system. The point is:

> *Because automation shifts the focus from a human manager to application programs, automated systems emphasize a programmatic interface.*

As the example architectures demonstrate, a variety of programmatic interfaces can be used. For example, in a monolithic architecture, all application software is linked together when the system is created. In an extensible framework, some modules can be replaced after the system has been built. However, replacement is usually more difficult in a framework architecture than in a software backplane.

A key concept that determines the flexibility of an automated system arises from the binding between the system and pieces of application software. We use time to classify approaches, and refer to bindings as *early* or *late*. An architecture that uses early binding is *tightly coupled*: a designer links application software into the system when the system is created. In contrast, an architecture that uses late binding is *loosely coupled*: applications can be added after the system has been built. Thus, a monolithic system uses a form of early binding, and a system that follows the software backplane architecture uses a late binding.

Because it allows a designer to optimize the interaction among programs, early binding tends to increase efficiency. However, because it means that choices made during design cannot be changed, early binding is less flexible. For automated systems, which are new and not well understood, architectures that permit late binding are preferable (i.e., late binding provides maximum flexibility to make changes after a system has been constructed). To summarize:

In a loosely coupled architecture, the programmatic interface uses late binding which maximizes flexibility by permitting management applications to change after a system has been created.

15.16 Validation Of External Expectations

The architectures considered in this chapter are not exhaustive; others are possible. For example, one unusual architecture arises from a separation of control and validation. To understand the approach, consider the following four assertions:

- Network management is so complex that programmers will not be able to produce perfect management software.

- Because management systems contain many pieces that operate autonomously, interaction among the pieces can have unintended side-effects.

- Because policies can overlap, it can be difficult for a manager to predict the effects of policy combinations.

- Small decisions made in an implementation can have a large effect on the overall system behavior.

Because all four assertions are plausible, an automated system may not be able to prevent all problems — even if a management system is constructed carefully, complex networks may behave in unexpected ways.

If we accept the hypothesis that no management system will prevent all problems, which architecture should be chosen? How can we minimize unexpected outcomes? One possibility consists of arranging for an independent validation system to examine the underlying network. Figure 15.7 illustrates the overall architecture.

As the figure shows, the idea is straightforward: a validation system operates independent of the management system and examines the outcomes. Because it has access to the entire network, the validation system can examine the global behavior of the network. The point is:

The complexity inherent in network systems may mean that even if a management system operates correctly, the network may exhibit unexpected behavior. One approach to handling the problem uses an external system to check expected outcomes.

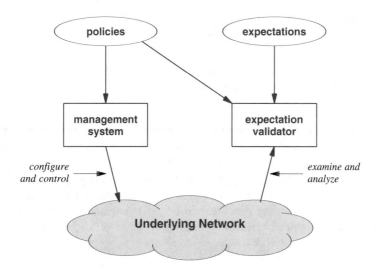

Figure 15.7 Illustration of an architecture that uses an independent validation
system to check outcomes. The network management system
can use any of the architectures described previously.

The figure does not show any direct interaction between the management system
and the validation system. The reason is important: to validate outcomes, validation
must not depend on information that has been obtained from the management system.
In particular, if information about the network that is internal to the management system
becomes inconsistent with the actual state of the underlying network, validation that
derives data from the management system will not be able to detect the problem. It
might seem prudent to allow a validator to check the internal management system data
(e.g., to verify that the information agrees with reality). However, the goal of an external validation system is to examine outcomes, not to assess whether the management
system is operating correctly.

As Figure 15.7 shows, a validation system has two forms of input. First, it uses
the set of policies that are used to control the management system. Second, it reads a
set of *expected outcomes* that should be checked. Expected outcomes can contain both
positive and negative statements. For example, a manager of an enterprise network
should be able to state a positive expectation equivalent to:

> *Routing is expected to provide a path to the external Internet from any
> point in the network.*

Similarly, a manager should be able to state a situation that is not expected to occur, such as:

> *The use of the network during the evening and nighttime is not expected to exceed the use during working hours.*

Rather than focus on individual links or network elements, an ideal set of expectations will specify global network conditions. Furthermore, to provide the most comprehensive validation, expectations should be orthogonal to functionality in the management system. Thus, if a manager has stated routing and firewall policies separately, an expectation might specify outcomes that involve both. Similarly, if a management system allows the specification of traffic engineered paths, an expectation might refer to the combined effect of traffic on all paths or to the effect of traffic engineered paths on other network traffic.

> *To check for interactions, a set of expectations should specify global network conditions and encompass multiple policies or subsystems.*

15.17 An Architecture Of Orthogonal Tools

The discussion of architectures above presumes that a single, distributed system will be constructed to cover all aspects of network management. A large, integrated system may indeed be possible and even optimal. However, many questions remain about the viability of a system that spans a wide scope of functionality and power. Even if a comprehensive system can be built, questions remain about the correctness, flexibility, and efficiency of the resulting code.

Does an alternative approach exist that does not lead to a single, large distributed system? The software backplane architecture suggests one possibility: a set of independent tools that each solve one part of the problem. The central question is whether a backplane is needed at all. Do management tools need to communicate? That is, can a management system consist of tools that operate independently, or do tools need to coordinate?

If coordination of tools is needed, exactly what functionality is required? There are two broad possibilities:

- Run-time coordination
- Coordination of data formats and interpretation

Run-time coordination. Even if tools perform independent tasks, coordination may be needed to prevent one tool from interfering with another. Run-time coordination refers to synchronization among tools to ensure that updates and changes are atomic across multiple elements and to prevent two tools from attempting to manage the same element at a given time.

Coordination of data formats and interoperation. Data coordination refers to agreement on data formats and the meaning of data. Even if the only exchange of data occurs through files on secondary storage (i.e., no backplane is needed), tools must agree on a standard representation for the data they consume and produce.

15.18 Summary

Two broad paradigms can be used when designing a network management system: a bottom-up approach that generalizes from existing network elements or a top-down approach that starts with requirements and derives a set of abstractions. A top-down paradigm offers the potential for powerful, new functionality, but can become impractical. A bottom-up paradigm guarantees that the resulting system will work with existing elements, but may be limited to making incremental improvements. As a compromise, a top-down approach can be used if abstractions are accepted only after an efficient implementation is found.

The FCAPS model provides abstractions that define the problem, but does not give abstractions that can be used to implement a management system; no model has been created to fill the need. Ideally, a set of abstractions should be limited, orthogonal, sufficient, intuitive, and practical.

Conceptually, a management system is separate from underlying network elements. An interface connects each element to the management system. Data traveling from the system to an element is said to be southbound, while data traveling from an element to the system is said to be northbound.

We reviewed several architectural approaches, including: a monolithic system, an extensible framework, a software backplane, a tiered hierarchy, and a database-centric architecture. Several techniques are available to increase the flexibility and efficiency of a management system; examples include automatic replication, data caching, and code migration. As an alternative, an architecture can be defined as a loosely-coupled set of orthogonal tools.

Because applications have a more significant influence on automated systems than human operators, the binding between an application and the system is crucial. A system that uses early binding fixes the set of applications when the system is designed; a late-binding mechanism offers more flexibility because late binding allows applications to be added or changed after the system has been built.

Networks are complex; the interaction among policies and autonomous pieces may lead to surprising outcomes, even if a system is operating correctly according to the policies. A macroscopic architecture that includes an external validation system can be used to check for unexpected outcomes.

Chapter Contents

16.1   Introduction, 283

16.2   Data For Management Software, 283

16.3   The Issue Of Data Representation, 284

16.4   Internal Representation And Programming Language, 286

16.5   The Effect Of Programming Paradigm On Representation, 286

16.6   Objects And Object-Based Representation, 287

16.7   Object Representation And Class Hierarchy, 288

16.8   Persistence, Relations, And Database Representation, 288

16.9   Representations At Various Points And Times, 289

16.10   Translation Among Representations, 290

16.11   Heterogeneity And Network Transmission, 291

16.12   Serialization And Extensibility, 292

16.13   The Need For Semantic Specification, 293

16.14   Semantic Validity And Global Inconsistency, 293

16.15   Information Models And Model-Driven Design, 294

16.16   Information And Data Models, 295

16.17   Class Hierarchies In An Object-Oriented Model, 296

16.18   Multiple Hierarchies, 298

16.19   Hierarchy Design And Efficiency, 299

16.20   Cross-Hierarchy Relationships And Associations, 300

16.21   Prescriptive Models And Generality, 301

16.22   Purpose Of Models And Semantic Inference, 303

16.23   Standardized Information Models, 303

16.24   Graphical Representation Of Models (UML), 304

16.25   The Issue Of Complexity, 306

16.26   Mapping Objects To Databases And Relations, 307

16.27   Representation And Storage Of Topology Information, 307

16.28   Ontology And Data Mining, 309

16.29   Summary, 309

16

Representation, Semantics, And Information Models

16.1 Introduction

Chapters in this part of the text discuss the future of network management by considering systems that can automatically configure, control, monitor, and operate networks. Chapter 14 presents overall goals and characteristics, and asks fundamental questions about how much automation can be expected. Chapter 15 examines possible architectures, including a database-centric architecture.

This chapter continues the discussion of future possibilities. The chapter focuses on the issue of an internal representation that an automated network management system can use. It discusses the question of timeliness, and asks whether an internal representation can be updated frequently enough to be useful for management tasks. In addition, the chapter examines information modeling technology and the proposed use of modeling as an aid in building future management systems. Successive chapters consider design tradeoffs and research questions.

16.2 Data For Management Software

When it performs a computation, computer software uses data values that are internal to the program (i.e., stored in memory). Thus, a software system that performs network management must obtain data values that correspond to conditions in the network. That is, management software follows a basic paradigm:

- Import information about a network from the underlying elements, and store the information in memory.

- Use the imported information to perform the necessary computation.

- Display results of the computation for a manager, or export the results to the underlying network elements.

The point is:

> *Because computer software can only manipulate data items that are stored in memory, a network management system must import information from underlying elements and must export results to both elements and managers' displays.*

16.3 The Issue Of Data Representation

The discussion of architectures in the previous chapter describes the bidirectional information flow between network elements and a management system: a northbound flow carries information from a given network element to the management system, and a southbound flow carries information from the management system to a network element. However, the discussion does not examine details. In particular, two fundamental questions arise:

- What information should be exchanged with other entities?
- How should the information be represented?

Information To Be Exchanged. The functionality of a management system is inherently linked to the information that the system exchanges with network elements. That is, the information available to a management system determines the scope and limitations of the system†.

In general, imported information defines the set of items a management system can monitor, and exported information defines the set of items a system can control. In terms of imported information, for example, a management system cannot assess network performance unless the system imports measurements of capacity and traffic from the underlying elements. Similarly, a management system cannot correlate faults across multiple network elements unless the system imports events from each system. In terms of exported information, control of routing requires that a management system must be able to export updates to forwarding tables.

---

†Information can also be exchanged with various support systems (e.g., a *RADIUS* server used for authentication.

In addition to limiting functionality, the choice of items to be exchanged can impact the flexibility of a management system. To see how, consider the time at which the choice is made. Although it can lead to higher efficiency, choosing a set of items early (e.g., before a system has been designed and implemented) places limits on potential functionality before experience has been acquired. Deferring the choice until after a system has been built increases flexibility, but leads to a less efficient implementation.

The points can be summarized:

> *The set of items that a management system can exchange with underlying network elements determines the functionality of the system; the time at which the set is chosen determines the flexibility of the system.*

We will revisit the question of flexibility in a later section; for now it is sufficient to keep the general principle in mind.

Representation Of Information. It may seem that the question of representation is an implementation detail that is irrelevant to the overall design of a system. As we will see, however, the choice of representation is pertinent to both the overall architecture and the efficiency of a given design.

An automated management system must import two broad types of information defined by their source:

- Information entered by human managers, such as a set of policies that a management system uses to govern decisions about overall behavior

- Information obtained from network elements that gives the current state of the network

Because the two types of information differ in origin, the representations usually differ. For example, policy information is stored in a form that is suitable for humans to enter and read. Information about current conditions in the network arises from underlying network elements. Therefore, such information is generated in an efficient, binary form. Neither form is appropriate for all management data – each form has advantages in some circumstances.

The point is that at some level a management system must contend with multiple data representations because management information originates in multiple forms. We can summarize:

> *Because some management information is entered by humans and other information originates from network elements, a management system must accommodate multiple representations.*

Later sections discuss an important consequence of multiple input representations: the need for translation among them. For now, we consider the question of internal representation, and assume that the system can convert an arbitrary input representation to an internal form as needed.

16.4 Internal Representation And Programming Language

One of the key issues surrounding the choice of an internal representation concerns applications that will use the data. In the ideal case, a consistent, uniform, internal representation can be found that is sufficient for all management functions. In particular, an ideal internal representation should:

- Offer a format that can accommodate all management data, including status information gathered from network elements

- Minimize the total space required to store management information

- Provide data in a form that is both convenient and efficient for management applications

In practice, of course, no representation can maximize all three goals. Thus, the selection of a data representation is a compromise — a designer must choose which goal(s) to optimize and which to concede.

The third goal, a representation that accommodates application programs, is especially difficult to optimize because convenience and efficiency depend on the programming language and programming paradigm. For example, programs written in C use *array* and *struct* as the fundamental data aggregates, and programs written in C++ or Java store data in objects. The point is:

> *Because a variety of programming languages and paradigms exist, no single internal representation is optimal for all situations; the choice is a compromise.*

16.5 The Effect Of Programming Paradigm On Representation

In addition to a programming language, a designer must choose a basic programming paradigm; the choice can influence the selection of data representation. For example, Figure 16.1 lists a set of programming paradigms and a technology that each uses.

Besides defining an access mechanism, many programming paradigms specify a corresponding data representation. For example, an SNMP MIB defines the type, size, and meaning for a set of MIB variables.

Paradigm	Example Technology
Operational API	OMG Internet Inter-Orb Protocol (IIOP)
Object API	Java Remote Method Invocation (RMI)
Remote Variables	SNMP Management Information Base (MIB)
Relational Database	Query Language (SQL)

Figure 16.1 Example programming paradigms and an example technology used with each.

The use of a *Service Oriented Architecture* (*SOA*) has been proposed to help overcome the connection between data representation and communication technology. In general, an SOA provides a set of definitions that can be used over an arbitrary transport (e.g., RMI or IIOP). The point remains:

> *The selection of a data representation and programming paradigm are not independent.*

That is, choosing a programming paradigm or technology can restrict the choice of data representation, and choosing a data representation can restrict the choice of programming paradigm. As the next section describes, data representations and programming paradigms are especially interwoven in technologies that are object-oriented.

16.6 Objects And Object-Based Representation

Object-oriented languages such as Java and C++ use a paradigm in which data and operations are collected into *objects*. An object includes a set of data items with a set of methods that can be invoked to operate on the data.

Although a management system can impose the view that the system maintains data and applications merely implement transformations, doing so decouples applications from the management system. That is:

> *To maintain a close coupling with object-oriented applications, a management system must offer an object-based representation of management data.*

When considering an object-oriented interface, several issues arise. In essence, because applications and a network management system share data, the details of objects affect both. If an object-oriented abstraction extends to underlying elements, a designer must consider:

- The set of data items that are present in each object
- The set of methods that an object provides
- The names used to reference objects, data, and methods

16.7 Object Representation And Class Hierarchy

One of the fundamental choices surrounding an object-oriented interface involves the organization of a *class hierarchy*. Unlike a procedural interface, an object-oriented design arranges object definitions in an abstract hierarchy. Successively lower levels of the hierarchy refine a class definition by giving additional detail. The result is known as a *subclass*. For example, a designer might choose to create a class:

NetElemConfig

that defines configuration parameters found in all network elements, and might choose to create two subclasses:

RouterConfig

and

SwitchConfig

that specify additional details for routers and switches (i.e., two specific types of network elements).

As we will see, the ability to create arbitrary class hierarchies introduces an extra degree of freedom in an object-based representation. In particular, a designer must choose a conceptual scope for each class, which depends on the underlying abstraction the designer envisions. Later sections discuss the idea in more detail†.

16.8 Persistence, Relations, And Database Representation

One of the principal issues that surrounds the choice of data representation centers on the concept of data persistence. Two questions arise:

- Does a management system need to keep management information in nonvolatile storage?
- If so, what representation should be used?

---

†A recent idea in object-oriented programming, known as *aspects*, attempts to overcome the derivation constraints imposed by a class hierarchy — an aspect defines behavior that can be bound to an arbitrary class.

Under the first question, it should be obvious that some information needs to persist, even if individual systems reboot or power fails. For example, descriptions of management polices should remain intact at all times. Interestingly, some of the data gathered from a network and some of the information generated by a network management system may also need to persist. For example, keeping a cache of recent events and flow data in persistent storage can help a manager diagnose problems after a failure occurs.

Under the second question, two broad options are available for persistent storage, and the representation depends on the option selected:

- Files created by applications and written to disk
- Records stored in a general-purpose database system

The chief advantage of using files is generality and flexibility: rather than forcing all data to be stored in a single form (e.g., relations in a relational database), each application can choose a suitable data format and representation. The chief advantages of a general-purpose database arise from the ease of distribution and uniformity of data. Because they are designed to operate in a distributed environment, modern relational database systems handle remote access and data consistency well. Thus, many experts insist on using relational database technology as the basis for persistent storage. As a final benefit, a general-purpose database enforces a relational view on data and requires a schema to be stated explicitly, which provides a single, unified representation for management data that does not depend on any application.

The point is:

> *Although a management system can use files to store persistent information, a general-purpose relational database is usually preferred; when using a database, data must be represented as records that adhere to the database schema.*

16.9 Representations At Various Points And Times

Although the above discussion talks about alternative ways to represent management data, a practical system will need multiple representations. In particular, the representation used at various points throughout a management system can vary. For example, when it displays information for a manager, the system must use a representation suitable for humans, but when interacting with a network element, the system must use the representation the element requires. Thus, an optimal representation can depend on where in the management system the information is used. The set of points in a system includes the following:

- Within the memory of a network element
- When transferred between an element and a management system
- In the memory of a management system
- In the memory of a specific management application
- On persistent store
- On a manager's display

Of course, as was discussed above, the representation can also depend on the type of information being stored. For example, the representation used to store information derived from network elements usually differs from the representation used to store policies. More important, the representation used to store bulk information (e.g., flow data) usually differs from the representation used to store individual data items (e.g., records of alerts that are unlikely to occur).

We can conclude:

Because no single data representation is optimal for all purposes and locations within a management system, we can expect a comprehensive management system to employ multiple representations and arrange to translate among them as necessary.

16.10 Translation Among Representations

To understand translation among data representations, consider the following examples:

- Independent values for scalar variables (SNMP)
- Relations (database)
- Objects (management application)

Although the representations differ dramatically, a translation should preserve semantic values. Furthermore, to make the system efficient, translation should not require extensive processing or memory. We can summarize desirable properties of a data translation as:

- Computationally efficient in terms of CPU and memory use
- Mathematically 1-to-1
- Easily and uniquely invertible
- Semantics preserving
- Limited to a linear increase in size

Most of the properties are obvious. For example, the second and third items guarantee that a translation is unambiguous and that the management system can translate in either direction. We will consider semantics later. The last item in the list refers to the relative sizes of items — to be usable, a translation must guarantee that the size of a data item does not increase dramatically. Although some representations require more space than others, the size of a translated value should be a linear multiple of the original size and the constant multiplier should be small.

16.11 Heterogeneity And Network Transmission

One data representation arises from the transmission of values across a network (e.g., transmission between a network element and a management system or between management system components at two network sites). Although transmission may seem trivial, two features make it difficult: encoding of data types and heterogeneity.

Encoding Of Data Types. Transport protocols such as TCP follow a byte-stream paradigm: although they allow a pair of applications to transfer a sequence of bytes across a network or internet, the protocols do not interpret the contents of the stream. Instead, communicating applications must agree on an encoding for data.

Encoding is especially important for items with variable size or cases where the exact type of item can vary. For example, consider the transmission of a character string: the sender and receiver must agree on the string length. A sender can prepend metadata that specifies the type and size of each item. In any case, an application must convert both data and metadata into a byte stream for transmission. We say that the data is *serialized*†. The point is that in addition to giving the details of how data is represented for transmission, a serialization scheme determines exactly which data items can be transferred. For example, applications can only transfer complex data aggregates such as arrays, structures, and objects if the serialization scheme makes a provision for such items.

To summarize:

> *The serialization used for data transfer determines the type of data values that a management system can transfer across a network.*

---

†Some authors use the term *linearized.*

Heterogeneity. Most large networks contain a variety of network elements and server systems from multiple hardware vendors. Consequently, data representations used by the underlying hardware can differ, meaning that software cannot merely copy the bits from a data item on one system to the bits of an equivalent data item on another. Surprisingly, even basic data items such as integers or characters can differ. For example, some hardware uses a *big-endian* representation of integers in which the lowest memory address stores the most significant bits, and other hardware uses a *little-endian* representation in which the lowest memory address stores the least significant bits. Furthermore, the capacity of data items can vary: some systems use 32-bit integers, while others use 64-bit integers. The important point to note is that a serialization scheme alone is not sufficient for correct data transfer.

We can summarize:

> *Because the size of basic data items such as integers depends on the underlying hardware and because a large network often contains hardware from multiple vendors, a network management system cannot assume that a native data value on one system can be transferred to a native data value on another.*

16.12 Serialization And Extensibility

As we have seen, transfer across a network involves two aspects: syntactic encoding (i.e., serialization) and preservation of semantics. Later sections of the chapter consider the question of semantics; this section focuses on syntax.

Even if we restrict attention to the syntactic aspects of serialization, several issues arise. For example, as was pointed out above, merely sending a sequence of bits is insufficient — an encoding must be devised that identifies the beginning and end of each item. In addition, an ideal serialization mechanism allows the transmission of arbitrary metadata. In particular, to eliminate ambiguity and permit verification by a receiver, each item can be given both a name and type.

The *eXtensible Markup Language* (*XML*) has become popular as a serialization technology. The chief feature that makes XML attractive arises from its ease of extensibility — a data item can be encoded in XML without changing the base language. XML makes it possible for a receiver to parse a serialized stream and extract all items unambiguously. Of course, a data value will not make sense to a receiver unless the receiver understands the semantics of the item.

The chief disadvantage of XML arises from the use of textual encoding†. Instead of sending data values in a compact binary format, XML encodes values as text. Thus, instead of using bits, XML encodes each integer as a string of digits. Encoding and decoding introduce processing overhead, and the use of a textual representation means the resulting values are larger than necessary (i.e., encoding introduces unnecessary

---

†The use of binary encoding has been discussed and proposals have been made, but no binary encoding standard currently exists.

transmission overhead). Consequently, a designer must choose between extensibility and lower overhead.

We can summarize:

> *Although technologies such as XML provide extensibility, other serialization technologies may offer lower computational and transmission overhead.*

16.13 The Need For Semantic Specification

Because a network management system must collect, analyze, and summarize data from many underlying network elements, a designer must guarantee that the interpretation of data values remains consistent across all pieces of the system. We use the phrase *data semantics* to describe the meaning of data items. In addition to the data type (e.g., an integer), semantics encompass the range of acceptable values (e.g., 0 through $2^{16}-1$) and the interpretation of an item (e.g., number of packets received since the system booted).

As we have seen, guaranteeing absolute semantic consistency can be difficult, especially in a large network that includes heterogeneous hardware. Thus, one of the challenges facing designers is a precise specification of data semantics that adequately captures salient properties and can be implemented efficiently on most hardware. In particular, to guarantee correctness, the specification of data semantics must transcend individual programming languages as well as individual hardware mechanisms.

16.14 Semantic Validity And Global Inconsistency

How should data semantics be specified? Two broad approaches have been proposed. The first relies on a human to create and follow semantic specifications, and the second uses automated tools. To follow a manual approach, a designer specifies the semantics of each individual data item, and then honors the specification when implementing software. Unfortunately, imprecise specifications or errors in implementation can result in situations where two or more parts of a system apply different interpretations to a given data value. However, the most important problem arises from the independence of specifications:

> *If the semantics are specified independently for each data item, the resulting combination of values can be invalid, even if each data value is valid.*

To understand why, consider an example. Suppose a given network element can have one or more physical network interfaces and that each interface has a MAC address. Further suppose that the semantics for the values are as follows: an unsigned 8-bit integer counter is used to store the number of physical interfaces (which means the range of values is 0 through 255), and a 48-bit integer value is used to store the MAC address of each interface. Now suppose the MAC address of interface 4 is assigned the hexadecimal value 0xff0310de1504. Also suppose the interface counter is assigned the value 3. Because each value falls within the acceptable range for the data item to which it has been assigned, each value adheres to the semantic rules. However, if a device only has three interfaces, it does not make sense to have a MAC address assigned to a fourth interface. Thus, although each data value follows the semantic rules, the combination of values is globally invalid.

16.15 Information Models And Model-Driven Design

How can a designer guarantee consistency of data items across a large, distributed system? As we implied earlier, the key lies in devising a precise specification of information that exists independent of any software, and then using the specification to derive and verify all parts of the management system. Ideally, the specification should:

- Apply to an entire system rather than one piece
- Specify all aspects of data items (e.g., name, type, and semantics)
- Include a specification of relationships among data values

Software engineers use the term *information model* to describe a specification that adheres to the criteria above and the term *model-driven design* to describe a process of constructing software that begins with an information model and uses the model to create software.

Some software engineers add an additional criterion that makes an information model amenable to automated analysis, verification, and manipulation. That is, they insist that in addition to being used by humans, an information model be available for use by program generators or other tools. For example, if a model is stored in a form that is amenable to automated analysis, it is possible to build a tool to check the model to verify that definitions are consistent. The point is:

> *If an information model is expressed in a precise form, tools can be created that check the model for internal consistency.*

Some members of the modeling community take an extremist view: they argue that information modeling will solve all software engineering problems by achieving the illusive goal of automating software generation. They assert that if an information model provides sufficient detail about all aspects of processing, it will be possible to build tools that take a model as input and generate correct, reliable, efficient software systems as output. Thus, they assert that in addition to defining details of data values, a model should contain details about the processing and human interaction that is desired.

Opponents argue that although a model can serve as a tool that helps programmers understand a problem and plan a solution, and may even help handle some of the tedious tasks in the initial phases of creating a program, no model will be sufficient for automatic software generation. They assert that once a model contains all details about processing, the model becomes indistinguishable from software. That is, before it can contain sufficient details to generate the code for a large, complex software system, the model itself will become so large and complex that model development will have all the problems associated with development of software.

At present, no evidence exists that models help automate software generation more than other tools, and it seems unlikely that such evidence will surface. Thus, we can conclude:

> *An information model is a tool that can help programmers understand a problem and plan a solution; claims that models can enable automated software generation have not been justified.*

16.16 Information And Data Models

As we will see, information models are *object-oriented*. Object-oriented modeling is especially pertinent for a software system implemented in an object-oriented programming language or a system that must export an object-oriented interface. A model can help a programmer gain a conceptual understanding of the overall structure and choose an object hierarchy before coding. However, the ultimate goal of an object-oriented model is more than a vague specification of structure — a model can be sufficiently detailed to allow creation of a system that uses definitions from the model.

A second form of modeling, known as *data modeling*, specifies the form of data in memory or on persistent store. Often, data models are *relational*, with the ultimate goal of a relational model being a schema for a relational database that describes data items to be stored and retrieved. Furthermore, a data model can specify semantic relationships among items (e.g., that the *zip code* in an address record be consistent with the combination of *city* and *state* values in the record). Of course, to be useful, a data model must do more than merely catalog data and specify semantic constraints — the model must specify a form that is efficient for processing. Thus, in addition to documenting data items, a data model includes a specification of expected operations or queries.

As we will see in a later section, information models and data models are not mutually exclusive. In particular, even if an object-oriented programming language is used to implement a software system, the system may use a relational database as a persistent store. Thus, a data model may also be needed. More important, the interaction of the two models can determine how well the system scales and how efficiently the system can access persistent values.

To summarize:

> *In addition to creating an object-oriented information model, a designer may need to create a relational data model that specifies how the data is mapped onto a persistent store; interactions between the two models can affect overall efficiency and ability to scale.*

16.17 Class Hierarchies In An Object-Oriented Model

How should an object-oriented information model for network management be structured? A fundamental decision revolves around the choice of the class hierarchy. In particular, one can imagine a single, global hierarchy that includes all aspects of network management information or multiple, conceptually separate hierarchies. For example, we might envision a class structure that follows the FCAPS definition as Figure 16.2 illustrates.

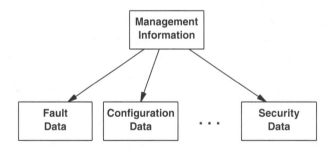

Figure 16.2 Illustration of the top layers of a class hierarchy that follows the FCAPS model. Each rectangle represents a class, and an arrow represents a subclass relationship.

Although it provides a convenient way to frame the problem of network management, FCAPS was not intended as a way to describe the structure of management software. Thus, using FCAPS as the basis for an information model may not result in an optimal organization of information within a working system.

Many alternative hierarchies exist, and several have been proposed for use in automated management systems. A model can be devised in which the hierarchy of information mirrors the structure of network hardware, or a model can be derived from the set of management tasks to be performed. For example, Figure 16.3 illustrates a hierarchy based on hardware.

In the figure, the upper-most level (i.e., the root of the hierarchy) is labeled *Network System* to indicate that the hierarchy models network devices. The subclasses each correspond to one type of device (e.g., *Switch*, *Router*, *Modem*). Further levels of the hierarchy can be used to distinguish among devices of a given type. For example, subclasses of *Router* might specify *Core Router*, *Access Router*, and *Wireless Router*.

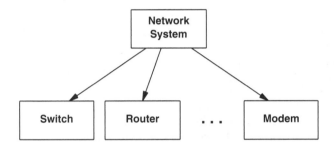

Figure 16.3 Illustration of the top layers of a class hierarchy that focuses on network hardware.

Alternatively, router subclasses might be used to divide routers according to the groups that use them: *Service Provider Router*, *Enterprise Router*, and *Consumer Router*. In any case, data items common to all types of routers are specified in the *Router* class; a data item that is specific to one type of router is specified in a subclass. Thus, a subclass is not needed unless at least one data item is unique to the subclass (otherwise, all data items belong to the superclass, and the subclass will be empty)†.

Other variations are possible. For example, instead of devising a model to describe network hardware, a broader hierarchy can be created that spans all computer hardware, with network systems forming a subclass. As an alternative, instead of restricting the hierarchy to network hardware devices, a hierarchy can be formed around *network elements* (i.e., include both hardware and software components, such as servers).

The point is:

> *Management information can be organized according to the problem being solved or according to the underlying facilities. Within each organization, variations exist. As a consequence, many information models are possible.*

---

†In some situations, a subclass is added as a place holder or to preserve symmetry. The term *moniker* is used to denote such a subclass.

16.18 Multiple Hierarchies

Although models illustrated by the examples above each consist of a single hierarchy, it is possible to define a model that uses multiple, independent class hierarchies. For example, consider a model that divides information into two distinct hierarchies, one that describes network elements and another that describes services to be configured and operated. Figure 16.4 illustrates the concept.

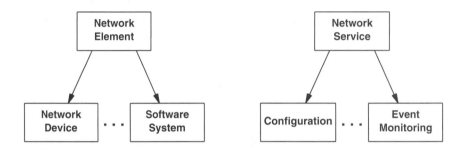

Figure 16.4 Illustration of the top levels of class hierarchies that correspond to network elements and services to be managed.

One of the advantages of multiple hierarchies arises from the ability to focus on aspects of information that are pertinent to a given problem without including irrelevant information. In particular, in a single-hierarchy model, the distance between two items can be arbitrarily large, even if none of the information between the items is used. Thus,

> *Multiple hierarchies can help avoid the pitfall of building an arbitrarily large model when only a few small pieces are needed.*

A later section discusses relationships across a hierarchy. The presence of multiple hierarchies does not necessarily eliminate such relationships. Interestingly, the combination of many hierarchies and cross-hierarchy relationships changes the fundamental character of the model: instead of being hierarchical, the model tends to become a *mesh* or *network*.

16.19 Hierarchy Design And Efficiency

Because an information model forms the conceptual basis that a designer uses to create a management system, the overall structure of the model often affects the resulting software. In particular, a poorly designed model can result in an inefficient system with unnecessary overhead. There are two main considerations:

- Depth of a hierarchy
- Interactions across a hierarchy

Depth Of A Hierarchy. In an object-oriented language, references are resolved by following a class hierarchy. Thus, when a method is referenced, the run-time system uses the most-specific instance of the method (i.e., the method in the class hierarchy that is closest to the point of invocation). The question arises: how deep should a hierarchy be?

Unfortunately, neither a deep nor a flat hierarchy is optimal for all circumstances. On one hand, a shallow hierarchy optimizes resolution by collecting information into a few objects. However, in a shallow hierarchy, each object is large, which means that the time required to retrieve an object is long. On the other hand, although small objects optimize retrieval time, small objects require a deep hierarchy, which increases resolution time.

The point is:

> *In addition to being designed to ease programming, an information model must be designed to yield run-time efficiency. One of the prime considerations involves the depth of a hierarchy.*

Interactions Across A Hierarchy. In addition to considering the depth of a hierarchy, a designer must consider interactions among objects that cross from one part of a hierarchy to another (or across separate hierarchies). Cross-hierarchy interactions are especially critical in the case where related information is found in distant portions of a class hierarchy. For example, suppose a designer places information about network hardware in one part of a hierarchy and configuration information in another. Before it can configure hardware, a management system will need to correlate objects. Similarly, if physical inventory information (e.g., the physical location of equipment) is placed in part of a hierarchy and logical descriptions of equipment (e.g., the servers operating on a given computer) are in another, giving the physical location of a fault requires correlating information across parts of a hierarchy. We can summarize:

If an information model separates related pieces of information into disjoint parts of a class hierarchy, interactions across the hierarchy can make the resulting system inefficient.

16.20 Cross-Hierarchy Relationships And Associations

The information modeling community has proposed a variety of mechanisms and notations that can be used to represent relationships and other information outside a strict inheritance hierarchy. For example, an information model can express:

- Multiplicity
- Identification
- Containment and composition
- Constraints

To understand the motivation, consider describing network hardware. Multiplicity allows a model to specify that an arbitrary router has zero or more network interfaces or that a given router has six interfaces. Identification mechanisms allow a model to have labels (e.g., to give an informal name to an entity or specify the organization that owns an item). Containment allows a model to express relationships such as *is a part of* or *is contained in*; composition inverts the relationship to *is composed of*. Thus, a model can specify that a router is contained in a specific equipment rack. Constraints further allow a model to clarify relationships: a given server can receive requests via TCP, UDP, or either.

Mechanisms that express relationships are known as *associations*. From a theoretical point of view, associations are aesthetically unappealing because associations break the strict class hierarchy. The question arises: how can information models avoid defining additional abstractions and unify all information under a class hierarchy? One solution, proposed by purists, involves imposing a hierarchy on associations — instead of viewing associations as bindings outside of a hierarchy, create a separate class hierarchy that holds the associations themselves†. The point is:

Because a strict class hierarchy is insufficient to document all possible relationships, additional bindings are needed. Modeling advocates assert that a hierarchical information model is sufficient for arbitrary information. Thus, rather than define associations outside the model, some modeling technologies cast everything into a single abstraction by placing associations in an independent class hierarchy.

---

†The inclusion of associations in a class hierarchy is reminiscent of work in recursive function theory where researchers became fascinated with mathematical structures that are each sufficient to represent all computable functions.

For example, the CIM standard that is discussed later in the chapter proposes a model in which network systems are described in one hierarchy, addressing is described in a second hierarchy, and associations in yet another†. Thus, the binding between an IP address and a specific router interface is described by an association, which is logically located in the association hierarchy. Figure 16.5 illustrates the concept.

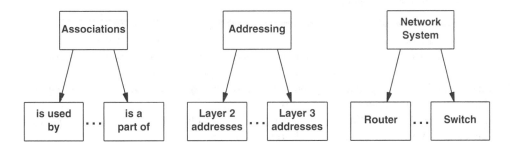

Figure 16.5 Example of an overall structure for an information model that places associations in a separate class hierarchy.

Although it provides conceptual unification, placing associations in a class hierarchy introduces a potential run-time inefficiency: whenever a binding is needed, the system must access the appropriate association object in one hierarchy to operate on objects in other hierarchies. Thus, the overall efficiency of a system that results from making associations part of a class hierarchy remains questionable:

Can an efficient management system be devised from a model in which associations are located in a class hierarchy?

16.21 Prescriptive Models And Generality

One of the primary questions about information modeling concerns the breadth and generality of a model. There are three broad approaches that can be characterized by the type of model produced:

- Solution-specific model
- Problem-specific model
- Domain-specific model

---

†Of course, it is possible to add a new root that links together all hierarchies; we depict them as separate to emphasize their conceptual independence.

Solution-Specific Model. A solution-specific model, which is small and constrained, serves as an aid in solving a specific problem. That is, a solution-specific model is devised to aid in the construction of a single software system. A designer who creates a solution-specific model knows the system requirements in detail and has a broad understanding of the overall software architecture that will be used. Thus, a solution-specific model focuses on data items that will be needed in one specific system, and can omit all others.

Problem-Specific Model. A problem-specific model is more general than a solution-specific model. Instead of focusing on a single software system, a problem-specific model documents information that is pertinent to a problem area, without restricting attention to a given solution. That is, a problem-specific model attempts to document information that may be used to solve a problem without assuming any knowledge of the approach that software designers will take. Thus, a designer who builds a problem-specific model understands the problem, but does not necessarily understand how software can be built to solve the problem.

Domain-Specific Model. A domain-specific model is the most general of all. Such a model attempts to codify information without knowing how the information will be used. That is, a designer proceeds to create a model without knowing the processing that will be required or the structure of the software system that will perform the processing.

Because it is restricted to a single system architecture, a solution-specific model is the least general. The disadvantage of a solution-specific model lies in its inflexibility — if a programmer decides to change the system architecture after a solution-specific model has been created, the model must be changed.

In theory, problem-specific and domain-specific models overcome the lack of flexibility by providing increasingly more generality. A problem-specific model attempts to provide a single model that can serve as the basis for multiple system architectures, and a domain-specific model appears to maximize generality across a large set of software systems. Thus, many model builders advocate creating a domain-specific model that can be used for arbitrary problems. They argue that a domain-specific model has the further advantage of unifying terminology (e.g., names of variables), which makes programming easier and code more reusable.

In practice, however, increased generality is difficult to achieve. Because an object-oriented model imposes a class hierarchy on information, the overall organization of the model determines how corresponding objects are organized in a software system that is derived from the model. To be totally general, a domain specific model must accommodate multiple run-time architectures. By definition, however, a model imposes a specific organization on information.

To put it another way: each model is *prescriptive* in the sense that the model dictates a specific information hierarchy. Because it is defined a priori and remains constant, we say that a domain-specific model is *static*. Interestingly, a static model that is devised before software is built exhibits a form of inflexibility because the model will either become so vague that it does not capture detail or so specific that it cannot adapt easily to new problems. In particular, defining a model a priori can lead to a static class hierarchy that produces inefficient software. The point can be summarized:

> *Although it seems appealing to devise a single information model that will be sufficient for arbitrary purposes, a static, predefined object hierarchy is inflexible and may not provide an optimal basis for any software system.*

16.22 Purpose Of Models And Semantic Inference

We have portrayed modeling as an aid for the creation of correct software systems. Defining a model means specifying semantic relationships among pieces of data. Thus, once a model has been defined and a software system has been constructed that follows the model, a programmer can be confident that the system obeys the semantic rules specified in the model. That is, by building and checking a model and then using the model to derive software, we can protect programmers from accidentally writing code that violates semantic constraints.

The software engineering community advocates the use of modeling as a tool to aid software construction, either to conceptualize a design or to help produce code; other groups take alternative views. In particular, the artificial intelligence community views models as a source of semantic information that can be analyzed. That is, a form of data mining can be employed: once a model has been devised, the model can be used to derive semantic inferences. The ultimate goal is to discover semantic relationships that are not obvious. Semantic inference in information models is related to work on a research effort known as the *Semantic Web*.

16.23 Standardized Information Models

A variety of information models have been proposed and used in the construction of network management tools. Solution-specific information models have been used to aid in the construction of specific software systems. In addition, groups such as the *Distributed Management Task Force* (*DMTF*) and the *TeleManagement Forum* (*TMF*) have each been working to create domain-specific models that will be sufficient for all management activities. The DMTF has created one domain-specific model, and the TMF has created two:

DMTF: Common Information Model (CIM)

TMF: Shared Information / Data model (SID)
              Multi-Technology Network Management model (MTNM)

Recently, the two organizations announced their intention to work together to harmonize various aspects of their models.

The question remains: will standardization help the models succeed? In principle, if the network management industry adopts a single standard, many of the difficulties in building software will be eased. For example, if a single model is used as the basis for building management systems, data items will be uniform across all management software, allowing systems from multiple vendors to interoperate. The interface between a management system and underlying network elements can also be standardized. In addition, serialization and persistent storage of objects can be standardized. As a consequence, standardization will make it possible to devise portable applications that can be used with multiple management platforms.

In practice, however, none of the standards has enjoyed wide use as the basis for management software, and the concept of a standard model raises an important concern: the implications of a static hierarchy. Each standard proposes to create a domain-specific model that can be used to create arbitrary management systems and applications. Thus, the standard models are extensive as well as static (i.e., the models attempt to capture full details about underlying network facilities as well as details about management services). Because the models are extensive, all aspects of information are captured, including associations. The open question is whether such a model can yield efficient management system software or whether an early decision about the structure will lead to inefficient software.

We can summarize:

> *Although they are standardized, the CIM, SID, and MTNM models each impose a static information hierarchy, meaning that they each exhibit the shortcomings of a domain-specific model. Consequently, it remains to be seen whether the models will yield efficient management systems.*

16.24 Graphical Representation Of Models (UML)

No discussion of modeling is complete without a consideration of the language used to express a model. Two possibilities have been explored: *textual modeling languages* and *graphical modeling languages*. The chief advantage of a textual language is ease of parsing. A textual modeling language specifies precise syntax rules that a designer must use, analogous to the syntax rules for a programming language. That is, a textual modeling language is defined by a formal grammar in the same way a programming language is defined — syntactic forms such as punctuation symbols are used to delineate items in the model. The resulting syntax is unambiguous. As a consequence, a model written in a textual language can be parsed by a compiler that checks the syntactic form, analyzes the specification, and translates the model into an efficient internal form.

The chief disadvantage of a textual representation arises from the difficulty humans have in reading and comprehending the resulting specification. Textual models, which tend to be large and filled with detail, use textual labels to denote relationships such as subclassing. The alternative, a graphical representation, can be much easier for a human to grasp. For example, figures in this chapter that illustrate hierarchies graphically are easy to understand.

Of course, the diagrams presented in this chapter only depict a few levels of hierarchy, and do not give the detail found in an information model. When used to specify an information model, each item in a diagram contains extensive specifications of individual items along with their type and meaning. In addition, most information models are large and complex — unlike the simplistic diagrams shown in the figures, the diagrams for an information model usually have extensive detail in each node, can contain nodes for hundreds of subclasses, and have extensive associations and other cross-hierarchy relationships. Thus, even though a graphical language can help a human understand the top levels of a small class hierarchy, an extensive model with many details is complex and can be difficult to understand. Presentation tools that elide details and provide navigation aids can help make a model easier to comprehend. However, we conclude:

> *Although a graphical modeling language can make a small model easy for humans to understand, tracing through a large model that spans screenfuls of diagrams can be as difficult as tracing through text.*

The concept of using a graphical language to represent a model has been explored extensively, and several graphical forms have been proposed. One graphical modeling language has received wide acceptance. It was created by the *Object Management Group*, and is known as the *Unified Modeling Language* (*UML*).

UML defines precise notation for items in the language, including ways to represent a class hierarchy and relationships among items in the hierarchy. For example, a solid rectangular box denotes a class, which has a name given at the top in boldface. A class rectangle can also be divided into subareas that contain a set of *attributes* and *methods* for the class. An open-headed arrow is used to depict generalization (i.e., subclassing)†.

UML is a surprisingly large language that represents more than class hierarchies and data semantics. For example, UML has notations to depict human actions, engineering requirements such as use cases, multiplicity (e.g., N-to-1), implementation, time-sequence diagrams, and other relationships. Thus, in addition to depicting static information and semantics, UML diagrams can be used to depict arbitrary interactions and relationships. Of course, in addition to diagrams, UML allows a model designer to specify textual information such as names for data and methods.

---

†UML provides alternative styles; subparts of a class can be shown in separate rectangles, with solid-headed arrows used to denote composition.

To summarize:

> *UML has emerged as a widely accepted modeling language that uses graphical diagrams. In addition to diagrams depicting a class hierarchy, UML includes ways to document arbitrary relationships, actions, interactions, and textual information.*

16.25 The Issue Of Complexity

One of the key issues in modeling and model-driven design focuses on the underlying complexity. One source of complexity arises from the complete generality of languages like UML. Because the language contains notation that can be used to document many aspects of information, a UML diagram can quickly become saturated with details, many of which are irrelevant to a given piece of software. Furthermore, because minor differences in diagrams can change the semantics in major ways, diagrams can be difficult to read. For example, because the form of an arrowhead (e.g., solid or open) can completely alter the meaning, an arrow between two entities must be examined carefully.

Taking a broader view, we can ask a question about the overall complexity: if the purpose of modeling is to serve as an aid in constructing software, how complex can a model become before the difficulty of constructing a general model is greater than the difficulty of building software with a solution-specific model or no model? In the case of domain-specific models, evidence suggests that the complexity of model construction is self-defeating — the task of creating a general model is so complex and time-consuming that construction can never succeed. For example, although the DMTF has worked on the CIM model for many years, the work is not finished and the model is not complete.

The point is:

> *Two aspects of complexity haunt information modeling. On one hand, a model can easily become so large and complex that humans have trouble comprehending it. On the other hand, a domain-specific model can be so difficult to build that the task will never be completed.*

16.26 Mapping Objects To Databases And Relations

An earlier section said that information modeling and data modeling can be used together. The combination arises from the need for persistent storage in a software system that follows a model-driven design paradigm. Although a programmer can write code that uses files to store objects on disk, doing so means choosing a data representation and building mechanisms for mutual exclusion and two-phase commit. The alternative to using files is a standard database system that supplies the needed mechanisms.

Before a database system can be used, however, a programmer must create a schema that specifies the items to be stored. Following a model-driven approach means a designer creates a data model and then uses the data model to derive a schema. In essence, model-driven design is applied at two levels of abstraction.

The combination of information modeling and data modeling raises several interesting questions. On one hand, we can ask whether it makes sense to architect a system in which a data model allows values in the database to be manipulated independent of the information model (e.g., direct storage into a database by network elements). On the other hand, the existence of both an object-oriented run-time system and a database poses a problem in a distributed environment because both run-time systems contain facilities for control of distributed processing. Should the object-oriented run-time system copy each object to the desired location before storing into the database, or should the run-time system hand objects to the database at arbitrary locations and allow the database to move copies? In the worst case, after the run-time system sends an object to a remote location, the database system might choose to store the data back at the original site.

The point is:

Although a system can be created that uses both an information model and a data model, the combination raises questions about how transactions are managed and which run-time system controls data placement. Inefficiency can result if the two systems disagree about data placement.

16.27 Representation And Storage Of Topology Information

A management system needs accurate and complete information about the network topology. As we have seen, the topology information pertinent to a management system includes both physical topology that specifies the location of each entity and logical topology that specifies connectivity and data paths. We have also seen that intelligent fault correlation requires a system to understand the relationship between logical and physical topologies.

In terms of modeling, the issue of topology raises several questions. How should topology be specified in an information model? How should topology information be entered into a management system? Recall that there are two broad approaches used for acquisition of topology:

- Manual configuration
- Automatic discovery

Automated discovery seems like an ideal approach. Information derived from the network itself will be accurate because discovery avoids the problems of human error when entering information or failures of humans to update the management system records after the topology changes. The latter is especially important because managers view operational correctness as a primary concern; updating records in the management system is an afterthought.

Despite appearances, however, automated discovery has potential drawbacks. Tools that discover topology usually rely on a combination of network protocols and application programs to deduce connectivity and adjacency. As a result, such tools can only search routable paths when exploring connections among elements, which means that the tools only identify a logical topology. For example, consider a situation in which a transport-layer tunnel connects two routers across a long distance. Because probes appear to travel directly from one router to another, a discovery tool will identify the two routers as adjacent. Similarly, because they rely on protocols, discovery tools cannot distinguish between physical and logical devices. For example, a discovery tool may not be able to tell whether a given router is virtual (i.e., whether the router is an isolated subset of a larger physical device) or identify the computer system on which a given server is executing. The point is:

> *Although the acquisition of network topology information appears to be straightforward, the issue is complicated because automated discovery tools that rely on higher-layer protocols can only deduce logical topology imposed by routable paths; the tools cannot easily distinguish between physical and virtual elements.*

Besides being limited to logical topology, some automated discovery tools prepare their output for direct deposit in a database. Thus, the topology description can be described by a data model that gives the appropriate schema, but the description does not fit easily into an arbitrary information model. We can conclude:

> *Discovery tools that are designed to deposit output in a database make it difficult to use automated discovery with an arbitrary model-driven design.*

16.28 Ontology And Data Mining

The discussion of semantics for network management is part of a larger, ongoing discussion about semantics in general. We know that it is possible to classify and structure information, but the central question for software designers is whether information can be organized in ways that make it easier to create correct and efficient programs. Intuitively, we can understand that no structure is optimal for all possible applications, so the choice of structure depends on the expected uses.

Interestingly, the artificial intelligence and data mining research communities have each examined the question of information structure from alternative points of view. Data mining research asks: given a database of information, what additional information can be gleaned by combining or correlating items in the database? The AI research community uses the term *ontology*, and focuses on the semantics of information. AI research asks: what semantic inferences can be drawn from a specification of information semantics? In each case, the research looks for relationships that are not apparent in the initial specification.

The point is:

> *In addition to considering specifications that aid programmers in creating correct and efficient software, related research considers how such specifications can be used to expose hidden relationships.*

16.29 Summary

Because software can only operate on data values, information about a network must be imported into the management system and results must be exported to the network. Imported information can come from human managers as well as directly from network elements.

The choice of a data representation is complicated because no representation is optimal for all situations. A management system must export information in a form that management applications can use, and may need to store information in a relational database. A typical management system employs multiple representations and translates among them, with serialization used for data transmission. XML offers extensible serialization.

Translation of data values must ensure that semantics are upheld. One technology for specifying semantics is information modeling. An object-oriented information model defines a class hierarchy; many hierarchies are possible. Important considerations for an information model include the depth of a hierarchy and the interactions across hierarchies. A model uses associations to express interactions, such as *is part of*, that cross hierarchies; associations can be stored in a separate hierarchy.

Information models can be solution-specific, problem-specific, or domain-specific. In practice, generality is difficult to achieve because a domain-specific model tends to prescribe a structure for software without knowledge of problems the software will be created to solve.

Two standardization efforts are working to develop domain-specific information models for all management activities: the DMTF organization has created the Common Information Model (CIM), and the TMF organization has created the Shared Information / Data model (SID) and the Multi-Technology Network Management model (MTNM). Each model imposes a static hierarchy; it is unclear how well the standardized models can work in practical systems. The Unified Modeling Language (UML) has become the de facto standard for specifying information models. UML uses graphical notation, but also requires textual information to be specified for some items. Because they are complex, information models are difficult to create and understand; whether models will reduce the overall effort required to create management systems software remains to be seen.

Acquisition and storage of topology information presents a special challenge. Although topology information entered manually is subject to human error, discovery mechanisms that use higher-layer protocols are limited, and can only identify a logical topology. Furthermore, discovery tools cannot easily distinguish between virtual and physical elements.

Chapter Contents

17.1   Introduction, 313
17.2   Tradeoffs Involving Scope And Overall Approach, 313
17.3   Architectural Tradeoffs, 315
17.4   Engineering Tradeoffs And Costs, 317
17.5   Tradeoffs In Representation And Semantics, 318
17.6   Summary, 321

17

Design Tradeoffs

17.1 Introduction

Previous chapters in this part of the book discuss desirable properties of a comprehensive, automated network management system, enumerate possible architectures, and consider the complex question of representation and semantics.

This chapter presents a set of engineering tradeoffs inherent in creating software systems that automate network management tasks. The chapter is intended to raise issues, not to provide answers. Thus, each section poses tradeoffs, lists possibilities, and assesses consequences without attempting to resolve questions or make choices.

To help organize the discussion, the chapter divides tradeoffs into several broad categories, beginning with the problem being solved and the general approaches that can be taken. It goes on to consider tradeoffs surrounding the choice of a network system architecture, software engineering and design tradeoffs, and tradeoffs that focus on representation and semantics. Obviously, the divisions are not absolute — we will see that choices in one category can affect possibilities in other categories.

17.2 Tradeoffs Involving Scope And Overall Approach

- **Extant Systems That Solve A Subproblem Vs. A Future Comprehensive System**

Perhaps the most significant tradeoff involves the overall scope of the problem to be solved. On one hand, we know from existing commercial and research systems that it is possible to build management tools that each solve one part of the management problem. On the other hand, although a comprehensive system is desirable, extensive research and development efforts will be needed to achieve such a system.

- **Autonomy In Decision Making Vs. Coordinated Policy**

    One of the fundamental tradeoffs focuses on autonomy, especially in a large multi-campus network. How much autonomy should each site be granted? Although autonomy is important, granting autonomy means relinquishing control. Even trivial details such as assignment of names can lead to overlap or inconsistency.

- **Tuning For A Fixed Set Of Known Elements And Services Vs. Generality To Accommodate New Elements And Services**

    If all network elements and services are known in advance, it is possible to design a system that is optimized to handle the particular set. If the goal is to accommodate arbitrary new elements and services, however, a system must be designed to emphasize extensibility rather than efficiency.

- **Support For Connection-Oriented Vs. Connectionless Network Routing**

    Although control of routing is a fundamental part of network management, a system can be designed to impose a connection-oriented or connectionless structure. The use of a connection-oriented technology, such as MPLS, for traffic engineering introduces more overhead, but gives the management system more control than dynamic IP routing. At one extreme, placing most of the intelligence in a management system means all control and configuration originates in the management system and network elements can be dumb devices. At the other extreme, if each network element contains sufficient intelligence to self-configure and adapt to network conditions, a management system only needs to provide global policies, monitor network status, and gather reports of equipment failures. A practical system usually chooses a boundary between the two extremes, with some intelligence in network elements and some in the management system.

- **Functionality Designed To Accommodate Human Managers Vs. Functionality Designed To Accommodate Network Elements**

    In general, a system that uses paradigms appropriate for humans may be inefficient for underlying devices and vice versa. For example, if the management interface on a device exports HTML that is appropriate for humans, it may be difficult for a computer program to parse and understand. Similarly, if a system allows a manager to specify a broad, global policy (e.g., to give priority to business functions), it may be difficult to translate the policy into parameters that achieve the policy.

- **Automated Topology Discovery Vs. Specification Of Topology**

On one hand, because it does not rely on humans to update a database when topology changes, automated discovery can produce a more accurate and timely record. On the other hand, discovery uses protocols, which means that discovery tools can only report logical topology and follow routable paths.

- **Recovery From A Snapshot Vs. Recovery From Reconfiguration**

A management system must provide a way to restart a network after a manual shutdown or power failure. Two broad approaches can be used: a copy of configuration commands can be saved as a manager configures elements, or a snapshot of the state from each network element can be saved on persistent store once the network is operating correctly. Although it can be more efficient, a snapshot may include temporal items such as timestamps that are meaningless after a restore. Using configuration commands to reconfigure a network avoids temporal discrepancies, but can be inefficient and may require a global order on configuration (i.e., it may not be possible to complete the configuration on a given network element until other elements have been configured).

17.3 Architectural Tradeoffs

- **Integrated System Vs. Separate Tools**

An integrated system provides a consistent, uniform mechanism to solve the entire management problem, but is not easy to change. Separate tools usually lack consistency, may duplicate data items or processing, but can be upgraded or replaced without affecting other tools.

- **A Single Network Vs. A Separate Network For Management Traffic**

Using a single network to carry both production traffic and management traffic has the advantage of lower cost and does not require a separate facility to administrate the management network. Using a separate infrastructure to segregate management traffic from production traffic has the advantages of noninterference and immunity to faults. Immunity means that a fault on the production network, such as a routing loop, does not prevent management activities from proceeding; noninterference means that management activities do not impact the production network. Noninterference is especially important for performance assessment because traffic such as flow data can place a significant load on a network.

• **Plug-And-Play Vs. Specified Configuration**

One of the most significant architectural decisions concerns the general question of configuration: should network elements interact directly to configure themselves, or should a management system configure each element? The advantage of centralized configuration lies in the ability of a manager to control precise details; the advantage of automated configuration lies in the ability of elements to function without the need for direct control.

• **Integrated Management System Vs. Scripts Used With A Standardized Element Interface**

On one hand, an integrated management system that provides all functionality can reuse information for various aspects of management and be designed to be more efficient. On the other hand, if each network element follows a standardized interface that allows software to interrogate or control the element efficiently, each manager will have the freedom to devise applications and scripts that provide the exact functionality an organization needs.

• **Standardized Element Interface Vs. Platform Plus Applications**

An architecture that uses a standardized element interface allows applications or scripts to be built that interact directly with the underlying elements. As an alternative, it is possible to build a generalized management platform that interacts with elements and applications. That is, the management platform gathers information from elements and makes it available to applications, and accepts commands from applications and applies them to elements. A platform architecture offers the advantages of hiding device details and eliminating replication of data, but has the disadvantage of limiting the functionality of applications.

• **Direct Manipulation Of Persistent Store Vs. A Separate, External Database**

An architecture in which a management system directly manipulates persistent store has the advantage that storage can be optimized for the data items to be stored. Although it may not provide an optimized representation for data, an architecture in which the management system is separate from the external store can incorporate standardized database software that provides direct access and control of individual data items by external applications.

17.4 Engineering Tradeoffs And Costs

- **Higher Traffic Overhead Vs. Less Accurate Information**

Many functions in a network management system require the system to gather and analyze data. Gathering data more frequently improves the accuracy of the analysis, especially in cases where the management system uses incoming data to assess network performance. However, increasing the frequency of observations increases the total traffic a management system transfers across the underlying network. Because the bandwidth consumed by management traffic is unavailable for production traffic, more accurate analysis results in a tradeoff of increased overhead.

- **Functionality And Power Vs Ease Of Use**

A tradeoff exists between the overall functionality that a management system offers to a manager and the complexity of the human interface. To permit a manager to specify details or select among many possibilities, a management system must offer more choices. Consequently, the interface will take longer for a manager to learn. That is, a system that allows a manager to perform the widest variety of functions and gives the greatest control of a network necessarily imposes an interface that is more complex.

- **Immediate Feedback Vs. Complete Analysis Of A Problem**

On one hand, a management system can notify a manager immediately when suspicious behavior is first observed. Doing so alerts a manager to a potential problem early, but can have the drawback of deluging a manager with unnecessary detail. On the other hand, a management system can wait until information is gathered from multiple sources, correlate the reports, analyze the results, and notify a manager of the root cause of the problem. Of course, it is possible to do both by notifying a manager early and reporting the results of deeper analysis when the results are available. From a manager's perspective, however, a tradeoff exists between rapid notification and more complete analysis.

- **Facilities For Remote Consolidation Vs. Management Traffic**

An important tradeoff in large networks centers on the distribution of management functionality, especially fault detection and analysis. A centralized management system arranges for all information gathered from network elements to be forwarded to a central point for analysis. A distributed design chooses to place consolidation points at various locations in the network. Each consolidation point collects from surrounding networks elements, analyzes the data, and forwards a summary back to the central management system. Thus, a tradeoff lies between additional facilities for remote consolidation and increased management traffic.

- **Scalable Addressing And Routing Vs. Automatically Assigned Addresses**

The key concept behind a scalable addressing and routing system is a hierarchy. However, hierarchical addresses must be configured (i.e., assigned in a meaningful way). The alternative to hierarchical addressing, known as flat addressing, allows addresses to be assigned automatically (e.g., fixed permanently with no configuration required), but leads to inefficient routing for sufficiently large networks. Thus, a tradeoff lies between the overhead of configuring addresses and limits on scaling.

- **Large Absolute Names Vs. Smaller Relative Names**

When choosing names for data items, a designer has a choice between absolute and relative naming schemes. Although it is unambiguous and can be used anywhere within the management system, an absolute name is large and usually unsuitable for humans. The alternative, a relative name, is smaller and often easy for humans to recognize or remember, but a relative name can only be used in a given context. Thus, the tradeoff is between large, absolute names that are unambiguous and smaller relative names that are ambiguous, but easier for humans to remember.

- **Extensible Systems Vs. Run-Time Efficiency**

A software system that is designed to be extensible contains provisions to make additions and changes easy. For example, a server can contain hooks that permit a manager to invoke scripts that perform specialized processing or tailor the server's actions to specific needs or situations. However, software systems that contain provisions for extensibility incur additional run-time overhead, even in cases where no external scripts are invoked. Thus, a tradeoff occurs between extensibility and run-time efficiency.

17.5 Tradeoffs In Representation And Semantics

- **Space Taken For Data Vs Time To Store Or Access**

The classic tradeoff in data representation, which is known as the *time/space tradeoff*, arises from the relationship between the amount of storage used and the processing time. In general, a representation that reduces processing time requires increased storage space, and vice versa. For example, to save storage, management data can be summarized or raw data can be compressed. In each case, however, processing is required before data can be stored.

- **Implicit Vs. Explicit Data Typing During Serialization**

A tradeoff arises when choosing a serialization scheme. On one hand, including type information along with data increases safety because a receiver can verify that the types of incoming data items match the data types that are expected. On the other hand, type information increases overhead in two ways. First, transmission overhead increases because more bits are transferred. Second, processing overhead increases because data type information must be created (and possibly checked) for each data item. Thus, a designer must choose a tradeoff between more safety and more overhead.

- **Efficiency Vs. Ease Of Inspection**

When storing or transferring data, a management system can choose between a binary encoding or a readable encoding. A binary encoding is dense and saves space, but a readable encoding has two advantages. First, readability makes it easy to debug software and identify problems, especially when data is created by a piece of the system built by one vendor and used by a piece of the system built by another. Second, readability avoids assumptions about binary representation that can make it difficult to move data across heterogeneous systems. Thus, the tradeoff lies in choosing between lower overhead and higher ease of data inspection and verification.

- **Extensible Transfer Representation Vs. Lower Overhead**

Technologies, such as XML, that allow a designer to include a name and type with each data item make it easy to extend the set of items being transferred. However, sending additional metadata along with each item increases both computational and transmission overhead — a binary representation that does not include metadata is more compact and takes less time to generate. Thus, a designer must choose between a representation that can be extended easily and one that has lower overhead.

- **In-Memory Data Model Vs. External Data Model**

One of the primary questions surrounding the representation of management data focuses on where items are stored. Which pieces of management data should be kept in main memory, which should be kept on secondary store, and which should be kept in both? The advantage of using main memory is speed of access: a typical RAM operates orders of magnitude faster than a typical disk. The advantages of secondary storage are persistence (data is preserved after a crash) and universal access (applications can access the data directly). Thus, the tradeoff is a choice between speed and increased permanence / access.

- **Object Size Vs. Hierarchy Depth**

    An information model in which the class hierarchy is relatively flat has the advantage of faster search time, but the disadvantage of longer load times because each object is larger. Alternatively, a model that has a deep hierarchy has the advantage of smaller objects, which means the time needed to load an object is lower, but the disadvantage of requiring more time to search the hierarchy.

- **Single Class Hierarchy Vs. Multiple Hierarchies**

    When building an information model, it is possible to define a single, global class hierarchy that encompasses all aspects of information pertinent to a network management system or to define multiple, independent hierarchies that each focus on one aspect. The advantage of the former is conceptual unification in which all management information is organized in a strict hierarchical manner. The disadvantage of a single hierarchy arises from the overhead that arises because a single model must include additional items that go beyond the scope of information needed for network management (e.g., definitions of metalevels inserted in the hierarchy merely to connect items that are otherwise independent). By comparison, multiple hierarchies allow a software system to be designed that only includes items pertinent to management, but has the disadvantage of seeming less organized. Thus, the primary tradeoff is between conceptual unity and run-time efficiency. A secondary aspect of the tradeoff arises from the increased space required when extra items are added to a single hierarchy.

- **Unifying Or Separating Associations And Class Hierarchies**

    Because information modeling is sufficiently general to accommodate arbitrary information, a model can hold metadata such as a set of associations that specify relationships among items in the model. Although it is possible to include associations as a separate part of the class hierarchy, doing so introduces additional run-time overhead because the management system must access an association object as well as data objects to which the association applies. More to the point, because they are conceptually unlike other data items, associations must be placed in a portion of the hierarchy that is completely independent from data items, which means that a system must first use the hierarchy to extract the association and then use the hierarchy again to locate the items to which the association refers. Thus, the tradeoff lies between conceptual unification of metadata under a class hierarchy and run-time efficiency.

- **Domain-Specific Model Vs. Solution-Specific Model**

    A domain-specific model offers the potential advantage of providing a definitive answer that suffices for all software systems in the domain. However, domain-specific models have proven difficult to construct, and the resulting class hierarchy may not be efficient for any given application. As an alternative, a solution-specific model that focuses on one particular problem may not be applicable to other software systems, even for related problems. Thus, the tradeoff lies between generality and feasibility and/or efficiency.

17.6 Summary

This chapter presents examples of tradeoffs that underlie the design of a comprehensive network management system. The large set of tradeoffs highlights some of the difficult decisions involved in selecting an overall approach, choosing an architecture, designing a system, and choosing data representations and an information model. The tradeoffs also help illustrate why no single approach has emerged as the key to building a next-generation management system.

Chapter Contents

18.1   Introduction, 323

18.2   Fundamental Abstractions For A Management System, 323

18.3   Separation Of Control And Validation, 324

18.4   Boundary Between A Network And End Systems, 324

18.5   Taxonomy Of Network Management Architectures, 325

18.6   Extent Of Functionality Offered By Existing Systems, 325

18.7   Management Of Routing And Traffic Engineering, 325

18.8   Automated Address Assignment, 325

18.9   Analysis Of Routing, 326

18.10   Security Policy Enforcement, 326

18.11   Infrastructure Redesign For Automated Management, 326

18.12   Peer-To-Peer Propagation Of Management Information, 327

18.13   Routing Failure Analysis, 327

18.14   Limits Of Automated Topology Discovery, 327

18.15   Data Mining Of NetFlow Data, 327

18.16   Storage Of Network State, 328

18.17   Anomaly Detection Using Bayesian Filtering, 328

18.18   Cost Of Protection In Scripting, 328

18.19   Late-Binding Interface Management Applications, 328

18.20   Boundary Between Management System And Elements, 329

18.21   Summary, 329

18

Open Questions And Research Problems

18.1 Introduction

Previous chapters in this part of the text describe properties of an ideal network management system, consider possible architectures, examine data representation and semantics, and discuss tradeoffs inherent in designing and building comprehensive management systems. This chapter continues the discussion by listing a set of issues and questions to be investigated.

The scope and difficulty of the problems listed in the chapter varies significantly. Some are appropriate for a graduate student to undertake as a project in a course; others represent long-term research that requires the effort of multiple investigators over a span of several years. In any case, most of the problems are amenable to incremental work — it is possible to define a small subset of the problem that is suitable for a single person to undertake in a fixed period of time.

18.2 Fundamental Abstractions For A Management System

What are the fundamental abstractions around which a comprehensive management system can be constructed? To understand the question, consider operating systems in the 1960s. Each hardware vendor built software to load programs and control I/O devices. The hardware on each computer differed dramatically, and basic abstractions were derived "bottom up" from the underlying hardware. Thus, one vendor had an

I/O module to read or write blocks on a specific disk drive, and another vendor had an I/O module to read or write data on a specific drum device. Computing lacked general-purpose abstractions that applied across devices and across vendors. Project MAC at MIT helped consolidate thinking by focusing on high-level abstractions such as *processes*, *files*, and *address spaces*. Although the Multics system that emerged from the project did not enjoy commercial success, the abstractions survived and remain the basis for building or discussing operating systems. Network management needs an analogous revolution: instead of building abstractions that generalize current hardware, software, and protocol facilities, researchers need to find a small set of orthogonal, high-level abstractions that will enable new thinking about the architecture of large, comprehensive management systems.

It is important to distinguish between abstractions that are helpful in describing or characterizing the problem and abstractions that are used to build management systems. We have an example of the former: FCAPS. New abstractions are needed to help designers construct management software systems.

18.3 Separation Of Control And Validation

Is it better to build a single, unified network management system that handles all tasks or to separate functionality into two independent systems, one that configures and controls a network and another that validates the results? The use of separate systems may be important because policies are often easy to state and verify, but difficult to implement. The separation allows an independent software system to monitor the network and verify that it adheres to policies.

As a subquestion, we can ask whether a single policy statement works best for both control and validation. As an alternative, it may be desirable to allow a manager to specify validation conditions independently. In either case, how should policies and validation conditions be represented?

18.4 Boundary Between A Network And End Systems

Exactly where is the boundary between a network and a computer system that uses the network? The question is fundamental in any discussion of network management because the boundary determines what items must be managed. Prima facie, the boundary appears impossible to define precisely. To understand some of the issues, observe that although they are implemented in end systems, protocols like TCP can have a tremendous impact on a network. Also observe that it is possible to define network services (e.g., web services) as part of a network or as services that use a network.

One particular aspect of FCAPS stands out as blurring the distinction between a network and end systems: security. Although a network is involved, an organization's information security policy usually includes actions and responsibilities of end systems. Thus, the question arises whether network security can be managed independent of end systems.

18.5 Taxonomy Of Network Management Architectures

What can be learned from a bottom-up analysis of network management system architectures? Do existing commercial or research systems use architectures other than those covered in Chapter 15? If so, what are the advantages and disadvantages of each?

In addition to answering the broad questions above, we can consider whether relationships among architectures can be quantified. That is, we can consider whether a taxonomy can be created that classifies systems by dividing them into groups according to major architectural features.

18.6 Extent Of Functionality Offered By Existing Systems

What combinations of FCAPS functionality are not covered by existing network management systems? Although systems exist that handle each of the five aspects of FCAPS, the question is focused on combinations (e.g., configuration plus fault detection). One might conclude that combinations not covered by existing research prototypes or commercial products are the most difficult.

18.7 Management Of Routing And Traffic Engineering

Is traditional IP routing or traffic management easier to plan, configure, operate, debug, or monitor? To be more precise, is it possible to construct a quantitative assessment of the management costs associated with each of the two approaches? Of specific interest are the costs of initial deployment, continuous operation, and recovery after failure (i.e., when backup routes are needed).

18.8 Automated Address Assignment

Is it possible to build software that automatically devises an addressing scheme for an entire organization? That is, can a program be devised that takes as input a network topology, a list of external connections, and an estimate of future growth, and generates as output a plan for assigning address prefixes to each physical network?

If solving the general case is too difficult, can the problem be solved by limiting analysis to specific topologies? For example, a network that consists of a single Local Area Network segment is trivial. How many additional networks need to be added before the problem becomes complex?

18.9 Analysis Of Routing

Can we build software that automatically assesses the routing infrastructure across an entire network? That is, can a program be devised that takes as input a description of a network topology plus a description of routing, and generates as output an analysis of the routing infrastructure, including correctness, efficiency, and ability to recover from node or link failures?

As a subproblem, consider software that automatically probes routers (e.g., using SNMP), constructs a topology, imposes a routing overlay, and analyzes the resulting graph for reachability, black holes, and asymmetric routing. Does such software handle all possible routing problems?

18.10 Security Policy Enforcement

Can software be devised that takes as input a statement of security policies and verifies that the policies are administered correctly and uniformly across an entire network? A language will be needed that allows a manager to express the security constraints to be verified. Is there an advantage to using two languages: one to express policies that should be implemented and one to express verification conditions?

As was pointed out above, verification is especially difficult in the case of security because many aspects involve end systems instead of network elements. As an alternative, consider the limitations that a boundary imposes. That is, consider the question: what security items cannot be verified if one is only given the ability to interrogate network elements and not end systems?

18.11 Infrastructure Redesign For Automated Management

Can we redesign network elements to make automated management possible? As an example, consider adding a management processor to each switch so that when a new connection is made, the management processor interrogates the device at the other end of the new connection, enters the information in a topology database, and configures the device. Assume that no configuration can be performed except through the management processor on the switch (i.e., there is no way to bypass the management system and manually change an element).

As an extension to the idea above, consider what happens when two switches interconnect. The management processors on the two switches should exchange topology and configuration information and agree to form a distributed management system. To how many switches can the idea extend? What happens at an autonomous system boundary?

18.12 Peer-To-Peer Propagation Of Management Information

Is there any advantage to using a peer-to-peer paradigm to propagate management information across a large network automatically? We observe that managers currently install a set of management nodes, and manually select consolidation or aggregation points. The question is whether an automated system can do a better job of adapting to conditions. Thus, the question is whether a system can be devised that automatically forwards copies of data to points in the network where the data is needed, without sending unneeded copies.

18.13 Routing Failure Analysis

Is it possible to devise software that automatically interrogates a network and analyzes routing weaknesses? That is, can a software system be constructed that probes routers, finds both the physical topology and routing mechanisms that are in use, and then computes behavior of the routing system for various combinations of node and link failures to determine where the network is most vulnerable?

18.14 Limits Of Automated Topology Discovery

Topology discovery tools that use applications and higher layer protocols to probe a network can only follow routable paths. As a broader question, consider a discovery mechanism that can interrogate network elements: if a management system has access to all information in each network element (e.g., via SNMP), is it possible to discover complete physical and logical topologies? If not, is it possible to characterize the topology information that cannot be discovered automatically?

18.15 Data Mining Of NetFlow Data

What information can be extracted from NetFlow data? Many systems that analyze NetFlow data produce statistical profiles of traffic (e.g., the percentage of packets that carry a given protocol, such as TCP, or the percentage of packets destined for a particular application, such as the web). The broader question is whether data mining techniques can be used to extract more than basic statistical information.

18.16 Storage Of Network State

How much space is needed to store network state? More specifically, can we estimate the amount of space needed to store the information that will be needed to reconfigure all elements in a network after a failure? There are two possible approaches: a snapshot of configuration parameters from each network element or a copy of the commands that were used to configure each element.

As an extension, consider redundancy in the state information (e.g., a set of routers that are each configured with the same management metadata (e.g., login ID, password, and authorization list). If redundant information is removed from network state, how much space is saved?

18.17 Anomaly Detection Using Bayesian Filtering

Is it possible to use Bayesian filtering to detect anomalous behavior in a network†? More specifically, in addition to looking for anomalies in normal network traffic, how can a Bayesian filter help identify anomalies in management data (e.g., status and fault reports)?

18.18 Cost Of Protection In Scripting

Scripting technologies that allow managers to write scripts to control processing often insert a layer of protection: instead of allowing a script to manipulate internal data structures directly, the system provides a copy of data to the script and translates changes back into internal data structures when the script finishes. What is the overall cost of such protection in terms of computational overhead? Are alternative methods available that provide equivalent protection efficiently?

18.19 Late-Binding Interface Management Applications

Can a management system offer a late-binding interface that allows new applications to be created dynamically and achieves low overhead? To understand the question, consider a software backplane architecture as described in Chapter 15. What interface should a backplane use to permit applications to manage network elements? Specifically, can an interface be designed that allows a manager to add new applications easily and quickly, while keeping the overhead of accessing management data low?

---

†Bayesian filtering is related to machine learning — it uses statistical techniques to identify unusual input by comparing observations to a baseline.

18.20 Boundary Between Management System And Elements

At what level should the boundary between a network management system and individual network elements occur? That is, how much management functionality should reside in network elements and how much should reside in the management system? The question has two parts. On one hand, we can ask whether placing more intelligence on one side or the other will affect the overall functionality. On the other hand, we can ask whether changing the locus of intelligence will affect the performance of the system (e.g., dramatically changing the amount of management data that must be transferred).

18.21 Summary

Because little is known about the design of future network management systems, many open questions exist. This chapter presents examples of topics that can be studied. The chapter explains questions without attempting to pose answers. Although many of the questions are suitable as projects in graduate courses, some will require coordinated long-term effort.

Bibliography

BABCOCK, B. and C. OLSTON [June 2003], ''Distributed Top-K Monitoring,'' *Proceedings of the ACM SIGMOD International Conference on Management of Data*, San Diego, California.

BLUMENTHAL U. and B. WIJNEN [December 2002], ''User-based Security Model (USM) for version 3 of the Simple Network Management Protocol (SNMPv3),'' RFC 3414.

BROWN, A. B. and J. L. HELLERSTEIN [July 2004], ''An Approach to Benchmarking Configuration Complexity,'' *SIGOPSEW 2004 - 11th ACM SIGOPS European Workshop*, ACM SIGOPS.

CASE, J. D., J. R. DAVIN, M. S. FEDOR, and M. L. SCHOFFSTALL [March, 1988], ''Introduction to the Simple Gateway Monitoring Protocol,'' *IEEE Network*.

CASE, J. D., J. R. DAVIN, M. S. FEDOR, and M. L. SCHOFFSTALL [March, 1989] ''Network Management and the Design of SNMP,'' *ConneXions: The Interoperability Report 3*.

CASE, J. D., R. FRYE, and J, SAPERIA [1999], *SNMPv3 Survival Guide : Practical Strategies for Integrated Network Management*, John Wiley & Sons, New York.

CLAISE, B., editor [2004], *Cisco Systems NetFlow Service Export, Version 9*, RFC 3954.

COMER, D. E. [2004], *Computer Networks And Internets*, 4th edition, Prentice-Hall, Upper Saddle River, New Jersey.

COMER, D. E. [2006], *Internetworking With TCP/IP Volume 1: Principles, Protocols, and Architecture,* 5th ed., Prentice-Hall, Upper Saddle River, New Jersey.

DILMAN, M. and D. RAZ [April 2001], ''Efficient reactive monitoring,'' *IEEE Journal on Selected Areas in Communications (JSAC),* special issue on recent advances in network management.

DIMITROPOULOS, X., D. KRIOUKOV, G. RILEY, and K. CLAFFY [August 2005], ''Classifying the Types of Autonomous Systems in the Internet,'', *SIGCOMM 2005* (poster), Philadelphia, Pennsylvania.

EIDE, E., L. STOLLER, T. STACK, J. FREIRE, and J. LEPREAU [February 2006], ''Integrated Scientific Workflow Management for the Emulab Network Testbed,'' *Flux Technical Note FTN200601*, University of Utah.

FEAMSTER, N., H. BALAKRISHNAN, and J. REXFORD [November 2004], "Some Foundational Problems in Interdomain Routing," *Proceedings ACM SIGCOMM Workshop on Hot Topics in Networking (HotNets III)*, San Diego, California.

FELDMANN, A., N. KAMMENHUBER, O. MAENNEL, B. MAGGS, R. DEPRISCO, and R. SUNDARAM [October 2004], "A Methodology for Estimating Interdomain Web Traffic Demand," *Proceedings of the Internet Measurement Conference 2004 (IMC)*.

FOX, A., and D. PATTERSON [June 2003], "Self-Repairing Computers," *Scientific American*.

FRANCIS, P. and R. GUMMADI [August 2001], "IPNL: A NAT-Extended Internet Architecture," *SIGCOMM 2001*, San Diego, California.

GREENBERG, A., G. HJALMTYSSON, D. A. MALTZ, A. MYERS, J. REXFORD, G. XIE, H. YAN, J. ZHAN, and H. ZHANG [October 2005], "A Clean Slate 4D Approach to Network Control and Management", *ACM SIGCOMM Computer Communication Review,* 35(5).

HARRINGTON D., R. PRESUHN, and B. WIJNEN [December 2002], "An Architecture for Describing Simple Network Management Protocol (SNMP) Management Frameworks," RFC 3411.

HASAN, M. [May 1995], "An Active Temporal Model for Network Management Databases," *Proceedings of the IFIP/IEEE Fourth International Symposium on Integrated Network Management,* Santa Barbara, California, 524-535.

HERNANDEZ, A., M. C. CHIDESTER, A. D. GEORGE [December 2001], "Adaptive Sampling for Network Management," *Journal of Network and Systems Management* 9(4).

HUNTINGTON-LEE, et. al. [1997], *HP OpenView*, McGraw Hill, New York, New York.

JOURNAL OF NETWORK AND SYSTEMS MANAGEMENT [2002-2005], Special Issues on: *Internet Traffic Engineering and Management*, 10(3), *Policy-Based Management*, 11(3), *Security and Management*, 12(1) and 13(3), *Distributed Management of Networks and Services*, 12(3), and *Self-Managing Systems and Networks*, 13(2).

LEE, S. J., P. SHARMA, S. BANERJEE, S. BASU and R. FONSECA [April 2005], "Measuring Bandwidth Between PlanetLab Nodes," *Proceedings of the Workshop on Passive and Active Measurements*.

MCCLOGHRIE, K., D. PERKINS, J. SCHOENWAELDER, and T. BRAUNSCHWEIG [April 1999] "Structure of Management Information Version 2 (SMIv2)," RFC 2578.

MORRIS, S. [2003], *Network Management, MIBs and MPLS: Principles, Design and Implementation*, Prentice Hall, Upper Saddle River, New Jersey.

NORTON, W. B. [2002], "The Art of Peering: The Peering Playbook," white paper, Equinix Corporation.

OZMUTLU, H. C., N. GAUTAM, and R. BARTON [March 2002], "Managing End-to-End Network Performance Via Optimized Monitoring Strategies," *Journal of Network and Systems Management* 10(1), 107-126.

PAGE-JONES, M. [2000], *Fundamentals of Object-Oriented Design in UML*, Addison-Wesley, Reading, Massachusetts.

PERKINS, D. [1999], *RMON*, Prentice-Hall, Upper Saddle River, New Jersey.

PRAS, A., T. DREVERS, R. VAN DE MEENT and D. QUARTEL [December 2004], "Comparing the Performance of SNMP and Web Services-Based Management," *IEEE Trans. on Network and Service Management*, 1(2). 11.

ROSE, M. T. [1991], *The Simple Book: An Introduction to Management of TCP/IP-based Internets*, Addison-Wesley, Reading, Massachusetts.

ROSE, M., editor [March 1991], "A Convention for Defining Traps for use with the SNMP," RFC 1215.

ROSE, M. T. and K. MCCLOGHRIE [1995], *How To Manage Your Network Using SNMP*, Prentice-Hall, Upper Saddle River, New Jersey.

SAPERIA, J. [2002], *SNMP At The Edge: Building Effective Service Management Systems*, McGraw Hill, New York, New York.

SCHULZRINNE, H. [July 2005], "Do you see what I see," 18th NMRG meeting, France.

SPRING, N., D. WETHERALL, and T. ANDERSON [March 2003], "Scriptroute: A Facility for Distributed Internet Measurement," *Proceedings Fourth USENIX Symposium on Internet Technologies and Systems (USITS)*.

STALLINGS, W. [1998], *SNMP, SNMPv3, and RMON 1 and 2: Practical Network Management*, 3rd Edition, Addison-Wesley, Reading, Massachusetts.

SUBRAMANIAN, M. [2000], *Network Management: Principles and Practice,* Addison-Wesley, Reading, Massachusetts.

SUBRAMANIAN, L., M. CAESAR, C. T. EE, M. HANDLEY, Z. M. MAO, S. SHENKER, and I. STOICA [August 2005], "HLP: A Next Generation Inter-domain Routing Protocol," *ACM SIGCOMM 05*, Philadelphia, Pennsylvania.

WIJNEN, B., R. PRESUHN, and K. MCCLOGHRIE [December 2002], "View-based Access Control Model (VACM) for the Simple Network Management Protocol (SNMP)," RFC 3415.

YEGNESWARAN, V., P. BARFORD, and V. PAXSON [November, 2005], "Using Honeynets for Internet Situational Awareness," *Proceedings of the ACM/USENIX Fourth Workshop on Hot Topics in Networks (HotNets IV)*.

ZELTSERMAN, D. and G. PUOPLO [April 1998], *Building Network Management Tools With Tcl/Tk*, Prentice-Hall, Upper Saddle River, New Jersey.

ZHANG, Y., Z. GE, M. ROUGHAN, and A. GREENBERG [October 2005], "Network Anomography," *Proceedings of the Internet Measurement Conference (IMC '05)*, Berkeley, California.

Index

A

AANTS   140
absolute
    bandwidth guarantee   73
    name   153
Abstract Syntax Notation.1   151
acceptable use policy   102
access
    point   15
    router   32
accountability   111
accounting   67
activation   51
active
    flow capture   172
    probing   82
adaptable system   249
AddHostName script   231
administrator   3
agent (SNMP)   147
aggregate performance   132
aggregation   31
aggregation of flows   167
alarm   59
appliance   245
application service   12
architectures   257
area (OSPF)   198
array   154
ASN.1   151
aspect   288

association
    in a Wi-Fi network   60
    in a model   300
asymmetric routes   199
asynchronous
    message   148
    notification   127
atomicity of updates   156
attack   61
audit trail   112
AUP   102
authentication   99, 107
authentication (SNMP)   159
authorization   99
automation   240
autonomous system   188
awk language   208

B

backplane (software)   268
bandwidth guarantees   73
baseline measurement   58
Basic Encoding Rules   147
BER   147
BGP Wedgies   200
big-endian   292
billing   67, 68, 69
binding   275
black hole   61, 200
blade   13
bottleneck   83

bottom-up design   258
business rules   253

C

cable modem   16, 72
Cable Modem Termination System   16
CableLabs   16
cache timeout   181
Cacti   140
carrier   31
carrier sensor   121
CDP   125
channel bank   19
charging
    see billing
CIM   303
Cisco Discovery Protocol   125
class hierarchy   288
classification   174
CLI   126
CMIP/CMIS   146
CMTS   16
CNR   223
Command Line Interface   126
Common Management Information Proto-
    col   146
community string   159
comprehensive system   249
confidentiality   99
configuration   39
    default   47
    tool   133
connection   69
connection-oriented   73
connectivity   122
content control   104
convergence (routing)   197
coordination
    among devices   106
    of passwords   108, 111
core
    network   241
    router   32

count-to-infinity   200
CRC   63
Cricket   140
Cyclic Redundancy Code   63

D

dark addresses   200
data
    aggregate   154
    confidentiality   99
    integrity   99
    mining   309
    model   295
    semantics   293
database-centric   266, 272
DDOS   107
deep packet inspection   168, 175
default configuration   47
denial of service attack   61, 107
design paradigm   258
device   11
DHCP   12
DHCP server   21
dig   140
Digital Subscriber Line   17, 72
discovery
    of routes   124
    of topology   125
distance-vector routing   197
Distributed
    DOS attack   107
    Management Task Force   303
DMTF   303
DNS   12
DOCSIS   16
Domain Name System   12
domain of authority   250
DOS attack   107
DropDecline script   227
DShield   140
DSL   17, 72
DSL Access Multiplexor (DSLAM)   17
dumb device   245

Dynamic Host Configuration Protocol   12, 21

E

early binding   275
echo   122
Echo Request   122
edge   241
edge router   32
EGP   188
egress aggregation   167
EIGRP   189
element
    interface   265
    management   12
Element Management System   28
EMS   28
encryption   102, 103
end-to-end measurement   81
enterprise   241
enterprise network   31
Ethereal   124
Ethernet switch   14
event
    correlation   64
    log   59, 112
    monitoring   127
evolution of tools   118
exceeding quotas   70
expect script   210
expectation validation   276
Extended Interior Gateway Routing Protocol   189
extensible   266
eXtensible Markup Language   292
extensible protocol   145
extension point   223
Exterior Gateway Protocol   188
exterior routing   188
external segment   106
extra hop problem   199

F

failover   196
failure scenario   94
fast
    failover   196
    recovery   196
fault prevention   64
fetch operation   272
FIN   181
fine-grained flow   178
firewall   20
firewall unification   107
fixed field (NetFlow)   178
flash crowd   61
flat-rate billing   68
flow   132, 164
    aggregation   167
    analysis   166
    analysis tool   132
    cache   181
    capture   171
    data export   177
    identifier   176
FlowScan   140
forwarding   185
forwarding table   26, 154
framework   266
full
    duplex   165
    mesh   94
future planning   83

G

Get (SNMP)   148
Get-Bulk (SNMP)   148
Get-Next (SNMP)   148
global
    namespace   153
    state   45
Gnu Radius   140
gnuplot   214
graphical modeling language   304
group (RMON)   158

H

hash algorithm   108
head-end modem   16, 17, 72
header   173
header checksum (IP)   63
heterogeneous data aggregate   154
hierarchical
    architecture   266
    model   298
    namespace   151
    objects   287
    routing   198
homogeneous data aggregate   154
Honeynets   140
hooks   223, 268
hop   187
hop-count   191
HTTP load balancer   22

I

ICMP   122
ID   176
identifier flow   176
identity   99
IDS   103
IGP   188
IGRP   189
incremental configuration   48
information model   294, 295
infrastructure service   12
ingress aggregation   167
intelligent system   249
interface   19, 265
interface aggregation   167
Interior
    Gateway Protocol   188
    Gateway Routing Protocol   189
interior routing   188
internal segment   106
International
    Organization for Standardization   151
    Telecommunications Union   151
Internet Control Message Protocol   122

interpreter   208
Intrusion Detection System   103
inventory   254
inverse serial multiplexor   138
IP
    address   167
    forwarding table   26
    router   19
    routing table   26
IPFIX   178, 183
IPsec   108
IS-IS   189
ISO   151
ISP   31
iterative transaction   52
ITU   151

J

jitter   187

K

key   102
key management   112

L

LAN   14
language for modeling   304
late binding   275
latency   79, 187
Layer
    2 switch   14
    3 forwarding table   154
levels of urgency   128
linearization   291
link utilization   81, 85
link-status routing   197
load
    balancer   22
    balancing   196, 197
Local Area Network   14
local measurement   81
locality of reference   176

log   59
loosely coupled   275

M

MAC address   14
Management Information Base   147, 150
management workstation   136
manager   3
manual override   246, 254
matrix of traffic   90
measurement   81
mesh model   298
metric (routing)   186, 190
MIB   147, 150
Min-Cut Max-Flow Theorem   195
mirror port   171
model   294, 295
model-driven design   294
modeling language   304
modem   16, 17, 72
moniker   297
monitoring   57
monitorscript   215
monolithic   266
MPLS   12, 73, 94, 193
MTNM   303
Multi-Protocol Label Switching   12, 73,
      94, 193
multiple sites   250
multiplexor   138

N

netconf   135
NetFlow   178
Network
      Management System (NMS)   28
      Operation Center (NOC)   136
network
      administrator   3
      appliance   245
      automation   240
      devices   11
      element   12

element failure   60
fault   55
manager   3
model   298
monitoring   57
planning tools   134
services   11
state   45
NETwork DOcumentation Tool   140
NMS   28
NOC   136
non-selfreferential   339
nonoptimal routes   199
northbound interface   265
ntop   140

O

object   287
object identifier   151
Object Management Group   305
object-oriented model   295
offline
      flow analysis   168
      flow classification   174
one-time key   103
online
      flow analysis   168
      flow classification   174
ontology   309
open NMS   140
Open Systems Interconnection   146
OSI   146
OSPF area   198
OSSIM   140
overconstrained optimization   195

P

packet
      analyzer   123
      filter   123
      loss   79
      sampling   181
paradox

see non-selfreferential
passive
    flow capture   171
    observation   82
passmass   212
password
    rollover   109
    sharing   111
path protection   194
pattern scanner   104
peering point   31
per-message atomicity   157
perimeter control   103
Perl language   208
persistence   288
ping   122, 214
plotscript   220
polling   59, 127, 149
POP   109
Post Office Protocol   109
post-packet-decode   229
precomputation (of routes)   194
prescriptive model   302
principle of most recent change   117
privacy   99
privacy (SNMP)   159
programmatic interface   126
protocol
    analyzer   123
    failure   61
    type   167
provider   241
provisioned service   12
public   159
public key encryption   103

Q

QoS   192
Quality of Service   192
quarantine area   106

R

RADIUS server   284

Radius software (Gnu)   140
RANCID   140
RBAC   111, 159, 250
reachability   122
read-write paradigm   145
reboot   146
record   154
recovery   196
recursive transaction   52
redundant path   200
relational model   295
relative bandwidth guarantee   73
remote
    aggregation   139
    management paradigm   143
    terminal access   138
Remote MONitoring MIB   158
residential network   31
resource
    overrun   107
    record   21
RIP   188
risk assessment   100
RMON MIB   158
Role-Based Access Control   111, 159, 250
rollback   50
rollover of passwords   109
route
    discovery   124
    flapping   200
router   19
routing   185
    convergence   197
    distance-vector   197
    exterior   188
    hierarchy   198
    interior   188
    link-status   197
    loop   61, 199
    protocol choice   197
    table   26, 154
    tool   133
    update protocol   186
Routing Information Protocol   188

RRDTool   140
RST   181

S

sampling   181
scalable system   249
screen scraping   133
secret key encryption   103
security   196
    architecture   105
    policy   101
Semantic Web   303
semantics   293
serialization   291
server   21, 22
Service
    Level Agreement   68
    Oriented Architecture   287
    Set IDentifier   16, 110
service provider   31, 241
services   11, 12
session key   103
Set (SNMP)   148
setup (configuration)   51
shared
    passwords   111
    secret key   103
Shared Information/Data model   303
shell (UNIX)   208
shortest path   187
SID   303
Simple Network Management Proto-
    col   146
single point failure   94
SLA   68
slow convergence   200
Small Office/ Home Office   29
snapshot rollback   50
SNMP   146
SNMP agent   147
SOA   287
software
    backplane   266, 268

    failure   61
SOHO   29
southbound interface   265
spam filter   104
spoofing   108
ssh   138
SSID   16, 110
state   45
stateful firewall   103
static model   302
store operation   272
structure   154
subnet ambiguity   200
switch   15
    Ethernet   14
    Layer 2   14
SYN   181

T

tail-end modem   16, 17
Tcl language   208, 210, 229
TCP   156
TDM   12
TDR   121
technologies   117
Telecommunications Management Net-
    work   32
TeleManagement Forum   303
telnet   138
template (NetFlow)   179
temporal locality   176
terminated traffic   75
textual modeling language   304
throughput   79, 187
Tier-2 ISP   30
Tier-3 ISP   30
tiered
    hierarchy   266, 270
    levels of service   70
tightly coupled   275
time
    division multiplexing   12
    progression graph   130

Time-Domain Reflectometer   121
Time-To-Live   21
timeout   50, 181
Tivoli   136
TMF   303
TMN   32
Tool Command Language   210, 229
tools   117
tools as applications   118
top-down design   258
topology discovery   125
traceroute   125
tracert   125
traffic
    analysis   163
    engineering   94, 185, 193
    engineering tool   133
    matrix   90
    model validation   93
    policing   71
    scheduling   73
transaction   48
transit traffic   75, 190
transmission link failure   60
transport
    protocol   155
    service   12
Trap (SNMP)   148
trigger level   127
trouble reports   56
troubleshooting   56
TTL   21
tuning a traffic model   93
tunnel   193

U

UDP   156
UML   305
unidirectional flow   165
Unified Modeling Language   305
universal system   249
upgrade paradigm   206
use-based billing   68

utilization   85

V

validation   276, 277
variable in an SNMP MIB   150
vendor independence   249
versatile system   249
view-based access control   159
virtual LAN   15
Virtual Private Network   103
virus scanner   104
Visual Basic language   208
VLAN switch   15
Voice over IP   79
VoIP   79
volume of traffic   69, 70
VPN   103

W

web
    interface   126
    server   22
WEP   16, 109
Wired Equivalent Privacy   16, 109
wireless strength and quality tester   121

X

XML   292